Hedgerow

Hedgerow

ANNE ANGUS

Illustrated by
MICHAEL WOODS

PARTRIDGE
PRESS

Text copyright © 1987 by Anne Angus
Illustrations copyright © 1987 by Michael Woods

Published in Great Britain by
Partridge Press
Maxwelton House
Boltro Road
Haywards Heath
West Sussex

(Partridge Press is an imprint of
Transworld Publishers Limited
61-63 Uxbridge Road, Ealing, London W5)

Designed by Caroline Reeves
Typeset by BSC Print Ltd, Wimbledon
Reproduction by East Anglian Engraving Co Ltd.
Printed in Great Britain by Jolly & Barber Ltd, Rugby
Bound by Adlards/The Garden City Press, Letchworth
ISBN 1-85225-007 0

The advice and skills of specialist librarians, field study professionals and other friendly naturalists and historians have been invaluable in preparing this book.

I have also drawn heavily on the advice and skills of friendly naturalists and historians. I would like to give special thanks to: Adrian Bayley, of the Field Study Centre, Preston Mountford; Dr R. A. D. Cameron of Brimingham University; Dr Paul Whalley and his colleagues at the British Museum of Natural History entomology department; Julie Harvey, of the entomology library; the staff at the British Library's Science Reference branch, Kean Street, London; Dilwyn Roberts, county recorder, the British Trust for Ornithology; Heather James, of Dyfed Archaeological Trust; Ian Watt, of the West Wales Trust for Nature Conservation; the staff of the county archives, Carmarthen; Michael Francis, keeper at the department of maps and prints, National Library of Wales.

Contents

Preface

Writing about natural history holds many hazards and rewards. Chief among both of these attributes are the demands of observation. The best way to illustrate the problem is to quote the founding father of ecology, Charles Elton, who told the story of two boys being sent into a wood to see what they could see. After half an hour, they reported two birds, several spiders and some flies. Asked how many creatures they thought were there, one said 20, the other 100. The true number was around 10,000.

Much has been written about the practicalities of watching birds, collecting insects, luring moths or trapping mammals. But there are also psychological skills. Early in my hedge-watching career, I found that the usual journalistic impulse to rush out and answer this or that question would not work. To watch birds, you go out and wait. If ever I made a plan for the day's or night's observation, something entirely different happened.

Once these skills are more or less acquired, there is the long, detailed process of identification and recording. Plant and animal life is infinitely variable in its minutiae. The disciplines are entirely new to a casual observer, and I found them salutary. I would not have missed the opportunity to learn the skills of identifying grasses by the ligule (a small fragment at the join between the stem and leaf) or flying insects by their tiny wing-veins. I only wish I could have learned them sooner and better (see book list for the best detailed advice).

It does not do to be too full of humility, however, because the professional scientists keep on telling us amateurs that natural history is a subject in which many more observations are needed than all the highly qualified scientists available could make in their combined lifetimes. If progress is to be made in understanding the extent and interactions of the species sharing the environment with man, the matter cannot be left to the specialists. These matters are not always amenable to the disciplines of high science. A posse of trained observers and recorders is what is needed.

To try to compensate for the areas of ignorance in my natural-history background, I have drawn on literature of the past few decades to expand and interpret the events in my chosen study area. Some, where I found the explanation especially intriguing or necessary, have been quoted in detail, and these are credited either in the text or in the book list. Others have formed the background for the sensible stringing together of those delightful but tiny kaleidoscopic fragments that the observer in the field brings home. The book list on page 160 is organised by subject rather than located in the text, so that readers can satisfy any appetites for scientific enrichment that I may have stimulated.

Exploring

The lane wanders towards the morning sun along the north-facing slope of a gentle valley in West Wales. Deeply cut into the fields, the narrow road is bordered by high banks topped with broad hedges, shaggy now in August's final outpouring of summer leafage.

Here and there a full-grown tree – oak, ash or holly – marks a corner, and shades the twisting roadway. Gates give outlooks over a green interlocking of agriculture or nature, with small, many-shaped fields and hedgerows, copses and spinneys, reaching up into the nearby moorland.

At the upper end of the valley, where the stream is born out of mountain water, a stark castle ruin overlooks the farmland in jagged splendour. The scale of the pastureland of old Carmarthenshire is comfortable, designed as it was for the duties of man and horse.

The fields and hedges have not hugely changed in the 500 years since the castle was methodically demolished, although the woodlands have drastically receded. Welsh fields got small because of the laws of Hywel Dda (Howell the Good), which decreed in the 11th century a system called Gavelkind. Land was to be divided equally between a man's sons instead of being handed over entire to the elder, as under England's primogeniture laws.

Farms have stayed small partly because the hilly land is unsuited to large-scale cereal production. The quality of the patchwork fields also varies greatly because of changing drainage and soil. It is the kind of country where a rabbit can make it across a field from one sprawling hedge to another without actually getting eaten. And many of those hedges were already made when the castle fell to the sledgehammers.

While I walked today, as on most days, from the western end of the lane along its length of slightly more than half a mile, the hedgerows once again revealed themselves as more than just a pretty landscape. After seven years of part-time hedge-watching, I have come to view the inhabitants, plant and animal, of these venerable shrublands with increasing wonder. Always a new species of insect, some strange facet of bird behaviour, a disgusting orgy of slugs or a frustratingly hard-to-identify fungus presents itself during the stroll between banks and hedges higher than my head. Mysteries pile up as I peer into the depths.

One kind of habitat gives way to another, as one scattering of pink flowers is succeeded by a great splodge of nettles or hogweed. Here, near a couple of cottages and a chapel, grasses and sparrows play in the wind. A little further on, by my own cottage and garden, hazel and sycamore have grown thick enough to hide lurking robins and wrens, who click their warnings to their recently fledged young. Looking up into a giant beech tree which someone, years ago, allowed to grow up out of a hedge, I can see the reason for the alarms: a pair of carrion crows have paused on their cross-country flight.

Where hops twine and dangle on the hedge, a host of insects preen and munch – weevils, beetles, caterpillars. Unfolding a damaged leaf, I find a white-spun nursery web where several dozen spiders' eggs are gently incubating. A treeless stretch of straight hedge, which I know as the favourite haunt of dunnocks (hedge sparrows) and water voles, is quiet today; only snails are busy recycling the herbage in the sultry damp. One of them demonstrates the extraordinary power of its slime by crawling over the rose thorns. At the gate to a fallow field behind this part, where brambles, hawthorn and dog-roses tumble confusedly, I am drawn to stopping and looking over the cross-hatched countryside untidy with patches of trees, streams lined with shrubbery and relics of a hanging wood along the river.

Farther on, by the copse where the nuthatch nested, my eye is caught by the newly-formed hooked fruits of sanicle, and the new-green leaves of wood sorrel. Both are woodland plants, and I wonder why these beauties survive only here. Just beyond the copse, downhill, heavy nectars of honeysuckle and perfumes of meadow sweet attract a buzzing clientele, and chaffinches fly into the holly trees.

Now, at the halfway point, the hedges take on a subtle change as the lime-rich soil becomes more acid. Lime-hating foxgloves light the bank with brilliant, coloured spikes. At the same spot, lime-loving polypody ferns abound. Another mystery. Just past a stream that crosses underneath the lane, attracting cresses and willows, is a huge oak tree, allowed to grow to maturity perhaps as long as 75 years ago. Blue tits are calling and flying between its giant arms, pausing to pry out and grub up a few insects. Opposite, a new splattering of pink blooms has appeared: it looks like great willow herb, encouraged by recent building activity in this area which has churned up the banks and deposited stray seeds. A narrow line of trees and shrubs, which I call the spinney, runs back from this point to some tall trees, where that

pair of carrion crows have nested, and are honking now while marshalling their young for a flight.

The next stretch curves uphill. Behind a cascading growth hide a multitude of holes in the clay banks. Here is a new hole dug by a returning mammal which has spent the summer nesting in the field behind. I can see many well-trodden mammal runs, some of them protected by the bent-down trunks of the very old hedgerow trees and shrubs. They form strange shapes, these distorted tree-stems, and make fine refuges where they run horizontally on the banks.

On top of one of these high, steep banks, a rustle betrays the colony of wood mice. The stems of the hazels and hawthorns in this hedge are thin, and form a miniature bluebell wood along the top of the bank. Are the mice interested in the strawberries still hanging on to the plants across the lane?

Wood sorrel

Wood anemone

Winding through a deeper cut for a few dozen yards, the lane darkens as an overgrown section topped by two full-grown trees, ash and oak, turns it into another kind of micro-habitat, very like a deep woodland glade. Red campion flowers and wavy wood-melick grasses move in the dappled light. The trees, clad in ivy, are big enough for a family of magpies to use as a base for their plundering of eggs and fledgling populations. There on the road is the evidence, a small blackbird, dropped hastily as I approached.

The last straight section of the lane before it meets a proper road leading to the castle, is unusual. On the right is the Hall, where English nobility once found a rural bolt-hole.

The hedges and a small copse are richer here in exotic shrub species, with a wild cherry among the delights. The wrens and finches love it here, and the thrush family exploits the Hall's lawns and paddocks. But, as if to contradict the cultivated garden atmosphere in this stretch of hedgerow, many lichen-covered stumps, and a few early autumn fungi, lend a pungent woodland smell.

In its full length, three water-courses cross the lane, and water runs alongside it for a while, then under it. Because this is wet western Britain, ditches often become rushing streams. Cattle cross the lane occasionally, bringing mud and dung and tearing down pieces of the banks. Dogs chase foxes and rabbits, cats hunt in the fields and farmers come along with various pieces of machinery. Machines and lorries sometimes dig into the banks of the narrow passage-way, altering the species of plant growing there. Four householders drive their cars along bits of the lane and back, once or twice a day, dodging into gateways when they meet, negotiating potholes in winter and mud in spring.

When I first became entranced with these hedges and banks as a small section of wildlife shelter, I knew nothing about their history. Clues indicated a great age: the meandering direction, the intricate interweaving of oak, beech, ash, elder, holly and hawthorn in the hedge itself, and the deepness of the lane under steep banks.

The dimensions and profiles of these hedgerows resemble descriptions found in early Tudor period estate books in the West Country: landowners dug a ditch four feet deep and four feet wide, throwing up the soil and stones to make a bank alongside it. Then they planted the top of the bank, partly for stock-keeping, partly to consolidate the mound of earth and keep it from falling down into the ditch. In the case of boundary hedges or lanes leading to estates and other fields, a double ditch was made and a double hedgerow like this planted, forming an eight-or-nine-foot-wide lane – just right for horse and cart.

This simple idea of drainage, bank and natural fence caught on, and covered Britain with miles and miles of linear scrubland. But it was not until the second half of this century that naturalists began to realise hedgerows had become the last resort of much of the dispossessed wildlife from felled woodland, drained wetland and ploughed-up heath and meadow.

Edges and glades in woodland areas have been richest in the kinds of wildlife we appreciate: wildflowers and song-birds, for instance. Hedges, three-in-one structures of cropped woodland, sunny bank and ditch, provide an unusually stable "edge" environment, kept under control by human hand (or machine). The contorted shrubbery would not stay shrubby if it was not cut or laid from time to time, for these are tree species, and quickly become leggy and useless as a fence. The banks would turn to bramble if they were not mown and sometimes grazed, while the ditches would fill with mud if the detritus that falls into them was not thrown up again on to the banks by the roadmen.

Naturalists travel long distances to explore the wonders of tropical rain forest or incredible desert life. But the intricate interactions in the 400,000 miles of native hedgerow of Britain are probably the most taken-for-granted habitat in the world.

One reason becomes clear when you pull out a 10x magnifying glass, or use a pair of field-glasses or a telescope. As our larger animals have become locally extinct (deer excepted because of their quasi-domestication), our wildlife has shrunk. The birds of the ancient forests were dominated by large predators; those of the hedgerow landscape are predominantly small, shy songbirds. Insect life in a hedgerow is nearly as rich as that in a woodland, with its three layers of habitat – canopy, scrub and ground. And botanising in the hedgerow, in these scientific times, is made much more rewarding by minute examination of the pollinating, seed-producing and distributing techniques evolved by plants along with co-operating animals. Even mice, shrews, voles, hedgehogs and rabbits, although held in great affection, have been slightly devalued as serious subjects of study because of our anthropomorphic literary tradition. We miss all these small things as we "flash" by in a car at 15 mph, and catch only a whiff of the hedgerow perfumes.

It was children who set me to hedge-watching. As a sometime primary school science teacher, and a mother, I found myself walking in the country with enquiring five-year-olds or demanding nine-year-olds and their relentless logic. I had to find out something about hedgerow life (and that of ponds and woodlands, too) in order to feed those enthusiasms through which we were trying to teach city children how and why to read and write and employ their logic.

Perhaps it was also partly because I was brought up on a farm in Pennsylvania where a hedgerow in British terms is unknown. Clipped privet or suburban barberry are a long way from the tangle of blackthorn and rose, or even the common hawthorn hedge, of Britain. But that American farm was in those days full of odd bits of woodland and overgrown ravines where we dabbled for crayfish, swung on giant Tarzan vines and set the dogs on rabbits, ground hogs and often, to our cost, skunks.

In the years since my childhood, most of the farms I knew have changed from rotated crops and animal pastures to monocultures lacking animals, short on trees. Transplanted now for nearly 30 years to a succession of leafier habitats (including London), I have tended to take seriously the warnings of damage to wildlife caused by farming efficiency and economic determinism.

I think of Britain in terms of scenes like a Roman road near Cirencester, where the full flowering of chestnut, hawthorn and cow parsley made a white almost-tunnel; of lanes in Sussex and lanes in Devon where traffic still comes last; of holidays, walking, which made wildflowers into a hobby. But I also think of it in terms of a place in Essex where suburbanisation and agribusiness have taken a terrible toll of the wildlife surrounding a village I knew.

Britain's hedgerows are said to make up more than 300,000 acres of linear refuge – bigger than all the officially designated nature reserves. The case for keeping them intact, or at least reversing the trend of hedgerow loss, now running at about 4,000 miles a year, has been thoroughly made out.

Scientists at the Nature Conservancy's Monks Wood station (in Huntingdonshire) studied the history, ecology and decline of hedgerow mileage in great detail during the 1970s. Although small improvements have been felt in the conservation of wildlife on farms since then, the scenario has turned sour on many occasions. Confrontation, politics and "green" antagonism have reached a point where some farmers who might have seen the light are seeing red instead.

In the part of Wales where I chose to create my own refuge, change has come slower in the countryside than elsewhere. Many farmers have kept their hedgerows and copses for a variety of reasons: conservatism, enjoyment of the ancient art of hedge-laying, lack of capital for fencing and grubbing-out, and lack of incentive, since cereal crops (with the premium they put on large fields) are not profitable here in hilly land. One 70-acre owner on the borders of the lane can point to the robin's nest in the bank, and greet the return of the lapwing, as enthusiastically as the most dedicated naturalist. And a local dairyman reaps a useful and rewarding harvest of walking-sticks from the materials of his hedges.

But few remember hedges as a source of timber or firewood; none has encouraged full-grown trees to interrupt the hedge-clipping machines. And some have slowly but relentlessly damaged the environment while seeking higher returns on small dairy and sheep enterprises. Grants for "improvements" have played their part; so has lack of knowledge of the newer grants for preserving cover.

Timber merchants eager for the profit from pitprops needed for coal-mines, have almost totally destroyed the remnants of old deciduous woodlands of the counties of Mid and West Wales. Motives like the fashion for the Crewkerne method of grazing cattle (by using electric fences to move them along a series of land-strips) are resulting in many minor hedge adjustments which add up to a continual impoverishment of plants and animals.

As the land is farmed with increasing intensity, otters and a heronry have vanished. Rooks have had to spread out over the fields instead of making large rookeries. Badgers are rare, and hedgehogs are seldom seen except dead.

In writing down events in the lane that I have chosen to study, my only aim is to find out about the wildlife that is there, but I will no doubt be documenting the effects of changes on the countryside as they come along. In the years I have been glancing at it sidelong, I have tended to become more amazed at how well agriculture and nature fit together. Many of the wild creatures we now enjoy are those which have adapted to man anyhow – the same birds you find in the city or suburbs, the same plants in large parks, waste placcs and riversides.

Hedgerows cannot be considered in isolation, of course. Few species live only in the hedgerow. The lane will merely provide a focus, acting as it does like some kind of Main Street in the immediate farmland neighbourhood, used at times by many, permanent home for a few. I plan to look, above all, for examples of the close dependence of one species on the other, of the way the snail and nestling, weed, shrub and flower fit – or does not fit – into the

The copse

teeming scheme; and the way the whole structure of this small piece of landscape responds to events.

I chose this particular double hedgerow after walking many miles of lane and pasture. The annual cutting makes a roadside hedgerow more interesting, and this one has just the right balance between rampant growth and management to produce a varied mix of common species, plus a few rarities. I often wish I could also study the little lane a few miles from here where in May a carpet of ramsons (wild garlic) blooms magically, or the busier roadside where unusual rarities – butterbur, squinancywort and early purple orchid – inexplicably thrive.

I am sure to raise more questions than I answer. The goal is not to list every living thing discovered, but to focus on as many interesting happenings as I am lucky enough to witness, and on the connections, the developments and the chains of life and death in this robust but responsive environment.

These are the concerns of the 20th-century naturalist, both amateur and scientist, and I shall be relying heavily on the back-up information of the latter's published works.

Scientific studies have failed to prove that hedgerows actually benefit human agriculture in the long run, although it is known that richly varied environments are more stable than monocultures. A single crop is prone to fall victim to explosions of a single pest. As the Monks Wood research pointed out, the presence of the enormous variety of insect life in a hedgerow could, for all we know, protect the crops of grass and cereals from plagues by single predators. Or the hedges could, as many farmers fear, provide predators with "homes in their larders", as in the case of rabbits. These are issues of such complexity that by the time the answers are learned in purely scientific terms, it could be too late.

Ecology is an untidy subject, and hedgerows are an anomalous kind of habitat where wild growth and human adjustments are in a delicate balance. The words of Gilbert White, the great 18th-century naturalist, who spent 30 years on his Natural History of Selbourne, are still apposite: "Though there is endless room for observation in the field of nature, which is boundless, yet investigation (where a man endeavours to be sure of his facts) can make but slow progress; and all that one could collect in years would go into a very narrow compass."

Twentieth-century science is prone to generalise. The specific lives and deaths of some of the creatures and growths in a half-mile of country lane may not have a high statistical significance. They are important, nevertheless, in creating an awareness of the interactions between all the elements of life on Earth. Learning to enjoy the variety and liveliness of it all could be the key to hanging on to what is beneficial in the countryside.

August-September

FIRST FORAGING

August 1. The air is full of alarm calls as young birds feed in family flocks up and down the hedgerow. A party of robins is on the sunny grass just inside the cottage garden. Startled, the parents fly into the hedge and click loudly, but one of the two young birds panics and takes shelter in an isolated bush. Squatting there, it fluffs out its new feathers and lowers its head, round robin eye peering out at me. The clicking reaches anguished proportions before, first the timid juvenile, and finally the whole family, fly to thicker foliage in a side hedge.

Opposite, in part of the hedgerow that borders a cow pasture, five wrens are feeding on an assortment of sheltering insects. They set up alarms, this time a faster set of clicking sounds, loud and agitated. One by one the young wrens, now in their fully fledged feathers, fly back to the overgrown hedge which serves as the chief roosting place. Then the two adults fly back too.

For a few weeks now, these early foragings by parties of young birds have been unfolding their small dramas. Five blackbirds, splodgy brown coats betraying them as young ones, are learning to use a fruit garden for their pleasure. As nearly always happens, one of the young males gets caught in the netting. Raucous *chinking*, along with a softer *pooh-pooh*, are exchanged between the older birds as they fly up to an overgrown patch of hedge.

Blackbirds go on looking after their young for longer than most birds, for there is perhaps more for these highly adapted omnivores to learn in the way of feeding strategies. A pair which bred in the copse often lead a family party in the cow pasture next door, searching the grass for invertebrates and moving and calling in an almost ritualised way. Another day,

eight blackbirds, young and old, are flying between the hedgetops and the edge of the lane to feed on a collection of seeds and insects which gathers there.

A little group of dunnocks, meanwhile, make their way on foot in the middle of the lane, zigzagging to eye each potential morsel directly from their side-facing eyes. The young have already learned the trick of picking up food easily from the hard surface where it has crawled, rolled or been deposited by hoof and tyre.

Down by the copse, another loud robin encounter sounds like about ten birds as I approach. The rhythm of these alarm clicks is quite different from the normal alarms of autumn and winter or later in the spring. This loud and continual alarming turns out to come from only two birds, apparently the still-paired parents of young ones whose flutterings I could just glimpse through the foliage.

Only a few days ago I saw these robins still feeding young in the thick hedgebank bordering the copse. I know the male because it exhibits a form of melanism, a few dark, almost black, feathers among the light grey underbelly feathers.

The hedge is a fine place for young fledglings on their earliest outings. Last month I witnessed the fledging of four young wrens, although I cannot say I actually saw them. Passing the hedgerow, I heard a wren alarm and some food-calling notes (piping, soft sounds). As I put my face to the hedge-bottom (the top of the bank is just slightly higher than eye-level here), I could barely see the fluttering of wings in the deep growth of the hedge while an adult perched on guard in the protruding ash shrub overhead. The fledglings were having a "walk" inside the hedge about ten feet from the nest I knew was there from the frequent visits of feeding adults. When another adult arrived with a beakful of food, the calling stopped.

Fledgling robins

There is so much bird food around at this time of year that they only need feed for a few hours a day, and unless I get up early I can hardly catch them at it. The seasons for caterpillars, adult insects, invertebrates, seeds and a few first fruits are all coinciding just as they are needed by the birds.

Other resident birds are forming flocks, and ranging far and wide to establish new feeding grounds for enlarged populations. Chaffinches, long since finished their brood-raising, scatter to the woods and back, using their characteristic roller-coaster flight down the hedgerows. Goldfinches continue to range through an enlarged territory to spot their specific seed foods from high points in the hedges and trees. And greenfinches make themselves scarce as the moulting carries on.

Suddenly a pair of marsh tits fire off their explosive call, *pitchooo*, from the hedge-top. They take off, calling, down the lane. These are not the only visitors from the woodland. While the garden warblers head down to the scrub oaks from the hedgerow, a pair of wood warblers peer out of a hawthorn bush beside the lane, on the same sort of all-change principle. Six jays come out of the wood to tear up the

peace with their harsh calls. A chiffchaff recently joined the abbreviated dawn chorus on a day trip from the beech woods.

Large numbers of starlings have absorbed the pair which bred in the buildings at the Hall, and their recently fledged young, into a flock; and willow warblers which bred in the thicker taller hedges of the nearby farmland suddenly achieve large numbers, flying straight at me now and then with their distinctive *phooeet* calls.

All these comings and goings are recognised as having more than one function. Birds do learn how to feed from other birds – witness the way tits have learned how to open milk bottles, and magpies follow milk floats to prey on the eggs. More complex is the settling of population questions, allied as they are to the availability of food and space.

Blue tits seem to have exploded, and the local wren population has more than tripled. Robins, they say, can live as long as 11 years. If they did, and each pair were to raise, say, ten birds from three broods a year, it would take only six years to produce a million robins! A study in the 1920s indicated the actual average length of a robin's life to be around two years and ten months (Burkitt 1924-26, from Lack,

Chaffinch

Robin

Nuthatch

Starling

Song
thrush

Blackbird

Juvenile and recently fledged birds

Garden warbler

Wood warbler

Willow warbler

Marsh tit

1965). But later studies have found even higher death rates. For the blackbird population, just fewer than two young per pair out of the four that reach fledgling stage will survive to breed on. The percentage of this species which dies each year fluctuates between 35 and 65 (Simms, 1978).

Researchers agree that one thing which keeps bird populations fairly steady is the business of territory, related as it is to the availability of food and, later on, breeding space. At this time of year, breeding is a long way off, but you can watch the species working out who gets a piece of the family homestead, and who migrates out to some other part of the countryside. Those that lose out entirely, die.

I watched the other day while a wren flew out of a hedge on the garden side, and flew to the intersecting hedge – a shaggy, overgrown place with two giant beech trees growing out of it. This hedge, with a deep ditch on one side of it and lawn on the other, is the epicentre of a large wren territory extending from the cottage to the copse.

The wren I was watching flew back to another hedge behind the cottage, then quickly back to the exact part of the lane hedge where I first saw it. A few minutes later the triangle was traced again, then again and again. The bird kept this up for more than half an hour, and was joined part of the time by another wren. The two of them explored boundaries for several days, much as chaffinches do in the breeding season.

Soon the wren population begins to decline, and the resident wrens put together their fragments of summer song. The wren answer to population pressure is to carve up the large territories into smaller ones. Wrens and robins are the first among our residents to establish an autumn territory, and they are the only birds in the hedgerow community to sing right now.

Most species, like the finches and tits, approach the immediate problem of food by foraging in flocks, or ranging widely over the countryside. Blue tits and great tits have already begun to form flocks and move around. A day or two ago, about fifteen of them, small yet as tit flocks go, flew down the hedgerow like so many vacuum cleaners, inspecting every bud and leaf-axil.

Efficient feeding over a large territory is a matter of life and death to these small creatures, which desperately need to increase their bodyweight before winter. Many will go elsewhere, perhaps in an irruption, one of those mass movements that bring dozens, or even hundreds, of tits flitting excitedly into the garden, and pecking at everything from window-putty to bark before whirling on.

Watching these tits, most of which bred near the lane this year, as they practise their calls, and experiment with different feeding niches, one thing becomes clear. All parts of the hedgerow landscape are necessary to birds like these as the different species of insect come and go, the different twigs and branches become rich with food.

August, when the new bird community is sorting itself out, and food is plentiful, is almost like a rehearsal for the survival strategies of winter. The new generation will survive only by exploiting all the features of the farming landscape — hedges, tall trees, ditches, grass and lane, as well as the remaining small relics of woodland.

RIPENING

August 6. Everything is happening at once. The hedges are at their fullest and shaggiest, the banks an outpouring of flowers and ferns and shrubbery, while climbers tumble over the whole untidy mixture, brambles cascading down and hops curling upwards. The sound of the bush-cricket, encountered but never seen, and the overpowering nectar of honeysuckle and perfume of meadowsweet, endorse the sultry fecundity, while caterpillars, snails and slugs rasp silently at the dark foliage.

End products are competing with beginnings: seeds are shed on to drifts of new seedlings from earlier growths; buds and new-formed nuts swell up on the same hazel twigs, and late blooms catch the light among the dense foliage. The hedgerow in August is a starting, finishing, budding, reproducing, eating-up and recycling organism.

Most spectacular of all right now are the seeds. In the cycle of flowering plants, seeds are the beginning of a year-long lottery for *lebensraum* in the fertile banks — a lottery that will determine the ground layer of the whole complex ecology.

Some plants seem bent on winning by buying up all the tickets. Conspicuous are docks and sorrels, with their plumes of blackening seed-carpels. Each plant of these Rumex species can have as many as 25,000 seeds, which simply drop from the triangular pods.

Umbellifers, cow parsley and hogweed, with upright clusters of white flowers turning now to flat seeds, play the numbers game as well. They too use gravity, with very little help from the wind, which is probably why they do so much better on main roads with their wide, flat verges, than on these hedgebanks beside a one-time cart-track. Most of their seeds fall from the tall, swaying plants on to the tarmac, and get eaten.

These weed heavies are in contrast to some of the prettiest miniatures of the hedgerow, which also go in for large numbers of seeds, but instead take to the air, with mixed success.

Common spotted orchids have appeared off and on through the years on the north-facing side of the cottage hedge bordering rough grass. The colony is small, and restricted to a strip of about 10 yards. The pale petals, marked by delicate purple patterns, are withering now, and the tiny, dust-like seed is setting. Orchid strategy for increasing is to make seeds so light that the winds can carry them to some faraway spot, where they may happen to find just the right amount of light for germination and prospering.

Alas, these choosy delights seldom increase. The well-grazed pastureland and crowded hedgebanks are too competitive, and this colony does not grow. In fact, a group of early purple orchids near a pasture where cows cross the lane and pause to graze, has recently disappeared.

The other miniature that specialises in wind dispersal is the familiar broad-leaved willow-herb, with small pink trumpets surrounding bright white styles. (It is a distant relation to the more flamboyant willowherb of railway banks.) Their successive blooms all along the lane have nearly finished, and long seed-pods like curved matchsticks have formed on their stems.

While I watch, the sections of the long pod split from the top and fall back, exposing and pulling taut a ladder-like arrangement of downy threads supporting small black seeds.

Meadow cranesbill

Suddenly a squally wind snatches them up, and the down floats along the lane trailing the seed.

Flowering plants which rely on a strategy of lightweight seeds and wind are often those which have strict requirements of light and shade, and thus need to travel far in search of it. Most hedgerow and scrubland plants which grow where competition is keen, go in for heavier seeds with more nutrition packed into them. The heavyweights can live on their own food materials packed into the large seeds until they grow big enough to beat out the competition for light and soil-nutrients.

Some slightly heavier seeds also have ingenious dispersal devices. Explosive techniques are favoured by some earlier flowering plants such as lesser celandine and the cresses, which shoot seeds like arrows. But the pea-like vetches that are blackening and drying now in the hedge-banks burst with some force when they are twisted corkscrew fashion. The pods of vetches are so constructed that they dry out assymetrically and twist open, spraying seed to the right part of the bank – at least some of the time.

The most subtle masters of the art of seed-popping in the hedgerow must be the violets. On this August day the early-flowering dog violets have long since made their bid for immortality, but not many seedlings result from their early flowers. To make up for this failure, the violets hedge their bets with a late-season cleistogamous flower. The capsule I found today on a dog violet is in effect an unopened bud where the flower has ripened and fertilised within the bud, producing seed from asexual reproduction. When I opened the capsule, I found 24 white seeds about the size of a child's pearls. When these are ripe, the capsule will split, making three small boat-shapes, which then dry at the edges first. As they dry, they put the squeeze on the pod and pop the seeds out.

The prize for flinging seeds about must surely go to the crane's-bills. The meadow crane's-bill, the bigger of our two geraniums in the hedges, has now dropped its intense blue cups, and made pods looking almost like onion-domes with spires. This perennial plant grows only on a side lane where chapel-goers turn in to worship, but in the lane itself, as in nearly every garden and waste space, is the annual herb Robert, its relative.

Again, the dispersal mechanism depends on a tension created by the drying-out process. The pods split from the bottom upwards, staying attached to the styles at the top. As they split in sections with a seed for each section, they create five spring-like strips, with the seed on the free ends. In due course they are flipped outwards by the springs, flying as far as seven yards, according to records. The long strip, or awn, stays with the seed, and helps to anchor it. When rains come, the moisture makes the seed's case unroll, and buries it.

The strange part is that the perennial members of the family which produce the winning toss of seven yards do not seem to spread widely, while herb Robert brightens the lane in drifts all along the way. As so often with botanic subjects, the variables and factors for success are tricky to calculate.

Some wildflowers hold their seeds in a form of pepperpot which spills them out gradually as the wind bends the plant. The fading petals of red campion, which still brighten the dark, woodsy section of the lane, grow on bladder-like structures. As the petals fall, the swellings at the base of the female flowers become receptacles for the hard, round seeds. Held upright until they are ripe, the seeds finally roll out to find a bit of *lebensraum*. They are like poppy seed-pods, but without the more elaborate escape holes.

Columbine has a cluster of five upright, elongated pods to hold black, oval seeds until they break apart and spill their interesting genetic mixtures where they may.

A spiller of seeds in championship numbers is the foxglove. Pointed pods are nearly ready now to open, this time held sideways until the pods dry and peel back, bursting to release hundreds of tiny sand-grain seeds. One plant has been recorded at 750,000 seeds. (Not by me!)

Seeds evolved to take advantage of animals are produced in these hedgebanks. Sanicle is growing on both sides of the lane by the copse where distinctly woodland varieties thrive. The flowers of sanicle, clusters of white star-bursts with long stamens and styles, have been giving way this week to small, hard fruits covered in hooks. The hooked fruits are designed for dispersal by the kind of mammals which made their holes and grazed in ancient beech woods, boar and badger among them, no doubt. The hooked seeds stay on the plants for many weeks, or until the flail comes to cut them down. The patch of sanicle, like the colony of orchids, never enlarges. In fact, over the years the sanicle and other old woodland flowers have dwindled, while the most prevalent hooked-fruited plants in the hedgebanks go on multiplying: wood avens are everywhere.

One clue to the difference is that wood avens' hooks are long relics of the styles attached individually to each seed in a bunch. Sanicle's burrs are single seeds with many hooks attached to the covers. Wood avens have an advantage in sheer numbers, plus ingenuity, although I doubt that either plant depends totally on mammal dispersal. If so, the wood avens' seeds must drop into the undergrowth to be picked up by small mammals, while sanicle seeds wither on the stem waiting for the locally rare larger mammals.

All this plant fecundity is just what the birds need when their populations are high. A seed that disappears inside a bird may never emerge, or may be ground to dust in its gizzard, but thousands of seeds, small and large, are dropped, or get through the bird, to plant themselves under popular bird perches such as gates and overgrown-hedgerow saplings. Before long, in autumn, a later crop of seeds will be distributed by birds. Hips and haws, blackberries and nuts, now just emerging green, ripen as the seeds of flowering plants are finished.

The fight for space in these lively banks involves a huge number of variables. Most of the plants there can reproduce underground vegetatively, and the roots and shoots of the hedge shrubs themselves thrive without maturing to seed. The proportion of seeds that live to grow on is as low as five per cent, anyway. But seeds play their part each year as the balance of plant life changes, and some old friends disappear, or others reappear. The basis of the hedgerow's resilience as a habitat is the very variety of plants and their mechanisms. In a bad year for one, another fills the gap.

Later the same day, the flail comes and cuts down the hedgebanks' luxuriant growth. Flowers, seeds, buds, tendrils and shoots are lying, greying, on the banks. It is an event of such proportions that I must let some days or weeks go by before trying to assess the effects of the holocaust.

Columbine

Wood avens

Garlic mustard

Herb Robert

Hogweed

Broad leaved willowherb

Violet

Common Vetch

BUTTERFLIES

August 10. A warm day follows a cool night. At 11am, after the birds have finished their morning feeding, two hedge brown butterflies are spreading their softly patterned wings on hazel leaves. They have chosen a stretch of hedge bordering an overgrown pasture near the chapel end of the lane.

There they stay for long minutes, and half-an-hour later, when I return, they are still there, still doing nothing. Their slightly clubbed antennae move occasionally; their shaggy scales reflect the species' inherited mosaic of warm orange and deep browns; their sharply outlined double false eyes are revealed to admirer and predator. One is a female, the other shows the diagonal slash of dark scales against the orange that hold the male pheromones, the scent it will release when it is ready to attract a female.

But now these insects are operating their all-important solar-heating system. As they sun-bathe, the veins in their broad wings are collecting the sun's heat, and letting it diffuse through their night-cooled bodies. Before they start on the most vigorous activity of the day, collecting nectar for energy, they see to their storehouse of heat, for a loss of heat wastes energy.

Later, I see the hedge browns again on crowded blackberry vines near the gatepost. Their wings are folded high above their bodies, and their long proboscis-tongues are extended on to the bramble flowers at the base of the stamens, probing the pollen-crusted flowers. Their traditional name, "gatekeeper", has a typical hedgerow explanation. Blackbirds have a habit of perching on gateposts, and dropping seeds, usually those of bramble, hawthorn and rose. So brambles grow by gates, and it follows that hedge browns forage at gates, flying methodically from flower to flower like bright, fluttering toll-keepers. Thus the interlocking of hedgerow species enters the folklore of names.

Why is it that I can predict not only the happenings at the gates, but which stretch of hedgerow the butterflies are going to be exploiting? Why do the exotic red flashes of the red admirals appear down by the stream or in the garden? Why are the bright tortoiseshells more likely in the overgrown shrubbery?

Butterflies have achieved a frivolous romantic image in human eyes, but they are just as intricately tied to the hedgerow's complex ecology as those seed-transporting birds, or the brambles themselves which provide food for so many different fauna.

These hedges are in the lightest, sunniest part of the lane, where all the mature trees have been cut down to stumps long since. The south-east-facing bank borders a derelict cow pasture, damp and weedy, sloping down to the remnant of a hanging wood and river. The long grass makes this field a mecca for all kinds of insects. But even before the field was left fallow, this stretch was a butterfly favourite, and almost the only place to see the various browns in large numbers: meadow browns, hedge browns and ringlets. Later on, skippers will come, too.

The morning sun falls on this bank at a near-perpendicular angle as the summer wanes. The opposite side of the lane is moist and shady, with a convenient muddy ditch where butterflies can dabble for their mineral needs. Both sides are especially rich in flowering plants, and the hedges are made of a variety of hazel, hawthorn, ash, oak, beech, elder and blackthorn.

The grass at the back plays the crucial part in the life history of the browns. All three species use it for egg-laying in September, then the young caterpillars use it for food before they overwinter in the depths, foraging occasionally on warm winter days. Finally, in early summer when they become "feeding and growing tubes", as Dr Paul Whalley calls them in his Guide to Butterfly Watching (1980), they start eating the grass in large amounts, and spin their cocoons to pupate among the stems.

Browns certainly fly in other parts of the lane, but in one summer's records the sightings were three times as frequent in the fallow-field stretch as in their other main territory, another south-to-south-east-facing section beyond the stream.

Butterflies do hold territories, defending them against trespassers of the same species, exploiting them for food and using them for courtship and egg-laying, as birds do. I have twice witnessed an "attack" by one hedge brown on another, and often see encounters between males and females, which could be courtship flights. This piece of hedge, about 20 yards straddling the gate, has provided the right combination of sun-angles, moisture, protection and food supply to encourage a colony of browns to thrive from year to year.

Hedge brown
(gatekeeper)

Ringlet

Meadow brown

Some kinds of butterfly do not move far from one generation to the next, unlike the migratory species or the stronger flying whites, which fly from smallholding to smallholding preying on the cabbages.

It is possible that the brown-butterfly populations are there partly for historical reasons, and that, like many of the plant colonies in old hedgerows, they would not be replaced easily if the environment were radically altered. An example of this hazard is provided by the brown hairstreaks, studied in Huntingdonshire in the 1970s (Pollard, Hooper, and Moore 1974). They were found to have declined to the point of near extinction locally as the post-war removal of woods and hedgerows in that area destroyed their habitat.

In the same piece of territory where I see the hedge browns, is a nest of wrens, at least one dunnock's nest, a chaffinch nest and a favourite roosting place for blackbirds. If the caterpillars of the browns escape these voracious feeders during the bird-breeding season, the adult butterflies face the blue tit population, and an even more deadly enemy, spiders.

The other day I watched a spider trying to trap them. One of the large, striped-legged Theridiidae struggled in the brisk afternoon breeze to fashion one of those untidy, random-looking webs favoured by this family of spiders. It was hurrying, and flinging its almost invisible silk between shoots of blackthorn and hawthorn, which protruded out of the banks, so that the web would become as efficient as a trawl-net fishing for butterflies and other insects flying along the hedgerow. The spider worked continually and rapidly, in spite of being buffeted about. A few feet away, a couple of hedge browns struggled too, keeping their folded wings edgewise to the wind like tacking sailboats.

I watched, convinced that the butterflies were doomed, but happily they gave up the struggle to feed and flew over the hedge to shelter for the night before they reached the spider's fine threads, barely visible now in the fading light. The spider had lost its frantic race.

Butterflies have two kinds of protection from their bird and mammal predators. They are adapted either to hide from them by camouflage, or to frighten them by flashing loud colour or startling patterns which the predator has associated with a bad taste or danger.

The survival tactics of the browns fall between these ruses. Not specially bright or nasty-tasting, they do sometimes resemble a brown leaf when their wings are folded upright, with the forewings' two bright little eyespots covered by the hindwings. If I come within vision of their compound eyes, which pick up small movements, the forewing spots appear in a flash.

Nobody has measured the adaptive success of devices like these, although the "eyes" of more flamboyant species, like the peacock butterfly, have been studied and found effective. It is hard to imagine what the ringlets, with their scattered spots, are trying to imitate. All these markings evolved over the long period of butterflies' history, and some of them may have been selected by an environment no longer extant.

The common butterflies in these hedgerows may not represent a particularly large bulk of food for the predatory food chain. Moths in their larval stage are in another category altogether. Perhaps the extinction of the butterflies would not remove a highly significant link in hedgerow life, although some day-flying creatures of this kind could be useful to certain species of bird, mammal or spider. Yet they fill a distinct niche in the temperate ecology, and have done so since the time of dinosaurs, and long before man. For all we know, they may be just as crucial to the survival of some of their fellow inhabitants as the grasses they feed on.

Do Not Pass Go

August 18. It is a little more than a week since the flail came and mangled the hedgebanks. Later on, the farmers themselves will cut the hedges with their own flail-cutters. Meanwhile, the steep banks have been mowed with a machine designed for masticating heavy shrubbery. In one pass along each side, the machine can do the half-mile in three or four hours. Until two years ago (we were among the last lanes in the county to be mechanised), a lengthsman used to come and spend a day or two in the neighbourhood with his sickle, hook and spade.

Each lengthsman, often arriving on a bicycle with his tools attached, had responsibility for a given ten miles of roadside, and managed it as if he were the owner. He cut the grass and herbs neatly and consistently at the same height, a few inches from earth. Tough shrubby growth, such as wild roses, blackthorn, bramble and hawthorn, which scramble down from the hedges, were kept in check. Plants with low overwintering rosettes, or other low-growth points, went unscathed, and occasional bright blooms would be left to continue their ripening.

The machine has done a different kind of job: where the bank juts out, it carves into the soil, stripping down to clay and hard roots. Many perennials are uprooted, marjoram, red campion and betony among them. When the machine comes to hollows and corners, shrubby plants are allowed to grow on. At the top of the bank where the ground levels off, the shoots of hedge plants, and runners of bramble, are hardly touched. Beech, oak, hazel and hawthorn are left to grow down from the hedge on to the bank, stimulated, if anything, by the slight pruning.

All along the banks, the colours of the climax season are gone. The purples, reds, blues and whites of foxglove, campion and columbine, of betony, sanicle and scabious, have been chopped off along with the grass, and lie rotting now among the remnants.

For a botaniser, it is shattering. The county council gets hundreds of complaining telephone calls every year as the flails make their rounds, 100-strong. But now, after a few rains and some warm sun, the danger of reacting too emotionally to any biological event is demon-strated. The mulch has washed down to the roots, and is being rapidly recycled by snails, slugs and insects. Flattened marjoram, for one example, has not only survived, but regrown in its former swathes, and is already budding again, ready to bloom. Other plants have simply shed their seed a little early, to ripen and germinate in due course.

Taking stock of the damage, I can work out some of the trends likely to be associated with the flail as the years go by, but it is a hazardous form of prediction because of the almost infinite variables of timing and environmental influences.

The most vulnerable plants should, in theory, be the annuals. If the head is chopped off a plant that reproduces only from seed before the seeds are set, it will obviously die out. My lists of plants in these hedgerows reveal only a handful of purely annual species. Wild flowers nowadays, almost by definition, are mostly perennials, with enough energy stored in their roots or rhizomes or bulbs to come back every year, for a few years at least.

Whether this is due to the years of hand-cutting, or the heavy competition from successful perennials, we cannot know. The surviving species include herb Robert, which was already spreading seed when the flail came; common vetch, a pinkish purple pea-like flower; nipplewort, a ubiquitous yellow-flowered upright plant, and a white umbellifer, upright hedge parsley.

The flail has not bothered these plants much. Herb Robert has a low growing point, and a long growing season. It blooms and seeds all summer and autumn, and already great swatches of pink blooms testify to its resilience. Common vetch is also low-growing enough to be sending forth new buds this week. On the other hand hedge parsley, the late-blooming successor to cow parsley and ground elder in the white umbellifer family, is rare here, and may well be affected by the timing of the cut.

Among perennials, there is another category of plant which is unhurt by the flail. Creepers or runners like strawberry and its lookalike, the barren Potentilla sterilis, both grow better after the cut. The key growth-points are at ground level, and shade from taller growths has been diminished.

All kinds of other creeping plants have been given a boost by the elimination of some of the light-snatching taller growths. Creeping jenny finds its way right out on to the paving, feathery silverweed leaves and vigorous creeping cinquefoil are thriving in the lower reaches of both banks. Violets (the dog violet has recently replaced the sweet violet, as it has done in many hedgerows) are so disdainful of the flail that they have even produced a bloom or two this week. Wood sorrel is making a comeback in an area opposite the copse where taller, thicker foliage has been cut.

All these plants which have simply dodged the flail, and other robust customers, will thrive on the new regime, but there is a category of wildflower whose range is already restricted, and will have little chance of spreading. Red campion, one of my favourite hedgerow plants, is in this group of worrying flowers. Down in the deepest part of the lane, under a shady oak near the Hall, is a bank where red campion and wood melick evoke a woodland glade in midsummer. The grass had shed its seed when the cut was made, but the campion

was almost all still in bloom. Already there is less campion this year than last. It seems likely that this is one plant that will dwindle, or certainly not increase, as it is forced to rely on its root renewal for next year's growth. The lengthsman's cut and timing were kinder to campion than the grinding blades.

Columbine had just finished blooming, and the seeds were not ripe, when the flail came and knocked them into the gutter. It seems likely that few of them will germinate, although the parent plants will survive. Searching the banks after the cut, I could not even find any seeds to save for myself. The pity is that the columbine flowers in this winding section of hedgerow near the Hall tend to sport some of the most beautiful colours I have seen, ranging from pale pink-and-white to a deep brownish purple. This variety depends on seeding, and many flying pollinators depend on the flowers.

Foxglove was at a crucial stage when the flail came. Limited already by the lime content of the soil (this lane is a mixture of basic and acid soils, ranging from more lime on the western end, to more acidic near the Hall), they are biennial bloomers anyway, with strict require-

ments of light, shade and drainage. The banks do seem to be liberally sprinkled with the leaves of future years' growth, so perhaps enough of the foxglove's thousands of tiny seeds will survive each year's cutting to keep them going. I hope so – not only for the sake of the sight of their fiery spikes as the red evening light strikes them, but because they are important to bees and other flying pollinators.

Butterflies at this time of year have little enough in the way of nectar-producing flowers. Hedge browns are pollen-lovers, satisfied with what they can suck from bramble stamens, but other late-brooded adults, like the speckled wood, may find short rations in a mangled hedgebank. Bees have good years and bad. In a rainy summer, the cutting down of the wild bees' nectaries at the only warm, dry spell in August, could be a disaster.

A few plants seem especially vulnerable. Betony, a favourite of the 19th-century herbalist, Richard Folkard, is losing ground every year. A tall, straight stem ending in a cluster of small purple flutes, betony is continually visited by insects. Another increasingly rare plant is the devil's bit scabious, which was just starting to bloom in a meadow-like stretch of bank. A few more may come later, but these bright blue pincushions are receding each year, to give

only an occasional sparkle among the brambles.

It is the encouragement of tough shrubby shoots by merely pruning the tops off them that leaves the heaviest mark on the hedgebank when the flail comes. I cannot remember seeing thickets of blackthorn on the banks themselves, or so many tree species from the hedge, spilling over to form dense mats in place of flowery banks.

Gradually, the shrub plants, especially bramble, seem to be overshadowing many of the tender, flowering things. Small delights such as the pale enchanter's nightshade, and sanicles, with their small white starbursts, could be doomed. It is all rather like a biological game of Monopoly.

In at least one county of England (Suffolk), the highway maintenance men and machines cut the grass verges on a schedule which suits the local wildflowers best. The dates are organised by the local Naturalists' Trust. Small differences in timing and method can make all the difference to the future of plant species. Even so robust a plant community as a hedgebank has its fragile members. Remembering that the banks must be cut (otherwise they would go back to scrub entirely), we still do not know enough about the delicate and complex balances of our farmland ecology to risk a policy of ruthless mechanisation without keeping tabs on its effects.

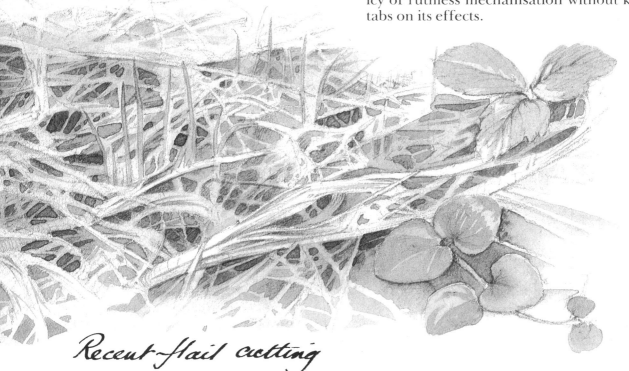

Recent flail cutting

BASKING

August 26. At the base of an oak-stump, a female common lizard lies curled up in a small depression she has made in the moss. Sheltered from the north-west wind, and screened from predators by surrounding leafiness, the creature evokes a blissful impression as it suns itself.

The lizards in the hedgebanks appear with astonishing predictability in April. They always show themselves first by the cottage gate, where a stony bank provides a warm reflecting surface facing the afternoon sun. During most of the summer, they spread out invisible in the grass, then retreat under the stones when the temperature gets too cold for even these hardiest of European lizards.

The lizards come out more in bad summers, when the brief appearance of warm sunshine gives them a chance to warm their cooled skin. The females must get themselves up to a temperature at which their hormones will flow, and reproductive organs swell, before they can breed. They can even adjust their breeding, and the gestation period itself, if the weather is unfavourable. But there is not much chance of seeing the young in the wild: the clever lizard finds deep shelter in these hedgebanks for launching its vulnerable live young. This is not an egg-laying species.

As far as I can tell, lizards have an easy life in this salubrious habitat: sun at any angle desired, plenty of deep foliage when it gets too hot, insect food in abundance and not too many predators since the stoat and weasel population has declined. The lizards do not seem to mind traffic passing a few inches from their noses, nor being stared at enviously by curious humans who enjoy watching their swift movements and languid basking.

LATE TREASURES

September 2. I love the way the dying summer produces some of the most interesting and delicate blooms – a few small, bright petals gleaming suddenly among the masses of deep leaves. For some time now, enchanter's nightshade has been gradually paling. When these flowers first bloom in August, they are a pale pink, the tiny trumpets only to be appreciated through a 10x lens. Then they fade to off-white. Marjoram is having a flush of blossom right now, too, with tall stalks of pink-purple florets clustered together. Being knocked down or cut by the flail has bothered these fragrant and colourful herbs not a bit.

It seems to be the season for the trumpet-shape in flowers, with betony reviving in a stretch by the fallow field. Slender purple florets are splendidly adapted to the long probosci of the wasps and flies of the season, which could explain the profusion of trumpets. Devil's bit scabious, a comparative rarity nowa-

days, has clusters of narrow tubes with protruding stamens to entice the late-season
insects. This plant only grows in the old lane,
while its relative, field scabious, grows on the
busier roadsides.

The other day I saw my first example this
year of the glamorous flowers of woody nightshade (bitter sweet). The deep purple bells,
with their bright yellow clappers, glow like
treasures among the shrubs of the hedge. They
quickly turn to luscious bright red, but highly
poisonous, berries. Waxy cups with feathery
stamens are cradled in the smooth broad leaves
of tutsan, a member of the St John's wort family, and a liberal sprinkling of new blooms of
creeping cinquefoil gives the banks some spots
of yellow colour.

Late blooms of earlier species are about: violets looking battered in the early gales, strawberry and Potentilla sterilis giving a vaguely
springlike look, and the odd single bloom of
purple common vetch. Bramble vines are
going through the whole sequence of deep
pink and white flowers with bright yellow stamens, clustered reddish fruit and seeds. Gardeners go to immense trouble to plant species
which will flower in sequence, and give pleasure at all times. The hedgerow does it
without thinking. I have even seen a
sad, battered orchid blooming in an
October Force Ten gale.

Devils' bit scabious

Betony

Tutsan

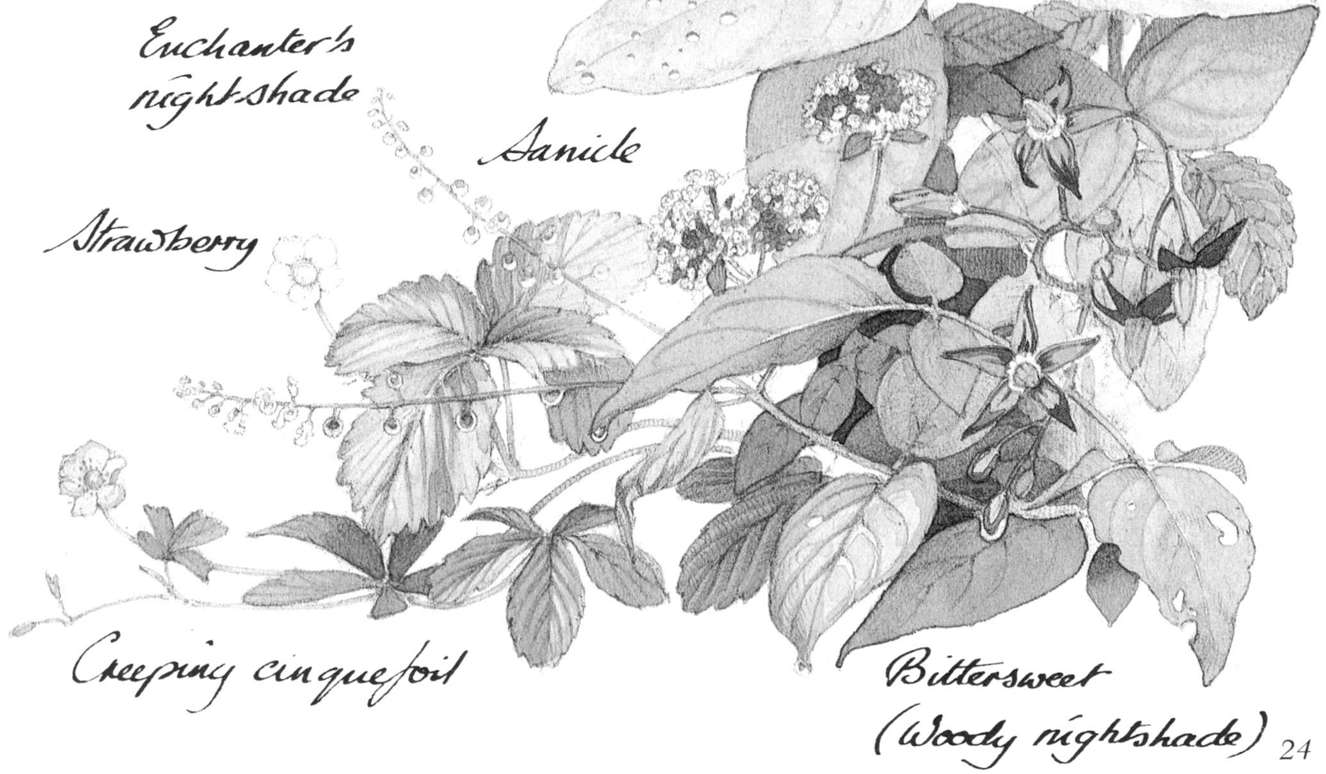

Enchanter's
nightshade

Sanicle

Strawberry

Creeping cinquefoil

Bittersweet
(Woody nightshade)

24

of old age – bad teeth. After 16 months of eating, eating, eating, it has ground down its teeth on a diet of snails and hard-shelled insects, along with occasional succulent worms and small slugs.

Its fast metabolism means ceaseless spending of energy in a compulsive search to replace the fuel. The old shrew could not slow down even if it had enough food given to it on a plate. Its physiology dictates the same habits and routine, month in, month out. Short rests, about ten times spread over 24 hours, punctuate the activity.

But the fight with the young shrew has taken its toll, and 16 months is old for a shrew. Coinciding with these stresses is the cooler, wetter weather which extracts energy in the form of body-heat. Suddenly, while running along the edge of the lane, not far from the place where it had left its tracks in the snow last winter, the old shrew has used itself up. I find the body, with its soft brown fur, dark brown on top, lighter at the edge and near-white underbelly, still remarkably clean; but all the characteristic red worn off its teeth.

Within an hour, a large black ground-beetle arrives, and starts to scavenge. No mammals will eat a shrew, dead or alive, because of its foul-tasting scent glands. But soon a host of invertebrate scavengers arrives, and within two days the tiny corpse is hollow, in three days, gone.

A Tale Of Two Shrews

September 6. A young shrew is making a new hole in the hedgebank today, confident, able to defend the territory, full of energy from the summer's flux of invertebrate life. This common shrew has just taken on the defender of a piece of bank opposite the copse, and won.

Now, as I watch, the young shrew bursts out of the detritus for a second, and quickly goes back again, feeling everywhere with its long whiskery nose, movements jerky and rapid, progress constantly interrupted by the need to explore left and right for food. Its eyes are little use to it, the smell-sense poor, but like so many of the quarry it delights in, the shrew has a form of antennae – long whiskers. Day and night, these wiggling sense-organs are at work finding food for an animal that needs to eat at least its own weight in 24 hours.

The old shrew, dispossessed of the best feeding ground in the hedgebank, is hard put to find enough food, and is suffering a further handicap

The hedgerow recycles its wealth fast. It is a place of quick metabolisms, of much food quickly eaten, many lives quickly lived, and nothing – no organic residues, usable minerals – going to waste.

The young shrew, meanwhile, is fighting again. Another survivor of this year's litter (18, on average, per pair) wants to take over this rich section of hedgebank. The squeaking in the depths is loud. I cannot see them, but the high-pitched sound is enough. They are grappling hard, each animal biting the other at the base of the tail. They roll over and over, squeaking. The defender rears up, the intruder scoots away and the fight is over.

Now all the young shrew has to do is keep out of the way of the tawny owl which comes and works the hedgerows at night, the only predator which does not mind the shrew's bad-tasting scent gland. (The cat kills the shrew, and leaves it on the path). If the young shrew succeeds, it will be one of only two of this year's generation of 18 to live to breed next spring. In its short life, it will have consumed hundreds of thousands of small creatures, from spiders and harvestmen to earthworms, beetles and small slugs – anything small enough for it to subdue.

AUTUMN GROWTH

September 19. Constantly changing light, sunshine and rain showers, mists and gales, flow over the land. It is September giving out stop-go cues to the plants and animals of the hedgerows. Wrens are briefly tricked by a warm day, and the equal day-night lengths, into exhibiting springlike displays. Violets bloom pathetically. But dead leaves slide scratchily over the roofs, and blow along the lane. A buff-tip caterpillar separates from the cluster, and goes to pupate in the deep undergrowth.

In the confusion, the embroidery of plants in the hedgebanks makes a *petit point* of small autumn seedlings and new growths. Many of them have sprung up where cows, sheep or machines have disturbed the soil during summer. Some of these small new plants are daughter clones of species which go in for vegetative reproduction, like strawberry, Potentilla or wood sorrel. Others are from seeds which germinate immediately without a winter dormancy, like garlic mustard, herb Robert or vetch.

Either way, autumn growth is a puzzling phenomenon. You expect plants to "know" that winter is coming, "know" that they will not survive unless, like herb Robert, they are hardy in most kind British winters. It is thought that some plants – violets, for example – are genuinely fooled by the day-length's being equal to that of spring, and that this explains their autumn blooms, if not the explosion of vegetation.

Germination of seeds is a highly complex matter, and a count of the seedlings growing down the hedgebanks raises more questions than it answers. First of all, the soil disturbance is the *sine qua non.* Cows and sheep tend to bring down turf and mud by pawing or scrabbling up the banks in search of greener pastures. The bare spaces left quickly sprout small seedlings and shoots, whatever the time of year. Strawberry and Potentilla send runners immediately. Garlic mustard has taken over several of these fresh grounds on the north-facing banks all along the lane. At a place opposite the copse, masses of young wood-sorrel leaves have appeared, and new campion growths are springing up even as the older generation is still in bloom.

Plants fight for space

Some of them will be short-lived, and give way to a natural succession of plant life with robust growth coming along to push them out. Others will thrive briefly, then pause invisible under ground while flashier members of the plant world take over. But meanwhile, the accidents of animal disturbance, propitious condition for early germination and vagaries of weather and climate have a profound influence on the plant populations. Annuals thrive in the early part of their young lives, perennials not till later; some, both annuals and perennials, bide their time and germinate only after a period of dormancy in cold weather. Others have to have cold, then warmth, plus the right day-length, before they put forth stems and leaves and finally flowers.

Scientists studying plant populations have recently identified three types of plant as far as growth rhythms are concerned. Some plants thrive early, putting about masses of seedlings and colonising open spaces quickly, then die back as competition, even from their own density of growth, destroys their light and nutrients. Dock and sorrel are like this.

The second type grows steadily and at the same rate, survives moderately well and may or may not be affected by its own density. Grasses are like this. Then there are the persistent plants which do not seed vigorously at first, or thrive in infancy, but bide their time and build up rosettes until the time is right for upward growth and final flowering. Biennials are the extreme example of delayed growth, but some, like mullein, may often lose out to other plants which have colonised the available space, while others, like foxglove, produce so much persistent seed that they can succeed in the long run.

It boils down to two basic strategies, according to Jonathan W. Silvertown (1982). One group of plants is adapted to rapid change, and colonises wherever space allows, thriving in an expanding environment; the other strategy suits plants adapted to a stable environment, such as a hedgerow, postponing rapid growth and reproduction until the time is right.

As I found when I examined the results of the flail-cutting of the banks a few weeks ago, the hedgerow's competitive environment certainly favours the plant which can store its nutrients in seeds or roots at ground level or below, then burst forth at a propitious time when the competing foliage has died down in spring, or when the animals and machines have provided a free seed-bed by accidentally gouging the banks.

These bare spaces attract the vegetative opportunists. Strawberry and Potentilla move in at this uninspiring time of year. One such space near the copse is a mat of tiny trefoil leaves which are attached to the old runners, and are busy forming crowns so that when the foliage dies down a full-blown daughter plant capable of blossoming and fruiting next year will survive.

The other most conspicuous opportunist, garlic mustard, has been making new plants to fill available space since the early plants went to seed last June. The north-facing banks tend to have more open spaces once the aggressive weeds like hogweed, dock and bracken begin to die down. Then this hedgerow speciality, also known as Jack-by-the-hedge or Alliaria petiolata, germinates and flourishes. Large round leaves with lobed margins show first, and at this time of year, these may be the last. Like many herbaceous plants, it has two kinds of leaf, and will only send up its long telescopic stem, and the sharp-toothed leaves with the gentle garlic flavour, when the time is right for forming buds and blooming.

The other prolific autumn growth is from wood sorrel, that delicate, woodland three-leafed perennial that grows in drifts near the copse. I find it impossible to tell whether the new young, light-green wood sorrels now growing and filling all spaces in that area are seedlings grown from last spring's explosive seed production, or whether they have sprung from old roots. The runners are very long in both cases, and the leaves as fresh and pale, What I do know from previous years' experience, is that every one of them will die down in winter, only to go through the whole process again next spring.

Autumn's rains and gales will mean that these light-sensitive plants spend much of their time folded up — hence, presumably, the pale colour for lack of chlorophyll — but they evidently achieve enough collection and storage of energy to make next year's display of delicate white, pencil-striped cups. The persistence of these fragile-looking, but clearly robust, colonisers is demonstrated on the north-facing banks, where they grow under dense mats of moss, penetrating the thick cov-

Strawberry

ing to the time of day: wise farmers cut hay around noon.

So, in many cases, these autumn growths of shoots and leaves are poor things, not just because the plants are cutting their cloth to match their ecological purse, but simply because the growth hormones do not stimulate a vigorous size in second or third growths. How this evolved nobody knows.

The red campion poses another mystery. When I took a few seeds and put them into compost to see if germination was immediate or delayed, they came up almost overnight, and produced a lush growth of springlike proportion, but on my windowsill. When I checked the banks in the neighbourhood of the Hall, where the red campion grows so vigorously in summer, I found some growths, but every one I pulled on turned out to be a vegetative growth, not a young seedling. These late bloomers need a warmth trigger to set off germination in the wild, and may suddenly bloom in a few warm winter days. A highly adaptable plant, campion evolved in Mediterranean countries to remain dormant in the hot summer. But it practices winter dormancy in Britain, so perhaps it will find new ways of prospering in the hedgebanks.

The springlike appearance of fresh young leaves, whether it is masses of nettles, profusions of dandelions or bright beds of violets, is in fact a kind of illusion. The underground systems of the plants are merely testing the air with a few shoots, and gathering what they can of energy, before the winter resting period — a far cry from the mixed seedling and vegetative climaxes of the early summer. I know from past years' observations that many of the plants I see now will be superseded or overshadowed when the summer heavies come out. Plants like nipplewort, a feathery yellow annual whose seeds lie dormant now, cow parsley and hogweed, bracken and the many bramble and rose shoots coming down from the hedges, will win the final battles. Only nettle and garlic mustard are prominent in the superficial view at all times of year.

For the rest, an ecological succession means that each plant has its time in the year for dominance and, like all things in the hedgerow, this variety means an assortment of food-plants for choosy insects and other invertebrates and mammals as they need it.

ering to reach the light from the gloom beneath.

Great swatches of herb Robert fill many of the vacant spaces, growing now from seed sown earlier this year. These annuals are a type of ephemeral which grow, seed, die back and grow again so fast that they appear to be perennial. The small pink, candy-striped blooms are still on the larger plants, giving a late-season suck of nectar to a variety of flies and bees. But the seedlings are spreading out from rosettes where the deeply cut leaves cluster.

As in the case of strawberry and its relatives, the autumn leaves of herb Robert are smaller than the springtime leaves. A mass of tiny vetch plants on the north-facing bank exhibits the same parsimony. This phenomenon is the reverse of the garlic-mustard pattern, where the autumn growth is large-leafed. It is well known that the first spring growth of any plant in a temperate climate is the richest. Farmers get their best grass then, rabbits wax fat and scientists can actually measure a higher content of natural sugars. Food value even varies accord-

SOMETHING IS ROTTEN

September 24. Under the tall oak that hangs over the deeply cut lane near the Hall, is a place where ferns and woodland plants grow on the steep banks, and a rank fungal smell greets the walker. Hart's tongue, polypody and dryopteris ferns mingle with the mossy sticks of the hedge, and the lichen-encrusted clay banks.

For the past few days, a flush of vivid fungi has been emerging, now in various stages of decay. Their tennis-ball-sized caps are shades of brownish pink, olive and grey. Underneath, their pores are a disgusting sulphurous yellow. They have been attacked from above by snails or slugs, and by what appears from the beak-marks to be birds. Their edges have been nibbled by small mammals, and they are riddled through and through by tiny mites and larvae. On top of these attacks, some of them have been visited by a white slime-mould which clasps their caps and stems. To the human nose, this gourmet dish of Boletus (impolitus is its second name) has an extremely rotten smell, nothing like the heavenly taste of the related ceps mushroom (Boletus edulis).

Plants which lack green chlorophyll grow all year round, of course, as networks of hyphae, an invisible lacework growing through the soil, especially among the roots of trees. This particular species is associated with oak trees, and although no special research has focused on the relationship this Boletus has with oak, the Boletus family has many members which form relationships with tree-roots.

It does not appear here every year, because fungi only sprout their so-called fruiting bodies when the summer has been warm enough to encourage the mycelia, as the networks are called, to reproduce themselves. It appears they have to reach a certain thriving state before they spend energy on the cell differentiation and growth necessary for the toadstool that we see above ground. Fungi are efficient producers of enzymes and other chemical messengers to trigger off these and other reactions within and without the organism. If the fungi have exhausted the food supplies, they do not trigger off the fruiting body.

The relationship these fungi have with oak, is called mycorrhiza. The fungus sends out special sheathed hyphae which cover the roots of the tree, take up sugars directly from the tree-roots and release minerals to them. Some kinds of fungi actually inhabit the roots themselves, and exchange nutrients.

Because this action does not destroy the tree, and benefits it to a certain extent, it is a symbiotic one. Down the lane at the gate where a bulldozer badly damaged a holly tree last year, a different story is being played out by fungi. A cluster of pale brown fruiting bodies has grown out of the dying roots in the clay of the bank. Great black rhizomorphs are even partly visible as this fungus interacts with its dying host, and sends out hyphae to attach to the roots. A parasitic honey fungus, this organism will speed up the death of the holly roots in the damaged bank. It is edible by humans, as is the unappetising Boletus, but oddly enough it is getting much less eaten by the hedgerow's other fauna.

On the hidden roots of a recently sawed-down oak at the corner of the copse, the presence of dead wood is betrayed by a huge flush of oyster fungus. These bracket fungi are growing directly on the old stump and roots, which they will gradually break down. The ability to digest lignin, the substance which makes trees woody and strong, is unique to the organism of saprophytic fungi.

A fourth kind of fruiting body has appeared in the grass on the garden side of the cottage-hedge. Lactarius pallidus is another exchanger of minerals and nutrients with the adjacent green plants. When the cap of this whitish mushroom is split open, it exudes white milk. One of the large family of milk caps, the pallidus is not only busy exchanging chemicals with the roots of the grass and the hedgebank plants, but also decomposing the leaf litter.

Today's flush of fungi is only the beginning of the autumn extravaganza. The hedgerow produces some fruiting fungi steadily throughout the seasons, not in the quantities found in ancient woodlands, but in a significant variety. In a nearby oakwoods I saw many new species, but it was interesting that the familiar hedgerow toadstools turned up in the forest clearings.

The species will unfold throughout the year, each in their own ecological niche where they can find their correct temperature, nutrition and plant structures for their odd individual chemical harmonies.

Boletus impolitus

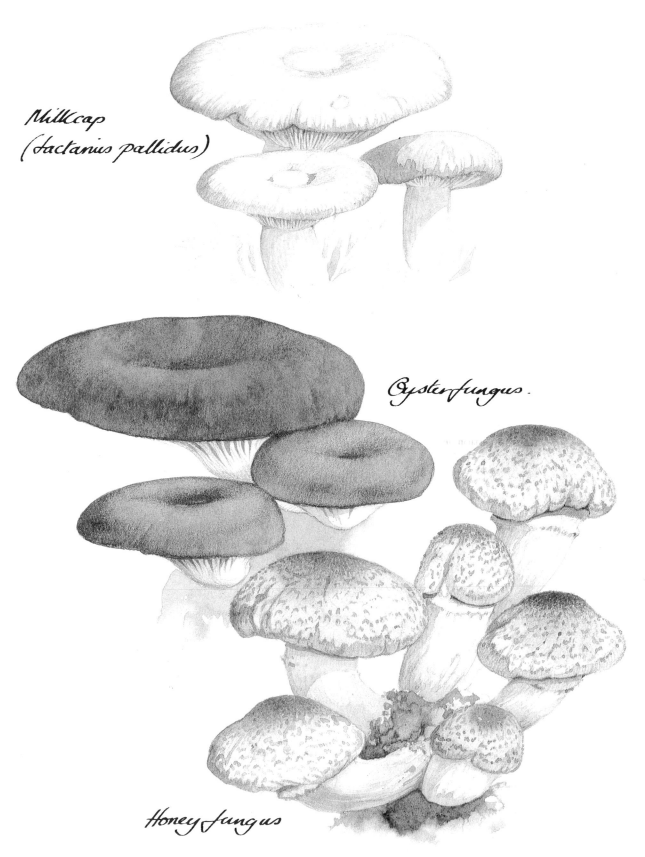

Milkcap
(Lactarius pallidus)

Oyster fungus.

Honey fungus

Rovers Return

September 26. Crouching in a leafy piece of hedge close to the Hall, I watch this morning for rabbits near the warren at the back hedge. The warren has been there for years, a small network of tunnels, with two large holes and a varying number of smaller ones, dug in the hedgebank 20 yards behind the lane. The hedge they use is an intersecting line which then runs almost parallel to the lane-hedge, but further towards the beech woods. The side I watch faces the sun, and provides the best grazing for the rabbits.

But no luck this morning, so I clamber out of the hedge, and continue up the hill towards the Hall. Out jumps a large rabbit, down the bank, up the other side and off towards a high, sunny field. It had been lurking in the hedge, and is off to graze farther afield, as they do this time of year.

Late in the day I see a large buck (I take it to be a buck because of its size and behaviour) grazing near the warren. In the afternoon sunshine it lollops along a bit, then pauses, alerted by the *pinks* and *chooks* of a touchy blackbird which had no doubt seen me. For a minute or so it sits perfectly still, using this rabbit device as a camouflage. When you stop to think, in the dusk and dawn times when one normally sees these animals, it is the movement that first betrays them, so keeping still is not a bad adaptation.

But soon the rabbit decides the danger is past, and starts to preen. First it licks its paws thoroughly then rubs them on its face and ears. Then it gives a series of jaunty, rapid little paw-rubbing movements, and sits there again, a magnificent specimen of rabbithood in its prime with glossy grey-brown coat and bright white tail. The tail shows up next as the animal bounds off to the hedgeside.

Back from its wanderings for the autumn breeding season, this rabbit and its mate, safely inside the underground passageways, are starting the whole yearly cycle again. It is the end of the neutral season now, and the rabbit pair, their reproductive organs active again, have returned to their breeding tunnels, their young having dispersed to find their own breeding territory. The hedgebank is a perfect site: well-drained, friable soil, sunny on one side and sheltered from the wind on the down-

hill side. I have never seen many rabbits at this warren, but they are always about, roving far and wide as the farmers graze and cut the pastures in rotation. Only one little family stays for the breeding season, using the tasty hedgerow shrubs for winter nibbles.

On the way home, I meet another occasional visitor to the hedgerows along the lane itself. At the overgrown section where a row of hazel saplings intersperse with hawthorn, I am aware of activity in the branches, and sure enough a grey squirrel is systematically raiding the barely ripe nuts from the bushes. Swinging almost monkeylike from branch to branch, the squirrel takes every single nut, demolishing its shell and eating or storing it as it wishes. The whole process, involving five trees, takes about 12 minutes, and then off goes the squirrel down the lane towards the Gweche oak, where the drey is hidden in the spinney along the stream.

The first succulent nibbles of the nut season vanish in that one efficient raid by one animal, leaving behind only a spattering of neatly halved shells.

October-November

SNAILS

October 5. As autumn brings painted grey skies, criss-crossing flocks and fading foliage, the underworld of the hedgebanks becomes more conspicuous. Taking a look with a 10x lens at the occupants of the heavy layer of litter, I come across a small yellow-and-brown-banded snail (Cepaea nemoralis by name) marching determinedly over the rotting leaves in the lane side of the cottage hedge. No bigger than a baby's fingernail, it nevertheless munches and rasps at the decayed plant material with snail-like persistence.

Snails evoke extremes of feeling in human beings. Inside the garden gate, the sight of them prompts a ferocious snatch, a fast overhead bowl into the hedge and a prayer for the first passing thrush to take care of the rest. Outside the gate in the lane, one's thoughts transform through curiosity, interest, fascination and finally admiration. The thick, smothering layer of detritus made up of dead herbage and hedge-clippings must be taken care of. Only man dumps his rubbish forever.

Delicate-looking, and vulnerable to a host of predators, snails are great stayers and performers. Yesterday I found just two snails' eggs when making a collection of litter inhabitants in the hedgebank. No doubt there were many more of these delicate soft-shelled pearls until the resident shrews, hedgehogs and mice made a feast of them. I saw a wood mouse approaching a tiny snail on the high bank under the Hall oak the other evening, but the mouse woke up to my presence before it had a chance to grab its slow-moving meal. I have often seen snail-shells pierced right through the spiral to be eaten in the manner of a mouse or vole at this spot.

These predators (and beetles, too) are as nothing compared with the depredations of the song thrushes later on in the year. Yet in spite of their gourmet qualities, snails survive in the hedgerows in their hundreds. I have counted as many as 47 in a 10-yard stretch without resorting to digging deep in the litter or surface soil, where still more snails are taking refuge.

Watching today as a large garden snail negotiates the stem of a rose bush, I can see one of the reasons for the snail's unexpected resiliency. The snail's foot (the part of its body which protrudes from the shell, and on which it walks by contracting in waves) is undulating over the most fierce of thorns. That unattractive but useful snailism, slime, has unique properties which allow it to coat the sharp prickle with a heavy viscosity. The slippery mucus undergoes a complex change in its physical structure (a change not completely understood by science), under the stimulus of the muscle-changes required to negotiate the thorn. A snail may move slowly, but it can go anywhere, even managing to right itself by flipping its shell over its shoulder when it gets into an awkward position.

Above all, snails are consumers and reprocessors of plant energy, converting the complex nutrients of plants, dead or alive, into palatable food for new plants and animals. To see a snail's mouth would require dissection and high magnification. A snail has not only a "jaw," which grabs the food plant, but a small tongue, called a radula, which holds vast numbers of grooves, and with which the mollusc takes a continuous succession of rasping bites out of the rotting vegetation.

After scraping their food in with their tongues, snails have extremely efficient digestive systems to go to work on the vegetation. Their stomachs are rich in enzymes and bacteria. In

Banded Snail

experiments to measure the efficiency of the digestion of various leaf-litter converters, including woodlice, mites, millipedes and snails, seven species of woodland snails were found to absorb and convert 50 per cent or more of the food, while the best any of the other orders (woodlice) could clock up was around 33 per cent, and most managed to digest only between seven and ten per cent. It is hard to measure the overall amount a snail eats, because so much of both the food and the animal is made up of water.

Their particular digestive skill is the ability to break down cellulose, and to decompose plant polysaccharides – those chemicals out of which they make their adhesive slime for hibernation. Some of the woodland species studied also have special enzymes that can cope with difficult leaf and twig litter from sycamore, oak and sweet chestnut. Other species have different chemical reprocessing specialities.

Snails, slugs and the other detritus feeders at work in the litter of the hedge-clippings release the simple small-molecule minerals into the soil in their droppings, or from their bodies when they die annually (or in two or three years in the case of large snails). Potassium and phosphorous are important nutrients released by snails and – in the case of at least 20 species, including those in these hedgerows – lime.

Arion Slug

Snails need lime to create their defensive shells, and they are equipped with a special digestive organ to store this vital nutrient. As the shells of dead snails are gradually weathered and shattered, this lime becomes available to new plants, completing the cycle.

While snails are probably responsible, along with slugs, for the largest volume of litter-recycling, there is a host of other creatures living in the top layers of soil here. A handful of rich leaf litter and soil from the base of the hedge always reveals an assortment of these rubbish dealers. So far I have counted more than 18 different kinds of insect, worm and woodlouse. And that is just the merest beginning.

Some of these creatures eat each other, some are eaten by snails and mammals. Many snails and insects eat the chief plant recyclers, fungi, so that in the hedgebanks there appears to be a constant, rich and rapid exchange of nutrients, quickly returning the benefits of all those cuttings back into the soil for the next generation of wildflowers, weeds and shrubs.

Meanwhile, it is no wonder that the hedgehog prefers the roadside hedge, with its huge crop of invertebrates, to the shaggier, less dangerous, field-hedges away from traffic, and it is not at all surprising that the robin and the dunnock grow tame as the invertebrate supply builds up. The hedgerow's damp vegetation is a man-made habitat, and ironically it is some of the creatures that man traditionally regards as enemies – insects, snails, slugs, worms, earwigs – which form the basis of this habitat as a wildlife refuge.

Garden Snail

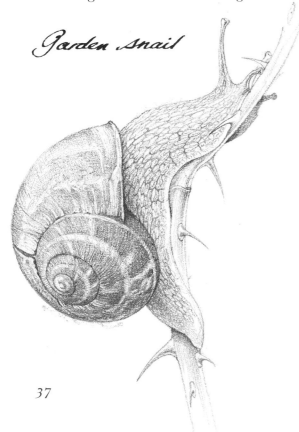

Trees

October 7. After a night of blustery gales and rain, the hedgerows lie battered, glistening and weather-beaten. Scudding clouds are roiling purple and grey over the landscape, and the birds are enjoying themselves.

As I leave the cottage gate, the first members of the bird community to chime in are the wrens, click-scolding in the lower branches of the beech trees and the overgrown hedge saplings. One of them does its outraged knee-bends at me while it clicks disapprovingly. The sight of this little bird cocking its tail up and repeatedly bending its knees, then stretching to its full tiny height, is always pleasing. It breaks into song, loud and trilling. No wonder that it is known by American Indians as "the little bird who makes a big noise".

Nearer to the chapel, robins are twarbling their truncated autumn songs, and answering each other from the high points in the hedge. At the copse, blackbirds are stirring up the population with their alarm *pinks* and *chooks*, hurrying in and out of cover like busy gossips while dunnocks flutter along the hedge, then over and out.

Here at the copse I pick up the sights and sounds of a flock of tits foraging in a party with some chaffinches and a pair of nuthatches. These birds are easier to recognise by what bird men call their "jizz," than by calls and field-marks. It is the way they fly, the constant movement, combined with the occasional sounds and sights of twitters and wings or peeps and whistles that identify the members of the troup.

This part of the lane and hedgerows is an important corner for bird life, not only because of the small, triangular copse, with its thick shrubbery and tall trees, but because of the line of scrub oaks straggling up the field boundary from the hanging wood down by the river. These trees form a corridor for woodland birds wanting to explore the open country. The tits, chaffinches and nuthatches always appear at this point.

Down the hedges they fly ahead of me, giving me a come-on with their flit-glide, flit-glide, taking them from leading shoot to leading shoot on the hedge shrubs. Beyond the copse, they assemble briefly in small groups on two holly trees which poke up like flags out of the

Chaffinch

Nuthatch

Marsh tit

Blue tit

Great tit

Flocking birds in hedgerow oak

hedges, one on each side of the lane. The nuthatch pauses to drum. Next stop is a good-sized beech tree at the corner by the Gweche stream where the lane lurches sideways to cross over. Here the morning sun's warm rays pick out the chaffinch reds as the clouds begin to part.

Now comes the climax. The tit party, and the other birds it has picked up in its travels, arrives at the giant Gweche oak. In a few seconds they fill its spreading branches with movement, colour and sound – some 30 birds all moving and fluttering. The puttering calls which they were using as if beckoning each other to fly along the hedgerows, change now.

The birds spread through the huge branches like some kind of performers on a multi-level Busby Berkeley film stage. They give voice to all their languages, calls and sub-songs, with fluttering movements played off against the calls tossed between them. Black and white, yellow and blue, flash and blink through the leaves as wings open and close, bodies tip. Here and there the chaffinch reds show up, and the gaudy nuthatch colours decorate the thick trunk. It is hard to imagine that the selective function of the tit display is anything but pleasure and fun. Three tit species take part in it: great, blue and marsh. But social behaviour in birds always has a biological benefit of some kind. Is it solely connected with communication about feeding sites and the various niches used by the different species in the flock? Or are there, perhaps, useful cues about populations, a kind of census-taking?

The birds soon fall to feeding on the oak's bounty, still calling and flying from twig to limb as they exploit their favourite habitat. After about 20 minutes, they move on to the tall ash and another big oak up the hill towards the old Hall. The show is over.

Before farmlands and the parks of great country estates were created, mature oaks in glades and on woodland edges would have performed this function for feeding flocks. In Gilbert White's day, the importance of trees to bird populations was taken for granted. He described 18th-century Selbourne: "The parish I live in is abrupt, uneven country full of hills and woods and therefore full of birds." Many species of birds have adapted over the last few centuries and decades to the spaced-out trees and copses of the farming landscape, some

long ago, others only recently. Small songbirds have even benefited by the decline of woodland predators such as sparrow-hawks, which are now relatively rare.

Watching, these last few years, the way the woodland birds use these hedgerow trees, and especially since the hanging wood down below lost nearly all its mature oaks to the timber merchant three years ago, I am beginning to get some idea of their value to wildlife, whether they are in a rural, suburban or agricultural landscape.

First, food. Hundreds of species of invertebrates inhabit a mature oak. If one moth caterpillar fails in a given year, another supplies the young nestlings. Today's feeding flock was exploiting an autumn harvest of eggs, pupae, gall-insects and larvae to build up their small bodies before winter. Without them, many marginal birds would lose their lives or go elsewhere.

True, the hedge shrubs themselves provide important food for birds and other species. Hazel houses something like 30 species of larger moths, and produces nuts even when repeatedly pruned back by the flail, or cut and laid by hand. Hawthorns and blackthorns are almost as valuable as short hedgerow shrubs as when they are full-grown. But beech and oak do not produce any nut crop unless they are allowed to flourish at full toss, and these crops are important to both mammals and birds.

Holly is another example. Few hollies in the hedge flower or make berries, but the fine holly pennants growing up out of these hedges have a massive crop of white flowers in spring which holly-blue butterflies fancy as a place to lay their eggs. Larvae eat the buds and young berries, and all year round the heavy leaves provide excellent cover for anything from pupating butterflies to courting chaffinches. Because the hollies are inevitably covered with a thick coat of ivy, they provide (as only one example among many) a place for the late crop of butterfly eggs whose larvae feed on the ivy buds. This chain, once broken, could prove disastrous to the local populations of butterflies, and their predators would suffer in turn.

Fifteen large stumps stand among these hedgerows, while only 14 remaining mature trees grow out of the hedges along the extended half-mile. Typical of the past two or three generations of farmers, the three local landowners have cut down trees for reasons varying from interference with farm machinery or electric wires to the shading of pastureland or the weakening of the hedge under the tall trees. (Hedge-plants grow poorly in dense shade, and hedges require filling in by fencing, barbed wire or old bedsteads.)

Not one farmer within miles has promoted a single hedgerow shrub by allowing it to grow to full height, despite a few stretches where the hedge is fairly tall. Hedgerow trees are a nuisance to the tractor-driver with the flail-cutter: it takes a few minutes to raise the bar and reposition it. Even where a farmer treasures his hedges, and goes in for hand-trimming and laying, he is still likely to cut back all the saplings. A champion hedge-layer who lives in the hills near here is the only man I know who allows a few to grow – and only because his absentee landlord insists on it.

Growing and harvesting timber in small quantities – an oak or an ash one year, a beech or two the next – is not an economic proposition. Local people can recall a time when hedgerow timber was valued, and grown purposely. As recently as 1965, the Forestry Commission did a national survey and estimated that hedgerow trees and parkland between them contained 946 million hoppus feet of timber (the measure of useful timber in the trees). That was more than the whole volume of Forestry Commission woodlands in the country.

But between 1947 and 1972, more than half the hedgerow trees were sawn down (Hooper, M.D. from Inst. of Terrestrial Ecology, 1981). The country as a whole has been doing just what my neighbours are doing, and soon these oaks, ashes and hollies will go the way of the stricken English hedgerow elms. A few people use the smaller hedgerow timbers for poles, fencing, firewood and walking sticks, but the likelihood of an economic timber business flourishing again, encouraging small-scale hedgerow growth, is remote to say the least. Ironically, it was the very fact that farmers were cutting the hedgerow timbers for regular use that motivated them to grow it and harvest it gradually, while providing a substitute forest habitat for wildlife.

On my way home today, I hear the nuthatch hammering again in the holly, see the chaffinches flying through the Gweche spinney and hear the resident robin singing from deep inside a garden conifer.

GRASSHOPPERS

October 10. A warm, sunny day brings two unexpected visitors to the grassy bank alongside the derelict Rock House field. I hear them before I saw them; two sets of chirpings, rapid bursts, then a pause of a second or two, then more chirps. They seem to be answering each other, as if in conversation and moving slightly away from each other, which I find puzzling even after I confirm that they are common field grasshoppers.

These cheerful insects are not the most regular inhabitants of hedgerows. They vastly prefer nice green fields or dry anthills, not too overgrown, but with some grass plants, at the roots of which they can bury their eggs. The mystery of their appearance in October in a damp hedgerow is compounded by the fact that only the males sing this loud, and here are two males singing to each other. They are moving away gradually, which might make sense if

they were females laying eggs, but all these poor males have to look forward to now is an early death. The female's eggs will have been laid by now to hatch out in the lee of the hedgerow next April.

One reason for the grasshoppers' taking temporary refuge in the hedgerow could be that intensive farming has resulted in fields either ploughed and reaped or closely grazed. The fallow field, with its long grass, is too wild for them, and the cow pastures probably to close-cropped. The females do come to the hedgebank to lay eggs.

So these amiable creatures have found a sunny spot facing the wintering sun where they can sing their final song, and burrow in the ground before the cold brings permanent silence.

Hips And Haws

October 18. The hedges are spangled with fruits, and the nut supply is reaching record proportions. It is going to be one of those memorable bumper years after a sunny summer, starting with the huge blackberries that have been fruiting in sequence since August, and ending near Christmas with a hail of acorns and holly berries lying on the lane.

Rose hips are displaying all the artists' reds, and going even deeper into black. Haws are gleaming in wine-coloured clusters, big as fists, and cuckoo pints (lords and ladies) are falling over and laying bunches of orange fruits on to the banks. The holly berries are still yellow, or faintly orange, and too hard for beak or tooth. A bumper crop of beech nuts is ripening on the boughs. Although most of the hazel nuts in places where the growth is high have been plundered by grey squirrels or humans, there are plenty left in the hedges for mice and voles, nuthatches, rooks, woodpeckers, magpies and even weevils, which drill entrance holes in them.

Hypericums (tutsan) have developed interesting red, yellow and black berries, and the honeysuckle which loads the hedge near the Hall end is bright with glistening red fruits. Here and there, where the hedges have been allowed to go uncut for several years, special delicacies are on offer – elder, rowan and guelder rose. A biennial cut, or even one every three years, and making a tall A-shape instead of the short top-and-sides favoured by en-

thusiastic flail-cutters, would do wonders for the variety, as well as the quantity. In the height of the fruiting season, I frequently count four or five times as many birds in the overgrown track which goes down to the river, as on the close-cropped lane hedges.

Today, near the copse, I watch a party of seven blackbirds go to work, not entirely without conflict, on a single hawthorn which has been allowed to grow about 15 feet high on the south-facing hedgebank. (It happens to be in an awkward place for the flail.)

With much *pinking* and *chooking* the birds fly to the tree two or three at a time, and pick off a berry, whole, flip it into their throats, pick another and perhaps one or two more. Off they fly back to the copse, calling again as their replacements arrive. A quarter of an hour of this leaves little impact on the hawthorn, which still glows like a legendary firethorn in the morning light. The birds then resume feeding in the copse, where fallen timber is undoubtedly housing a feast of invertebrate life, emerging now after overnight frost.

Underneath the hawthorn tree is a collection of leavings. There are whole dropped haws, pieces of the outer skin, clean whole stones, greenish, and bits of the outer fruits. Most puzzling is a collection of four of five fruits in a pellet-like mass, the haws partly masticated or digested, with the shiny stones still attached. It looks as if a bird has swallowed them whole, passed them on to its first stomach (where acid dissolves some of the softer parts of the fruit), sent them on to the crop (where they have undergone some grinding up), then regurgitated the lot.

The bare seeds could have been the leavings of a bank vole, which will strip the fruits and leave the seeds, while the fruits alone could have been a wood mouse's rubbish, as this hawthorn gourmet does just the opposite. Thus two similar mammals share the habitat amicably.

The habit of eating and dropping fruits has influenced the pattern of hedgerow plants for centuries. Every gate in this lane, with one exception where privet was planted, is surrounded by bramble, hawthorn and rose. Just here, by the hawthorn tree, is a section of hedge which has been lost through shading from a large oak. A post-and-wire fence has been put up to fill a 10-foot gap, and all along

Yew

Bittersweet
(Woody nightshade)

Hawthorn

Rowan

Ro

Black bryony

Honeysuckle

Cuckoo pint

Blackberry

the fence bramble twines, planted by birds sitting on the posts and defecating. My milkman, who lives across the valley, remembers when he ripped out a hedgerow and put in some fencing. Hawthorn sprang up and prospered at the foot of each fencepost. Soon he will have a new hedge. (Americans are even beginning to study the wildlife in their "fencerows" planted by birds.) I can see purple droppings along the hedgerow today, underneath some of the favourite perching places. They are loaded with bramble seeds and, when the next rain comes, will wash down among the rich detritus.

Yew is a species which pops up in odd places along the banks nowhere near a parent plant. This is a favourite of greenfinches, nuthatches, marsh tits and robins. The yew makes an aril with the fleshy part attached to the side of a hard nut instead of surrounding it. This enables more species of birds to enjoy and transport the seeds: greenfinches and robins eat the soft part, while nuthatches and marsh tits make off with the kernels and leave the sticky fruit behind. Some of the seeds are carried, and dropped to germinate in odd spots of clear, shady soil.

All these devices were evolved to transport seeds to the woodland edge, where they could germinate and grow in the partial sunlight. Shrubs which make succulent fruits simply cannot grow in dark, canopy-shaded woodland, or among· evergreen forests. As the number of gladed woodlands with their rich edge ecology has diminished, the hedgerows have become refuges for the plants and their bird predators. This man-made linear habitat mimics the old woodland edges.

The assorted feast of multi-coloured berries and nuts is not immediately snapped up, however. Many of them stay temptingly on the trees and hedges, then suddenly all go in one day. Others are treasured, and eaten one by one in the depths of winter. Colour is thought to be an important trigger for birds in choosing their fruit harvest. A comprehensive study of European birds found a strong preference for red, black and, to some extent, blue fruits (Turček, 1963). More species, when confronted with a choice, went for these, the usual colours of ripe fruits, than for yellows and greens.

But the situation in the wilds of my hedgerows seems more complicated. Soft, ripe blackberries which come in rapid sequence are eaten

quickly. That hawthorn tree has been worked systematically from the top down, although the haws are all dark red. The rose hips which have almost reached their final colour will still be hanging on the bush in dead of winter, although the mice and voles will have picked up any that drop. Holly berries stay on the tree long after they redden, then drop to carpet the lane after Christmas, and finally get eaten all at once.

Robins come late to the feast every time. They love cuckoo pint's orange berries, but right now they are too busy in the undergrowth of the copse and the hedge feeding on invertebrates. Worms have not yet taken to the deep underground; beetles, crane flies, gall larvae, spiders and centipedes are plentiful. The berries have been nibbled at, but by something much more dainty than a robin – more like an insect, or a snail.

Blackbirds seem to wait until the time, as well as the fruit, is ripe. Another hawthorn stands very close to the one I have been watching, but it is yet untouched. As the hedgerow's most eclectic feeders, perhaps they can afford to nibble a little of this and a little of that before feasting on a rich crop like this. Another reason for delayed harvesting: robins and wrens have distinct autumn territories; blackbirds are slightly more relaxed about it, but feed securely in their own areas. They have staked their claim, and can defend it until they are ready. A further possibility is that birds use trial and error in feeding. Fruits that look ripe may still be hard, and unripe haws do appear on the ground.

Ash keys are hanging like bunches of feathery grapes, but they will mostly hang there until late winter, when the bullfinches will have them to tide them over the hungry gap. One of those crops that fluctuates from year to year, ash keys are around in winter when the fruit buds are swelling on orchard trees. Scientists have tried to use knowledge about the timing of bird feeding to control fruit predation. Alas, if you plant more ash trees as a control on fruit-bud eating by bullfinches, you will, in time, get more bullfinches (Newton, 1985). When a lean bud eating by bullfinches, you will, in time, get

year for the ash comes along, your fruit crop will be devastated.

Beech mast has a similar relationship with the tit family. The fully grown beech trees in these hedgerows produce mast only sporadically, and this looks like a bumper year. In fact, beech trees are incapable of manufacturing many nuts in successive years because the energy for one year's ripening saps the strength needed for formation of next year's flower buds (which should happen simultaneously in late summer).

A bumper year will be followed by a completely fruitless year, then the supply will build up again until conditions are right for another bonanza. Scientists studying tit populations have found a distinct correlation between the numbers of tits in a given year, and the size of the beech-mast crop (Perrins, 1979).

But before I predict an invasion of tits for this winter, there are a few qualifications. The tits' numbers also fluctuate in the same way in areas where there is no beech; on the edge of conifer plantations, for instance. Tit survival rate is partly decided long before the beech starts dropping its mast. The two species, great tits and blue tits, are probably influenced by one or more other factors.

While there is no proof that the birds depend on the beech, there is another intriguing theory that the beech has evolved into sporadic fruiting habit as a defence against over-predation by tits. If the beech made mast in large numbers every year, this theory goes, the tits would eat them all, and more birds would prosper, to the cost of the beech. By fluctuating irregularly, the successful beech trees have kept the tit population down to a level where in bumper years there is plenty of mast to find good ground and germinate new beech trees. (Silvertown, 1982).

Further along the hedgerow today, I spot a newly dug mouse-hole in the bank near the Hall oak. A pile of earth gives it away, and a partly eaten rose hip lies beside it. Further down the bank is a hazel-nut shell chewed open in the manner of a wood mouse. At the end of the day, another marauder appears: a small flock of redwings visits the hedgerows, causing the blackbirds set up a raucous *chooking* of protest.

The farmland fruit which my predecessors among the smallholders and farmers turned

into jams, wines, pops, puddings and pies, is still bountiful. The same plant species make an old lane, or a woodland edge, a delicious habitat, both for humans and for the songbirds we have grown to love.

HAMMER AND TONGS

October 20. A nuthatch is hammering away in the holly. First it snatched up a nut from the beech tree that stands at the Gweche. But the beech has smooth, unsullied bark, so it flies to the holly that stands up about 20 feet out of the hedgerow, and finds a handy crevice in the scarred and gnarled branches of this older but smaller tree.

The bird wedges the nut, and sets to work with a systematic technique. I can see it all in profile through the field-glasses. The bird needs that crack in the bark because the pivot point in its body, where the legs join, is well aft of centre. If it tried to grasp the nut, it would miss by a couple of inches. This way, when it goes to hammer the nutshell, the full weight of its body goes into the stroke of the beak. The bird flings itself at the nut, using a little extra flutter of its wings to increase the force. *Rat-a-tat-tat. . . tat-tat* is the rhythm, the beak striking at such an angle that it points back towards the bird's body like a pincer movement. In about half-a-minute the nut disintegrates, and the nuthatch carries it to another shrouded holly branch to eat it.

This is a bird of fixed routine, taking advantage of the structure and food supply of the hedgerow. A favourite hammering place is the big oak tree opposite the copse, where it has a whole range of nuts within reach — the oak's own acorns, assorted hazels in the copse and the nearby cottage beeches. Every morning the pair fly out of the woods or copse, and range down the lane, using the various kinds of trees to practice the nut-cracking arts.

Later in the day another, less efficient, hammerer goes to work. A different technique is used by the rook which lands heavily on a branch of the pollarded oak behind the cottage. The bird's large claw clasps an acorn, which it holds against the branch and strikes, smashing the nut messily. A small gaggle of songbirds collects underneath the branch, ground-feeders (such as blackbirds) who have learned from experience that the rook will spill crumbs. They peck here and there as the rook finishes, wipes its beak on the branch ostentatiously, defecates twice, hunches its shoulders and flies off.

Following the blackbirds still later, I can see them at their more serious feeding, tossing aside the leaves at the foot of the hedge alongside the cottage garden to expose the invertebrate life hiding there. A wireworm (it appears) and some other kind of insect are discovered. I saw a dunnock doing this the other day, too.

In a tall piece of hedge near the derelict field, a blue tit did some acrobatics yesterday. It looked as if it was pecking spasmodically against the dead-looking sticks of a bush, but careful attention revealed that it was getting at some kind of invertebrate life, most likely eggs of one of the rafts of moth species harboured in these hedges.

Among the many feeding techniques to be seen in the hedgerows, the panache of one robin I saw recently is memorable. The bird perched in a high shrub on the south side of the lane, then flew fast and hard at the north bank, driving its beak right into the soft earth. After it did this twice without any apparent success, it gave up and flew into the copse.

The hedges not only have something for everybody, they also have a place for every different feeding mechanism. The birds that feed on many kinds of animals and plants thrive in this environment, and so do the specialists.

WILDERNESS

November 7. A copse is a lovesome thing. Not so deep in shade as to lose its undergrowth, yet bearing tall canopies to shelter birds and squirrels, a copse — even just a small triangle of trees left to grow in a corner between fields — is like a small-scale wilderness.

It is a place where, sitting still for half an hour or so, you can glimpse a shrew poking its head above the leaves, or hear a mouse wittering away under the hawthorn and ivy. Blackbirds love bossily to *pink* and *chook* in and out of them, and chaffinches play games among the stems. To most farmers they are useful small places to bury dead lambs, or dump rusty churns and worn-out bed-springs. Collectors dig up old crockery and bottles in them, and out-of-sorts youths drink cider there.

Of the 10 plant indicators of primary woodland listed by Richard Mabey in his book, The Common Ground (1981), this little copse and its hedges contain four: wood sorrel, wood anemone, early dog violet and sanicle. All plants that are slow to colonise new areas, these are not conclusive clues to the age of woodland, but such copses were often kept going down the years, originally to provide poles and fenceposts, firewood and beansticks; later to be used just as dumping grounds.

Today, the local coal merchant is starting to cut down the trees. Six oaks of one-to-one-and-a-half feet in diameter have come crashing down, and the rest will soon go; except, I hope, one tall ash which overhangs the lane, and possibly one mature oak at the back of the triangle.

It is not the first time the maturer timber has been harvested from this copse, but in previous cuttings there was management, with thinning, selected felling and replanting. Timber is not

now seen as a continuously useful renewable resource around the farm or estate, but as a quick emergency cash-crop. Economic pressures on the dairy farmers of Wales are strong. A small piece of unused land appears a wasted asset, and patch after patch of woodland is going under the chain-saw encouraged, still, by government grants. A long time has passed, and there's been a revolution in farming, since anyone grazed pigs in a piece of woodland, or searched it for edible fungi. The industrial attitude towards farming means: save time, waste resources.

It is not simple to predict the effect this will have on wildlife in the lane's aegis. This amputated copse is at a wildlife crossroads, where birds and mammals take refuge while foraging in the fields and hedgerows. Chaffinches and tits frequent it daily in their travels. Voles retreat there in summer to nest, returning to the hedgebanks in October. Foxes love it as they make their way across the countryside at night, and flocks of roaming birds use it regularly for spotting the best fields for food gathering.

The copse will be missed when it is cleaned up, its loss just another small step in the making of a naked landscape out of a rich, shrubby farmland habitat.

EMBROIDERY

November 10. Sun and mist give the valley an atmosphere of unreality this morning, with only the castle ruins sharp on their cliff, and the tops of the beech woods dark against the rest of the landscape, woolly and vague. By eight o'clock, the early alarm calls of the blackbirds and robins have died down, and the quiet business of feeding is well under way in the fields and hedgerows. The amputated copse is silent, and so are the great oak trees.

Now the morning sun lights up the burning orange of the Gweche beech, where a large male blackbird perches and *pinks* in alarm, its tail jerking up with each utterance. The mist-filled air transmits the sound of the huntsman's shouts from the farm as he struggles to box his horse.

The unusual mixture of moisture and temperature doesn't just magnify the morning sounds — it has had a startling effect on one

particular order of hedgerow fauna: the spiders. Hundreds of web-spinners have emerged in the dark, and performed an amazing orgy of random spinning on the roses and brambles at the cottage gate. A whole section of hedgerow is festooned with a mad embroidery of disorganised threads, thickly woven as if to obliterate the scene.

Along the hedge are more orderly webs — orbs, then sheets, more orbs, more sheets. I counted 18 sheet webs, and 17 orbs, in a scant 20 yards, plus more incomplete webs of both types. The oddest part is the association of the two spiders so close together in what are evidently favoured areas of the hedgebank. The variety of technique is also new to me. Some of the hammock type of sheet webs are unusually thickly made and elaborate, while some of the orbs are abandoned, unfinished; others are askew and incompetent. It looked as if the spiders were working in a frenzy to take advantage of some transitional climatic coincidence. Another odd aspect of the event is the complete absence of spiders. Usually at 8am they are still lurking in their hiding places just off the webs, or hanging upside down under them, or busily wrapping a victim in a deadly shroud. Had they finished, and returned to their earthy hideaways, or had some early party of starlings demolished them?

Fortunately, there exists an outstandingly thorough and well-written volume, W.S. Bristowe's The World of Spiders (1958), to tell the amateur spider-watcher what to look for, when and where, and to provide interpretation based on experiments. The festoons of random webs are the result of a change from cold to warm air, Dr Bristowe explains. The spiders become acclimatised to the cold weather, and get restless when it suddenly warms up. At the same time, the warm air flowing causes air currents which promote the aerial travels of these creatures. The urge is to climb upwards and spin out a thread into the air. When the thread pulls hard enough to support the spider's weight, it launches itself upwards, and floats wherever the breeze takes it — in this case, conveniently across the lane. Who has not felt these webs on their face on an autumn morning in a country lane? It is known as the gossamer season.

The species responsible for the explosive web-building of last night is Linyphia, one of the money-spiders. We have at least two of these species — montana, with hammock-like webs, and the commoner Linyphia triangularis, with domed webs. Both use their webs in the same way: an insect lands or crawl on to the sheet, and the spider rushes out from hiding, or from beneath the web, and bites the prey through the strands. It then pulls the insect down through the web, and finishes it off either there, or after storing it in the hiding place.

The orb-weavers, mostly the common garden spiders, have made their elaborate webs all over the place today, but most often I find them over the entrances to mammal holes. For a long time I wondered if they were interested in the various insect parasites carried by mice and voles, but I gather it is more likely the air currents caused by the holes. Insects waft into these webs as if carried on a tide, when the night air cools.

The engineering feats of spiders have been the subject of wonderment, myth and legend, but the real explanation is more intriguing than the superstitions. The spider starts by sending out a thread in the same way as the money spider does. When the thread catches, and is tested as being strong enough, the spider crosses on it, spinning a second, sturdier bridge line as it goes, and discarding the first. A second strong line is dropped from the bridge, and caught up and fastened at the first point, so that it droops below the bridge line. This line is then pulled taut by a line centred on it, and pulled downward, forming a triangle. The lower angle of the triangle becomes the hub of the orb-to-be. The sides form the first radials.

The spider systematically constructs radials until it no longer perceives wide spaces between those it has already made. In this way it always makes 25-to-35 spokes. To make the first spiral, a compact, strengthening spiral at the centre, the spider revolves around the hub, releasing thread. Next it forms a larger spiral working outwards, but this is only temporary: the final spiral, coated with the gummy substance that will trap the prey, is made by working inwards again. Finally, the spider pulls the spiral threads tight, and causes the gum to separate into small drops.

The spider itself never gets caught. Two adaptations see to that. One is an oil secreted on to its legs which prevents sticking. The other

Spider web construction

First radial lines

Temporary spiral is constructed from centre outwards.

is a special hook on one leg which prevents the spider from slipping, and helps it to manoeuvre round the sticky drops. Experimenters have dipped the spiders into ether to remove the oil, and the poor things stuck fast to their own traps.

You need to remind yourself that these invertebrates have no reasoning brains, and that all these adaptations to the laws of physics and mathematics are instinctive. The entire process can be analysed as a series of stimuli and responses, inherited through genes and evolved by natural selection over the long history of arachnids. They are helped by a special touch-smell sense which allows them to perceive chemicals through their palps. Out of a complex series of simple nervous reactions has been built their successful adaptive behaviour.

If a web is cut as the spider is spinning, the process breaks down. Young spiders are known to spin as well in the first try as their mothers, while only in old age does the ability to design and execute the orbs deteriorate. That is not to say the spiders cannot adapt and learn in relation to their environment. The choice of the mammal holes indicates a conditioning process of some kind, and the very fact that the hedges are a favourite habitat seems to mean the spiders have learned where to find the structure for web-building, and the prey that shelters there.

Last month I noticed several other kinds of spider-webbing. Egg cases appeared here and there, and on the bare clay bank under the Hall oak a tubular webbing turned up surrounding a small hole in the ground like a decorated tunnel entrance. Tubular webs, built originally to protect the spider's eggs and warn of danger, developed by chance the function of trapping prey at the mouth of the spider's retreat. Several species, the forerunners of the weavers I have been watching today, do this. Out of primitive responses made complex by selection of the successful species, has evolved what Dr Bristowe summarises as an "amazing array of automatic rules of behaviour to cope effectively and indeed brilliantly with all the usual sets of circumstances they are likely to encounter".

Because they are so successful in numbers, the spiders of the hedgerows play a key role in the food chains. Judging from the contents of their webs as I have seen them in the early mornings, for instance, the population of tiny moths would explode without spiders. Equally, spiders would explode without many of the other hedgerow animals. Their list of predators reads like a list of hedgerow fauna: swallows, swifts, tits (when the young are in the nest), wasps, beetles, ants, certain parasitic flies, centipedes, shrews, lizards, toads and starlings — and other spiders.

To supply all these hungry species, a garden spider lays as many as 800 eggs in each of two clutches. Money-spider populations can reach as high as a million-and-a-half an acre. Looking down the hedgerow this morning, I can well believe it.

FAIRIES

November 16. Glancing into the deeps at the foot of the hedges this morning, it is easy to see why legends of fairy folk spring up in woodland cultures over the centuries. Tiny white, grey, pink and brown toadstools lurk in the foliage, attaching themselves to sticks, springing out of moss or leaves and ranging under the umbrellas of larger fungi.

Individually, these fruiting bodies, which arise in season from the soil, and from interstices of rotting wood, make up very little organic matter. But if you add them all together, and include their networks of invisible hyphae, they form a huge mass of living tissue. Furthermore, like the fairies of legend which appear on the doorstep and leave sixpences or bowls of milk, or do the washing-up for Cinderellas, these minute members of the hedgerow population accomplish vast and important work in the ecological storehouse.

Once more, this order of plant life has its particular niches. At the eastern end of the lane, where the woodland and parkland nature of the surrounding countryside's history is reflected in the plant and animal species, some of the fungi have a distinctly woodland character, while others echo the meadow behind. *Mycena flavo-alba* is about the size of a shirt-button, and thrusts its white, smooth stem out of the litter. *Mycena galopus*, a slightly larger, greyish toadstool, also flourishes in leaf litter here. A bramble stick, left from the flail's depredations or from earlier hedge-laying, sprouts

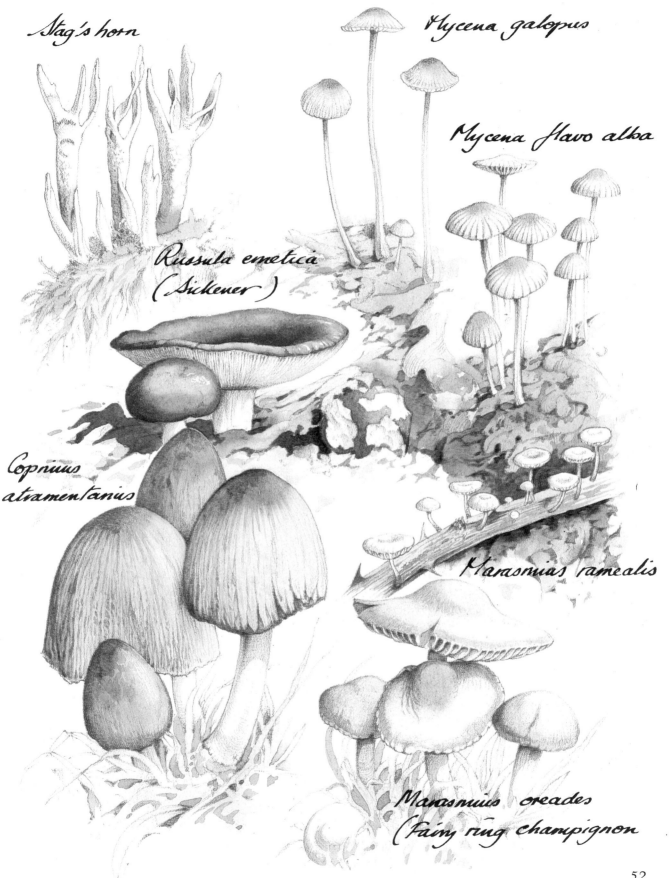

Stag's horn

Mycena galopus

Mycena flavo alba

Russula emetica
(Sickener)

Coprinus
atramentarius

Marasmius ramealis

Marasmius oreades
(Fairy ring champignon

52

a delightful fringe of Marasmius ramealis. A relative of the fairy-ring mushroom (which also grows on the garden side of the cottage-hedge), the Marasmius curves upwards from the stick, while its hyphae interlock in the bramble's tissues to break down and store its complex organic compounds as free nitrogen, phosphorous, potassium and calcium.

Another, more robust, wood-decomposer was lately having a go at the dead roots near the gate of the fallow field. Mycena tintinnabulum, with its dense tuft of skinny stems and a crowd of dark brown caps, is short-lived as a visible fruiting body, but the underground mycelium is still busy there sucking the nutrients out of the wood, and keeping them stored for later use.

Among the other fungi of this type are a cluster of Psathyrella on a stump between the copse and the Gweche, and an amazing cluster of fruiting bodies, with large brown cups and velvety black stems, growing out of dead wood near the cottage.

Various kinds of staghorn fungi are growing out of the litter and wood remnants, too. Near

the path where the rabbits cross the lane, a Clavaria rugosa has been quietly thriving, and today a patch of moss is sprouting some Xylosphaera hypoxylon, which has been working over the wood fragments underneath.

The oak which overhangs the lane near the Hall still harbours a multitude of little fungi around its roots. The great red Russula emetica's fruiting bodies have been severed at the base of the stem, and carted off by mice or squirrels, but Mycena capillaris, which grew in the shade of the earlier flush of Boletus, is still there, fading. Coprinus species are springing up in the meadowlike situations near gates, where luscious ink caps have opened up their scaly umbrellas in spots fertilized by pausing cattle.

Aside from feeding mammals and insects of the hedgerow with their rich nutritious flesh, all these varied fungal bodies, and their miles of underground hyphae, perform a massive recycling function. In a place like a hedgerow, where a rich variety of plant life jostles and thrives, then is cut down and dies, the need for recyclers is paramount. If the fungi and other detritus feeders were not present, the leaf-fall in an average oak wood, let alone a prolific woodland edge, would soon smother all growth.

It was not until about 10 years ago that researchers began to measure the high significance of certain fungi in the recycling of green plants (Frankland, Hedges and Swift, 1982). When they began to study the quantity of the standing crop (biomass) of the fungi which fall into the group of spore-producers (basidiomycetes), they found that they formed 66 per cent of the small flora of the forest floor. When they examined the dead oak leaves 18 months after leaf-fall, they found that 86 per cent of them were colonised by spore-producers.

More important, estimates of the part that fungi play in the metabolism of leaf-litter systems is in the order of 34 to 57 per cent. In other words, the networks represented by these tiny, fragile toadstools and mushrooms are workhorses capable of acting on that much of the plant material that falls to the ground, and breaking it down into chemical nutrients which can be re-absorbed in due course by new plants. They also make the litter itself more easily assimilated by other decomposers such as earth worms, nematodes, millipedes, spring-tails and mites.

It is not easy to study the quantities of these microscopic changes, but by patiently stripping the hyphae from oak and ash leaves and inject-ing them with a Mycena fungus, researchers measured amounts of nitrogen, phosphorous and potassium taken up by the fungus. They got results similar to those of other studies on wood decomposers. The concentrations of these vital plant nutrients were greater in the fungi than in any of the green-plant residues they were living on. Bracket fungi have also been found to concentrate minerals such as molybdenum and zinc. Iron, copper and sodium also accumulate in their structures.

They do the job by their extraordinary abil-ity to penetrate deeply into other plants' struc-tures, by their relatively large surface area in relation to mass and by their unique ability to move chemicals from one place to another, a considerable distance away. In contrast to wood-boring animals, which remove impor-tant nutrients altogether, the basids, or spore-producers, stay put and slowly release those key elements to the next generation of plants. In the meantime, they have broken down the large molecules of organic compounds into useable simple elements.

Timing is everything in the chemistry of recycling systems. If nutrients were to be released into the soil all at once, they could be leached away by rain into watercourses, and on to the sea. Basidiomycetes, including the deli-cate Marasmius and Mycena, hang on to these nutrients, then release them over a long period. Dr Juliet Frankland, who has reported at length on these studies, calls the basids the "habitués rather than opportunists" of the forest.

Sometimes they release nutrients spasmodi-cally, as in the case of a fruiting body that deliquesces, like slimy ink-cap, or when a fruit-ing body decays after the spores are produced and dispersed. But the fact that the root hairs of so many plants grow right among the nutriti-ous fungi must mean that they are taking up the concentrated elements of nutrition. The fairy-ring mushrooms in the garden confirm the fact that soil containing these fungi is much richer in plant foods. They create a ring of dense green grass as they move outwards each year from their original position.

Animals which graze fungi could also drop some of the nutrients back into the soil with their excreta. The clever human cook who dis-covers just where the mushrooms are growing is not the only one to benefit from these con-centrators of minerals. One set of fruiting bodies in the hedges was eaten into a fringe within hours of their appearance. Basids gather up plenty of calcium from the litter, which goes through further changes to be taken up eventually by invertebrates that need high quantities of calcium for their shells.

While contemplating all this invisible chemistry as I counted 17 different species of spore-producers in the lane hedgebanks, I came upon yet another kind of fungus, looking like some sort of crystal deposit, clustered round twigs and grass in the Hall section of the hedge. This turned out to be Exidia albida, a fungus which finds its niche in whatever collec-tion of woodsy material it comes upon, and holds together its own substrate while per-forming the alchemy of decomposition.

The variety of adaptations in the fungi I have seen are so vast and bewildering that man's imagination in creating such myths as fairies and gnomes seems a puny thing.

HOLES

November 22. In the hedgebank at the Chapel end of the lane, I can see a hole, well camou-flaged by grass and fern and with a leaf pulled into its mouth. By the cottage behind a clump of creeping buttercup in the shaggy bank, another hole lurks with a partly eaten rose hip lying beside it. In the steep, dark, north-facing bank opposite the fallow field, are four or five small-bore holes, ungarnished by grass or leaves, drilled deep into the clay. Still more holes can be detected along the derelict field if one feels around under the heavy foliage.

Near the copse, and under a stump opposite, are dozens more old and new holes of varying size and shape, some going straight into the bank, some at an angle, some with large piles of earth spilling out and covering up the opening. Around the crossing of the Gweche, where water converges into a gully, then runs under the road with the stream, a hole gives directly on to the watery ditch.

As the lane winds uphill to the Hall oak, the number of holes increases — this is a part of the lane which is not heavily travelled by humans — and it reaches a crescendo at a place where ash and oak overhang. On the north-west-facing side, at top-of-the-head level, where last spring a miniature bluebell wood appeared among the hedge-plants, two clearly visible runs show where small mammals cross the lane, trampling down the foliage. It is a kind of T-junction where a field-hedge intersects the lane-hedges in the shade of a tall, ivy-covered ash where overgrown hawthorn and hazel make a thicket. Here is a network of tunnels made by overhanging roots running horizontally along the bank. Under the oak near here are three more runs used by larger animals, and leading towards the rabbit warren. As the hedgebanks level down to the east, where they border the Hall's paddock and gardens, the holes and visible runs are more spread out, but still appear regularly.

The occupants of this network of busy runs and tunnels are elusive and mostly nocturnal. It is in the nature of a hedgebank to be a bad place actually to see small mammals, because it provides continuous dense shelter. They can also detect footfalls and other vibrations, and their sense of smell is good. The best we can do is catch a glimpse of a tail-end, or a face and ears, before the owner plunges, startled, back into the mini-jungle.

It is nearly always a wood mouse, but twice I have seen a bank vole cross the lane between a commodious hole and an old pasture gate, its stumpy shape, short tail and warm light colour betraying it. Moles are easily identified by the large earth piles they make, covering the entrances, and I have no doubt that a water vole has built its palace overlooking the ditch near the Gweche.

Shrews make small-bore holes so that they can squeeze out their wet fur as they enter, but they also take over other holes. And there is a large hole in the little-travelled section of lane between the stream and the Hall that I am sure is a rabbit's construction — not an attempt at a permanent home, but a temporary refuge when traversing the lane on the way to and from the hedge-warren just behind it. One evening, I peered into the hedge at this spot on hearing a slight rustle, and was more startled than the rabbit to see a flash of white cottontail, and a lolloping figure retreating into the field.

It has been raining for several days, and last night there was a deluge of almost biblical proportions. This morning the skies are washed pale and streaked, while ditches and watercourses are tinkling and splashing, and even mildly roaring with excess water. Some of the animal holes on the south side of the lane, where the fields are higher than the road, are acting like drainage pipes, and pouring water on to the swollen ditches. Any inhabitants must have been washed out during the night.

Come to think of it, there was an owl patrolling the hedges again early this morning, and although I have seen and heard owls at a few other times, I have noted five times in my diary that the owl has been hunting along the lane hedges after heavy rain. Whether the weather signals good pickings of newly homeless mice, I cannot tell, but there appears to be a noticeable link between the tawny owl's hedgerow hunting, and the flooding of holes.

Outside their holes and tunnels, the mammals of the hedgerows are vulnerable to a number of predators. The tawny owl gets (or has probably already swallowed) most of the shrews, as they venture out blindly for food. The bank voles spend the summer nesting in the copse and spinney, then return in October to winter in the banks, where they can find plenty of buds, fruits, leaves and sticks to chew. Dogs often spot these creatures, but they are too fast and too near their holes to be caught, and will be saved for the owl. The fox which crosses the lane at the cottage garden nearly every night these days is another successful predator, and there is another fox which crosses the lane near the Hall.

In an effort to count and identify the species and breeding condition of the small mammals in the hedges, I have set Longworth traps near the runs. (These are specially built wildlife traps which, if properly baited, provided with nesting material and emptied promptly, can do no harm.) Every time, I get wood mice, often the same individuals I have previously marked. If I put them in places where I know the mouse traffic is high, the traps are filled in a few hours; if I put them anywhere overnight, the mice generally find them before morning.

It will take several years and many traps before I can finish putting numbers to those studies of the mouse population, which increases dramatically in autumn as the fields become less leafy and fruitful, and the woodlands less covered. The effect of a high mouse population is to stimulate the numbers of predators in the lane. When I see a stoat (which is not every year), I believe the mouse and vole population is high. The foraging habits of the hedgerow mice and voles can be pieced together from evidence of runs and leavings, plus trapping and research. (See book lists).

This is the mouse's first taste of cold weather, and it spends the day deep in the bank, where the protected, friable soil has been dug to make a nest three feet along the tunnel. Instinct has prompted it to begin to store food in the tunnel. Certainly the pile of hazel-kernels will be needed when the snow comes. Emerging as the dusk turns murky, the mouse crosses the lane and makes a shallow hole in the opposite bank among the leaves. It moves quickly under the remaining foliage, runs to the deep hedge and climbs high into the shrubbery, finding a hawthorn in fruit. Working from the less thorny stem of an intertwining hazel, the mouse plucks a cluster of haws, and runs back to the shallow depression it has made earlier. But the smell of a snail interrupts this meal, and the mouse creeps along under the ivy leaves to a place where the snail is grazing on a fern leaf. The snail contracts into its shell, a pale, banded species about the size of a small marble. The mouse pounces, and seizes the shell in its long incisors, drilling it right through the spiral and removing the succulent prey.

Trying out the flesh of the haws, the mouse decides to press on for something more solid, and just along the bank it finds another hazel nut. At the feeding niche, the mouse props the nut on its wide end, tilting the sharp end towards its mouth, and holding it with its prehensile claws. Scraping those sharp upper teeth against the nutshell from the far side, it gets a purchase on it, opens up a minute hole, turns the nut and eventually bites the whole top off it, leaving tell-tale grooves on the outside of the shell from the grinding of the upper teeth.

This kind of foraging continues for an hour or so, until the mouse has had its fill of fruits and seeds. It then runs back to the hole, leaving a partly chewed rose hip in the feeding niche. Meanwhile, the vole has discovered some discarded haws, and is making short work of the fruit left behind by the mouse, which ate only

the seeds. The vole, too, comes upon a hazel nut and opens it, but this time the technique is different: the nut leans away from the animal, and the lower incisors do the work, leaving a much neater opening in the shell.

Two members of the rodent order are sharing this rich and rewarding habitat with only a partial overlap in diet. The two species of shrews (common and pygmy), the squirrels and the moles also find their own shares of food and times to forage among the concentrated plant and animal life in the banks and adjacent fields. Between them, all the mammals of the hedgebanks make important contributions to the general ecology by giving and taking: food, seed-transport, predation, soil-digging, excretion and finally dying. They are all part of the busy mechanism of the woodland edge.

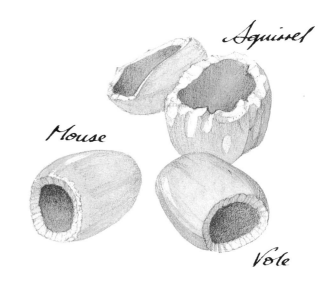

Squirrel

Mouse

Vole

Three ways to eat hazel nuts

On Stop

November 27. Problem: you are a soft-bodied hermaphrodite masochist with only a frail spiral shell between you and death by evaporation or freezing. Your many predators are beginning to develop a powerful hunger, and there seems little hope of your most recent clutch of offspring — already whittled down from 77 to six — surviving through the winter to breed on. What do you do?

The design of a common garden snail uses so many principles of mathematics and physics that when one is told that these unlikely scientists are also chemists *par excellence*, one can be forgiven for disbelief.

Yet there they are tucked into a deep hole, under and behind a thick root, stuck fast to the oak's trunk itself, a hen-and-chickens of a snail family: one large and six small. Try pulling them off — impossible; prying them — no go. These snails are glued to the trunk, already smoothed and grooved by previous years' hibernations, with a mucus that contains polysaccharides. It has taken the human species quite a long time to develop "superglue", using the same components and a brain that is capable of reasoning it out. How many million years it took the snail to hit upon this evolutionary miracle is unknown.

Hedgerows are full of crannies suitable for snail hibernation. I have seen a cluster of them clinging to each other in the recesses of an old vole hole. But an animal that spends (roughly) half the year on stop is vulnerable in the soil, and open sites could freeze the tender viscera despite the protective shell and sealed-up mouth. Where other than a hedgerow could it find exposed roots, gnarled branches scarred from frequent cutting, and double rocky banks? Not to mention unpolluted air, and the succulent lettuces which will be ready next spring in the smallholders' gardens.

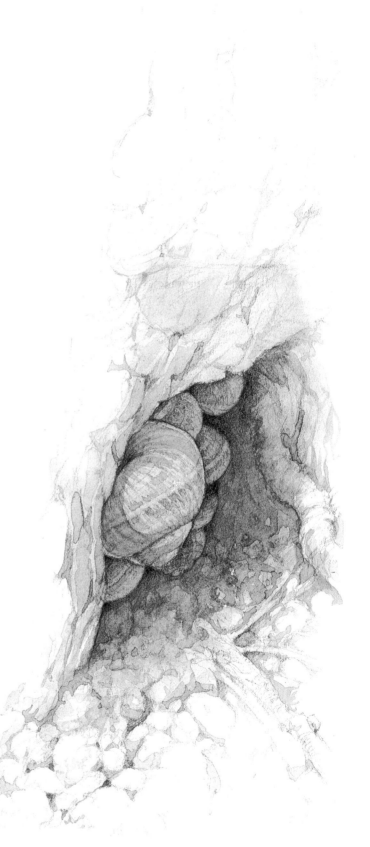

Hibernating garden snails

Rooks in aerial display

December-January

BIRDS IN THE WIND

December 6. Gusty winds have brought down the last shreds of autumn leaves, and rain has left the bare bones of the hedgerows glistening. Like a series of squalls at sea, the winds are coming over in repeated short gusts for about an hour at a time, followed by a period of dead calm, followed by another hour or two of furious gusts.

The occasional rook shoots by the window like a low-altitude jet, but all the small hedgerow birds are taking refuge deep in foliage, banks and woods. The only sound is the sad *seeping* in the hedge of a concealed dunnock. Not even a blackbird, which usually flies fast and low behind the hedge in windy weather, is ready to brave this kind of tricky wind pattern, and they too are lurking quietly in the copse today.

The birds of this farmland community have a variety of ways of coping with winds, some more successful than others. Aside from the blackbirds, many of the medium-sized birds react to wind by flying fast, and close to the hedges. Chaffinches and dunnocks often seem to fire themselves like bullets out of the hedge, from one side of the lane to the other. Magpies, whose long tails make them able to manoeuvre, at least awkwardly, on most days, fly low when it blows.

Birds with the shorter, broader wings in relation to body-length, are built more for dexterity in flying in the shrubbery, and cannot cope with strong wind. These are mostly birds with undulating flight, like finches and tits. Wrens and blue tits stay closely sheltered in low shrubbery on windy days.

The wrens sing early, as usual, from the heavy cover of the lower beech branches, surrounded by more hedge foliage; then, some-times after an attempt to find a cranny in a roof recess of the cottage, or flying at a window, they retire, invisible. I surprised a party of blue tits the other day during a veritable gale, foraging deep in an overgrown ditch, the perfect foul-weather feeding spot. Today, and all really stormy days, finds no birds at all in the higher trees, and none for the human eye to see in the hedge.

On the worst days, when cold as well as wind makes foraging impossible for long periods, the dependence on man rears its interesting head. The cottage compost heap and feeding post in the shelter of the building are visited by every kind of bird from rook to house sparrow. Better yeat is a barn. One day, when I had been wondering where all the chaffinches and sparrows had gone, I walked up the road past the cowshed, about 500 yards away. A loud twittering and peeping echoed under the metal roof of the cowshed, and answered my question. They must have gathered there from miles around. Thrushes and robins, it seems to me, are poorly suited to strong winds, with their bodies fatter than their wings appear to be able to support, except with every kind of aerodynamic advantage. This could be deceptive, of course, because the huge pectoral muscles that make up the fat "breasts" of birds are the driving forces for their wing-power, operating the wing-bones with the energy efficiency of a well-designed pulley system.

Blackbirds use the low hedges cleverly, and I have also seen a redwing fly over the lane in a roller-coaster movement, to take brief advantage of the hedges' shelter.

Feeding on the ground on cold frosty mornings, blackbirds and dunnocks also use the hedge's protection against wind, and choose the sunny slopes under the hedges, as do the sheep. Great tits, which have more direct flight than their relatives, the blues, stick to the short distances from copse to copse in heavily wooded areas.

Then there are the birds which positively delight in high winds. These species have an entirely different wing-shape, with longer wing-spans and ragged tips, so that individual primary feathers can be turned to allow air through, prevent turbulence and guide the bird's flight. The buzzards that visit the hedges for small mammals are able to use their wings to soar in circles over their prey before dropping down on them. Starlings, much smaller, seem to use fairly strong winds the way schools of fish use currents, simultaneously banking and changing the pitch of their wing-feathers to alter their course, tacking downwind across the fields.

But the greatest wind-performers in this farm world are the rooks. Several times in autumn, and again last week, I watched while these usually rather clumsy-looking flyers revelled in the wind, soaring and rolling, diving and plunging, launching themselves in every direction. Nobody knows just why they do this. It is a time of year when such behaviour would not appear to have any display function in a sexual context, and it seems to play no part in flock-formation or feeding strategy. It is impossible not to put it down to pure fun, like the macho display of a gymnast or a skier. Why they should leave off feeding on a cold, gusty morning and start playing about in the sky is anybody's guess.

Meanwhile, the wrens and tits are already searching out their deep winter retreats, where in the worst of the weather they will crowd together for warmth and shelter. Cold winds steal body-heat from small birds, for whom this energy is a matter of life and death. Those rook jokers can have the playground today; the wise little birds have gone to ground in holes under roots, in stone walls, in high banks covered with thick brambles, in places where even the most persistent bird-watcher will never find them. For small song birds, winter foliage (especially holly), man-made buildings and odd pieces of rough landscape are acutely important.

THE UNDERWORLD

December 12. The landscape has turned grey and dead-looking under the morning overcast. Winter has bleached it and immobilised it. But later in the day, when the sun comes through low down in the sky and picks out the red end of the spectrum, the illusion reverses. Drab hedges spring to life as reds and warm browns, berries are lit up shining and juicy looking. Winter tree buds appear fat and full of life, and the pale greens of the low hedgebank plants show up. Birds come out of their lurking for a few minutes and show their colourful markings, and a chance exposure of a rose root demonstrates the brilliant scarlet of underground growth that is going on all the time.

That dead look was an illusion after all. The hedgerow is full of life in winter, some of it suspended in a state of low metabolism, like snails and hedgehogs, some of it maturing slowly inside invertebrate eggshells, some of it waiting in an immature state for the warmth and day-length signals to crack open the pupa case, or unplug the nest hole.

A rotting log left lying on the bank from a long-ago hedge-laying reveals this slumbering life. Brought into a warm room on a cold December day, the log immediately begins to release moving creatures, and reveal an active plant life in its depths.

First to react to the temperature change are the woodlice, at least two species of them in these hedges. Moving fast on their 14 legs, they try to find deeper, wetter crannies. They range in length from a few millimetres to just over a centimetre. These are those tiny crustaceans that gobble up decaying animal and vegetable matter in all dark, damp places, indoors and out.

Tiny, thrip-like insects run about whenever a piece of the log is broken off. And, only visible through the 10x glass, many more springtails lurk in the soft parts. The white ones are especially fun to come across, as they obligingly flip their springs and jump a foot or two on to the kitchen table.

Each handful of rotting wood contains half-a-dozen worms of various kinds. White, transparent worms display the contents of their alimentary canals through their glassy flesh. A red worm, about two-and-a-half centimetres long, burrows tightly in a crack in the decaying

A rotten log and its inhabitants

Beetle larva; rove beetle; centipede; earthworms;
woodlice; insect pupa cases; pill millipede;
pot worms; round worms; snails and eggs;
spiders' eggs.

wood, and cannot be pried out, and an earth worm shifts soil through itself where earth has already filled a hollow part of the log. Four samples of yet another worm come wiggling out, about a millimetre in diameter and a mere centimetre in length, slow-moving, sleepy creatures. At first I thought the curled-up pill millipede was a snail, then I found three other specimens of this strange creature, about an inch long when extended. Unlike the black pill louse, which I have seen before in the banks, these are a light buff colour with darker, reddish spots in each segment, and they curl up into a tight, snail-like spiral, suggesting a defence mechanism. Confusingly, there were also half-a-dozen curled-up millipedes, hiding their many legs under their flat spirals. And, like nearly every log, this one has a hibernating snail and a handful of snails' eggs.

Spiders enjoy this environment, and are by now running about in protest at the disturbance. Tiny reddish and brownish money-spiders are the most frequent inhabitants of a log, and this one has three minute spiders with even more minute bits of debris encrusted on the backs of their abdomens.

Other spiders have come and gone, leaving behind webbing containing eggs firmly attached to the log's more solid pieces. Other cocoon-like structures contain larvae of over-wintering insects, and one finds all kinds of odd bits of lichen and woolly material, sometimes with decaying pieces of insects caught in them. A pupa or two nearly always fall out of a hedgerow log or stump, a favourite place for some species of moth and sawfly to pupate in autumn.

Plant life that thrives on the log includes two or three mosses, many lichens, fungi — two slimy cup fungi with soft grey, pink and yellow colours, and two kinds of staghorn fungi — and some seedlings of ground ivy, English ivy and dog violet. The earthy parts of the log are, in fact, interlaced with plant rootlets and many indistinguishable hyphae which make up the mycelium networks of still more species of fungus.

The community inside the log is also interspersed with the leavings of earlier inhabitants: sawdust by wood-borers, casts from worms, frass from larvae, eggs and droppings of various insect species, some half-eaten grubs and a liberal sprinkling of shattered snail-shells.

These remnants are mingled with rotting leaves, stem fragments and seeds. What is going on here under my lens is the manufacture of a beautiful, rich compost. It will take years, but between them the plants and animals that thrive in dead wood will convert it inevitably into useful soil, full of nutrients for later generations of trees and herbs.

It is the largely invisible, and not so attractive, inhabitants, along with a host of still smaller microscopic fauna, that make hedgerows such a valuable part of the farmland habitat. A woodland where logs are allowed to lie and rot may have more creepy-crawlies per square foot, but when so few pieces of old woodland and forest survive, the hedgerow becomes a crucial place for rich invertebrate life. The hedgerows are also most accessible to animals further up the food chain. The hedges along an old lane like this are richest of all in these species because of the continuity, the lack of grazing or ploughing close to the banks, and the continual cutting down of stems, trunks and leaves, which means the piling up of detritus. This explains why animals like hedgehogs, which feed in litter, prefer the lane-hedge to the hedges between fields.

When I finished with the log today, I was a little lazy, and threw it temporarily into the back garden instead of returning it immediately to its niche in the hedgerow. Within minutes a dunnock flew down to it, and started pecking away at this diverse assortment of invertebrates.

Springtail

REFUGE

December 23. Frost has turned the fields pale grey-green and put a pattern of crystals on each winter leaf. Hairy leaves like ground ivy, speedwell and nettle show the frost, but the hairs hold the frost away from the leaf, protecting its tissues from the ill-effects of freezing and thawing. The frost is patchy, showing where the hedgebanks give protection from cold winds.

Walking the various lanes and roads on the side of this hill, I can actually feel the shelter value of the hedgerows. On the worst cold and windy days it is unpleasant, almost impossible, to walk along exposed roads, but where hedgerows rise above my head, as they do in the old sunken lane, you can literally feel warmth as a contrast.

To test the mini-climates, I have done some temperature measurements in three locations, comparing the warm spot underneath a big oak with a more open hedgebank, and with a field with average wind exposure. While there is not a measurable difference in temperatures after a long warm or cold spell, the sheltered oak-shadow takes longer to cool down when there is a rapid fall. There is an average difference of one degree in overnight minimum temperatures. The hedgebanks, both the open sites and the sheltered ones, are warmer than the surrounding fields at most times, but during the day, the sunnier sites reach a slightly higher (less than one degree) maximum.

The warm spots under large oaks are favourite places for mollusc hibernation and mammal runs. Birds, too, use the oak-shadows as refuge in cold weather. The lane itself is providing a sheltered foraging site for resident and more far-flung birds now. The locals, blackbirds, dunnocks and wrens, can be glimpsed fluffing out their feathers in the deep foliage. A pair of bullfinches fly to the mangled copse, and search for winter fruits and buds, then fly on down the hedges, pausing on a hawthorn here and a holly there. The mistle thrushes have come back, bold and noisy as ever among the branches of ash and leaves of ivy, and a delightful little flock of long-tailed tits appeared yesterday out of the woods along the Gweche, flitting and showing off their colours while *click-twitting* in their cheerful, acrobatic way.

Fieldfares and redwings are flocking about, using the field that slopes away from the wind down towards the beechwoods for their winter foraging. A buzzard flies into a hedgerow beech, wipes its beak and preens for a few minutes before being seen off by a couple of rooks.

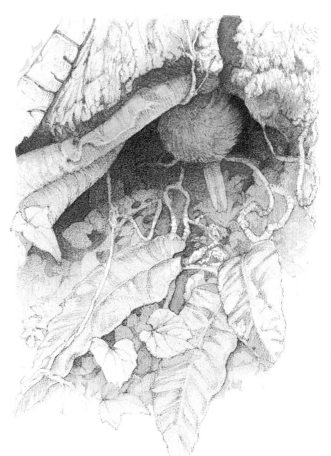

Overnight, while yesterday's raindrops were freezing on the hedge, the population underneath was busy and undaunted. I counted seven newly dug holes in the hedgebank in one section between the copse and the cottage alone. Just opposite the copse is a section which seems to have been colonised by moles. A large set of mole-runs and fortresses stretches through the field behind, and since autumn some of the animals, perhaps surplus males from the summer's breeding, have been coming into the hedgebanks.

Every time it gets cold enough to freeze the topsoil, when human logic would dictate a lie-in, the mammals of the protected hedgebanks liven up and make new holes everywhere. Piles of earth are deposited on the frozen ground, and new holes are made by the less conspicuous species, like shrews, too. The mouse-runs are often marked by a tell-tale trace of food leavings, or a leaf pulled in behind the occupant. There are obviously many reasons for this heightened activity: the need for wider foraging in cold winter, flooding or freezing of the original runs, movement to find less frozen ground deep in the hedgebanks; to name a few.

The fox-run that crosses the cottage garden goes through a gap in the lane hedge. The run is noticeable, and the fox leaves a dropping from time to time as it pauses under the hedge, also marking the hedge with urine. The lane, with its sheltering mammals, is a rich hunting ground for the fox. The owl is attracted to these hedgebanks, too, and I was startled on a recent morning by its strangled call from the hedgerow beeches at the cottage. It was using them as a launching pad for night attacks.

Yet the predators do not have it easy. Along the steepest part of the lane, under the Hall oak, is a haven for small mammals. The bank and tree give shelter from the prevailing south-west winds, and the roots running horizontally along the banks, combined with the heavy foliage, permit mice and voles and shrews to cover yards and yards of territory without ever emerging from the overhanging mosses and ferns.

Later in the day, when the frost has melted and the birds finished their late-morning foraging, I catch a glimpse of the rabbit return-ing to the warren on the well-travelled run which crosses the lane near the Hall. The hedgerows come top as a wildlife refuge as the winter deepens.

ROOTS AND BRANCHES

December 28. Skeletons of oaks spread crooked twigs against red winter-evening skies, and skeletons of hedgerow shrubs reveal the remarkable variety of species, along with the distorting effects of centuries of hedge management. The ability of a tree to suffer continual annual, biennial or triennial pruning, cutting down, or part-severing, and to grow again in a variety of branching, bending, shooting directions, is the fundamental basis of the hedgerow as an artifact. The structure and function of the hedge are determined by the growth habits of its particular species, and the treatment it gets from the owners.

Here at the cottage hedge, a mixture of hazel, holly, oak, beech, hawthorn, privet and sycamore forms the major structure, bearing a liberal sprinkling of roses, ivy, hops and bramble. Gaps let in sheep just when the ewes are heavily gravid, and hungry for the succulent garden shrubs. Beech makes the best thickness of hedge here with its contorted twigs and branches, and its held-on leaves, but it is slow-growing, and discourages its neighbours, thus creating gaps. Holly does the same, although at the eastern end of the lane there are places where large batches of holly mingle closely with oak, beech or privet.

Sycamore, the johnny-come-lately of the ancient hedgerows, tends to grow very fast, and send up tall shoots each year. It is of little value as fencing unless the main stems are "laid" every year. Ash shoots up quickly, too, on the top of the hedges, but responds to the cutting regime by forming a fairly thick branching from the cutting point.

It is easy to see why hawthorn is the most popular hedgerow shrub. (It completely took over the hedges during the rapid enclosures of the 19th century.) Where it grows in these hedges, it forms a tangle, wide at the bottom, of many stems and twigs, putting out new shoots in every direction. The flail positively stimulates this hedge plant to grow thicker in the lower parts of the hedge — one-up for the flail, from the farmers' point of view.

In the case of hazel, the situation is a little different. This tree grows fast enough as a hedge shrub, and cutting down does not deter it, but it never makes a low thicket of stems, so the winter hazels are likely to be gappy, and the hedges vulnerable to hungry sheep. The cottage hedge is especially sieve-like, because it has not been bent down and laid for many years. It would have to be allowed to grow tall and leggy for three to five years before laying, and no cottager has been willing to shade his garden thus from the south.

The Rococo Beech

Admiring the rococo beech-trunk along the eastern section of the hedge, I keep wondering why this species does well in hedges at all when we are told it does not take kindly to pruning. Beeches were long pollarded by landowners. who wanted to harvest their timber, yet keep their trees. They survive this treatment well, obligingly sending up new branches from the old stools, but they do not like occasional pruning or lopping. Unlike many other species, their response to injury is not a redoubled vigour of growth. Yet the beech is extremely widespread in hedges, where gnarled and scarred carcasses live to document the years of sawing and slashing. When the cuts come, the new shoots go in different directions until, finally, the shrub is a masterpiece of elegant zigs and zags.

The beech's habit of keeping its leaves in winter is another confusing phenomenon. The hedge beech, the pollarded beech and the young sapling all have beautiful bronzed leaves hanging on to their twigs even in the hardest gales, until the new green ones come to supplant them.

The answer to both these puzzles lies in the chemical messenger system circulating in trees' cells. All trees send out substances from their leaf-buds to inhibit growth of other leaf-buds close along the stem. This phyllotaxis, as it is called, determines the way a plant behaves when gardeners prune or nip out buds, thereby removing the inhibitor chemical and promoting growth in different directions. In the beech's case, a change in the chemistry of these messenger hormones comes with maturity, and changes the tree's response both to pruning and to the leaf-fall inhibitor.

Still more mysteries are posed by the places where different species grow along the hedgerows. All kinds of interesting historic, biological and ecological puzzles are growing there to be unravelled. Oak seedlings, and even oak shrubs, pop up here and there in the hedge's half-mile, but never within the immediate environs of a tall hedgerow oak. The obvious reasons for this would be the shade cast by the spreading branches — especially as these mature trees happen to be in otherwise shady parts of the lane — and the effects of the oak's roots in taking up needed moisture.

Not so, according to recent research (Shaw, M.W., The Reproductive Characteristics of Oak, from Morris and Perrins, 1974). Oak seedlings do best in a situation with half or less of the full daylight, and water stress is only likely to affect seedlings drastically in dry years. It now appears that the other culprits are the defoliating caterpillars, which have a habit of descending on long threads immediately below the parent tree, pausing to munch any seedlings they meet on the way to the ground. A mature tree is largely unaffected by these June larvae, but a seedling is quickly demolished, and will not sprout new shoots. They die because they are too small to compensate for the loss of important nutrients caused by serious defoliation. The wrong amount of lighting could add to the young tree's distress.

When I discovered 23 well-rooted small oaks in a stretch of about 30 metres, with no visible parent plant nearby, I began to wonder how they could all have been dispersed by immensely careless squirrels or nuthatches. Examining them carefully, and yanking on the roots, I discovered they were not young seedlings, but thickly stemmed little trees which must have sprouted up from underground stools. Since growing oaks do not throw out vegetative shoots or suckers from their widespread roots, it seems likely that this unusual crop of small trees in a grassy bank is the result of a continuing growth from the roots of vanished trees. The hedgebank, it seems, is a reservoir of growths ready to respond to small changes in the way the banks are cut, alterations in light and shade, moisture and the competition from other vegetation.

A lone holly about a foot tall grows out of another bank where no holly appears as a possible parent tree. Again it is thickly branched and strongly rooted, certainly not the product of a recently dropped berry.

Surprisingly little blackthorn grows in these hedges. This popular hedge species shows up along the best cow pasture at the western end, and as a few stems and spines elsewhere in the hedge. But if I want to pick the sloes, I have to go to the overgrown hedges intersecting the lane.

Lately there has been an explosion, almost, of young blackthorn suckers growing freely on the hedgebanks; not yet thorny, barely woody. The impression I get is that the near-perfect soil conditions and drainage are ideally suited to the promotion of sucker-growth. As the

flails cut the top growth drastically, and miss much of the shrub-growth in the banks, these former wildflower havens are becoming more and more colonised by shrubs of the kind that favour suckering growth from their rootstock.

The hazel population is another mystery here. A favourite of early hedge-planters because of its uses for hurdles and other agricultural needs of the Middle Ages and later, hazel was a good coloniser, when there were plenty of woodlands, because of the popularity of its nuts among birds and mammals. Smallholders liked it in hedges because it grew up quickly, and sheltered orchards. In parts of these hedges there is as much hazel as hawthorn, usually the number one hedge species. But there are almost no hazel seedlings or shoots growing anywhere in the hedge-banks. It has already done its colonising.

Wind-dispersed species, such as ash, syca-more and willow, are frequent in these hedges, although the willows are chiefly in the damp parts near the Gweche, where they have escaped from the spinney which wanders alongside the stream. A few other kinds of shrub, mostly animal-distributed, are rare colonisers here: alder, guelder rose, privet and the odd rowan and elder. But the most rampant of all, intermingling with any and all of the other tree shrubs, are the brambles and roses overflowing into the fields and banks, filling the gaps and rooting and shooting from branches that touch the ground. A great deal of honeysuckle, and a tiny sprinkling of wild gooseberry, complete the list of hedge-shrubs.

The various species grow in different proportions in different sections of the hedges. Sample counts moving down the half-mile reveal the same main species throughout, but in widely varying combinations. At the Chapel end, hazel dominates with hawthorn, elder, ash and a smattering of bramble and rose. Where the best cow pasture backs the hedge, huge old bent-down stems of hawthorn and ash are

The Hedge in Winter

exposed, where generations of farmers have created a living fence. Alongside the cottage garden, more beech and holly enter the scene, and the first sycamore and privet are found. A well-balanced mixture of all the common species carries on for the next 100 metres to the copse, where a woodland-edge ecology becomes more apparent than ever. Hawthorn, elder and rose grow thickly in this section.

Another micro-habitat takes over in a stretch leading down to the stream, with holly predominating and two hollies springing high from the hedge. Opposite the mature Gweche oak, a thicket of hawthorn thrives, but further on, where the other giant oak gives the lane a woodland feel, ash marches along with hazel and hawthorn. We are now running parallel to the hanging beechwoods by the river, so perhaps it is not surprising to find the common species of the edges of beechwoods here.

At the eastern end, where the castle view reappears, and the Hall's paddocks border the lane, the character of the hedges changes again. Privet and snowberry take over two quite long sections, logically enough, as these hedge-plants are often associated with houses.

The easternmost part of the hedge is different again. Holly and beech come in long swatches intermingled with hazel, hawthorn and oak mixtures looking like coppiced forest trees, and there is one nice rarity: wild cherry. Interestingly, the distribution of shrubs along both sides of the lane are roughly comparable; evidently the shading of the north-facing side is not enough to dampen these woodland-edge plants' enthusiasm.

A close look at the geography of the lane reveals a backward look at the history of land use, and a forward glimpse of the constantly changing mixtures of habitat for animals and plants determined by a venerable mixed-species hedge.

Moss covered Ash in Copse

MOSSES AND LICHENS

January 2. Four days of heavy rain have brought new life to the luxuriant blankets of moss, and the crustings of lichens, on the banks and barks of the lane. Just as everything else "goes on stop", the underworld of non-flowering plants takes steps towards reproduction. Especially conspicuous is a moss shaped a little like a miniature Christmas tree which has begun to display new pale green growth at its tips. A look through the magnifying glass reveals this to be a common moss of woodlands and hedgerows, Eurhynchium praelongum. It springs up here, at the copse, and in every section of hedgerow where the moisture reaches the right level, blanketing the soil.

Further along, another moss sports a thick fringe of spore capsules on reddish stalks. A woodlouse, a beetle and a strange, aphid-like insect fall out and run off as I examine it. After a pause to listen to a mixture of optimistic bird song in the winter gloom, I find some more moss growing low down on the horizontal trunks of old hedge-plants, with a crust of pale grey-green lichen growing on it. Another stump in the fallow-field stretch is covered with a pale, crusty lichen which is now growing inches-tall hollow stalks on which its spores are ripening. Beside it, a similar lichen displays cup-like soredia (spore mechanisms).

Everywhere it is the same: bare places of clay are being clothed in a dark green moss, or a flat pale liverwort; slime fungus, brown and rubbery-looking, grows all over a dead branch in the Hall section of the hedge; sticks and rocks are plastered with the various flat lichens, with their odd scribbles of spore-producing mechanisms aptly called Graphis and Opegrapha.

In any one day, I can count up to seven varieties of moss in the hedgebanks. Lichens are more restricted in kind, and are becoming less conspicuous over the years. Unfortunately, I have not made any early records, but lately I have noticed very few of the erect or bushy types of lichens. It seems likely that the combined discouragements of higher air pollution and moisture loss through repeated droughts and cruel pruning, have extinguished some of these lichens, famous as they are for indicating unpolluted air.

The mosses that grow along the half-mile include species of moorland, chalk downs, streamsides and mountains, perhaps indicating the wide variety of habitat provided by the linear woodland. They fluctuate with the moisture content of the soil and air, taking over the banks, fields and gardens along the hedges in very wet spells, drying out and waiting for their opportunity during the recent trends towards prolonged dry weather. They must have a moisture-conservation function, too, and young woodland plants grow quite happily under the thickest moss, bursting forth through the matted growths at their allotted time.

Near the moist banks of the Gweche, where the lane crosses, and large pieces of machinery have lately been operating, there are expanses of bare clay in the hedgebanks. The earth has been dug out so deeply that no seeds can land on the bank here, and only the odd dandelion and one brave specimen of yellow archangel have survived underground to grow again. But already, in the month or two since the damage was done, a greening can be seen here and there. A liverwort, Pellia epiphylla, has spread tiny leaves over some of the rougher spots, and a moss, one of the many Fissendens species, is growing on top of that. From simpler to more complex, as these plants form a carpet on the clay, perhaps new flowering plants will gain a foothold, too.

Lichens are not really hedgerow plants. I see many more species, and much more obvious growths, when I walk in the nearby woods, or up on mountains. Their basic need is for a suitable substrate — tree-bark, stone or soil — moisture and plenty of light. We think of lichens as plants of the dark woodland, but they must have a fairly high level of light, probably because they have so little chlorophyll, and thus must use the light to best advantage. These hybrid plants, made of a kind of layer cake of algae between fungus, have a relatively unspectacular role to play in the local ecology. They take no nourishment from their host tree, soil or rock. All of their metabolism involves the nutrients that can be plucked out of the air and sun by the algae, and exchanged with the fungus.

Nasty-tasting acids protect lichens from the foraging of large animals, with the notable exception of reindeer. But a host of smaller creatures with various kinds of protections against the acids feed on them. One reason the

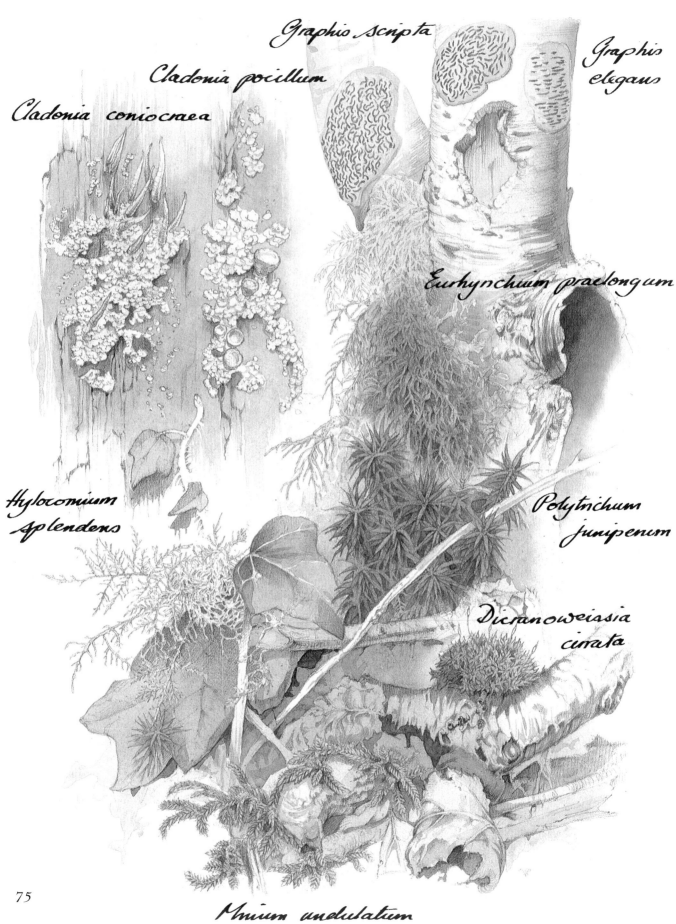

Graphis scripta

Cladonia pocillum

Cladonia coniocraea

Graphis elegans

Eurhynchium praelongum

Hylocomium splendens

Polytrichum juniperum

Dicranoweisia cirrata

Mnium undulatum

lichens in the hedgerow are rather forlorn imitations of the woodland growths is that the abundant snail and slug populations have been gobbling them up. Here, on a holly stem where a bare patch eats into one of the Graphis lichens, is evidence of insect predation. Many different kinds of mites and moths feed on some lichens, and in their seasons the caterpillars of moths and butterflies make short work of small discs, with spore-like soredia, the reproductive parts of lichens. Some creatures hate them — those woodlice were on their way out — but a particular lichen gourmet is a tiny insect of a psocid order, whose relatives include the book-lice and an array of dwellers in bark and dusty warehouses who live on algae and fungi in such dark and fusty places.

Moss and lichens are important to birds and mammals in another way. Mosses line the nests of just about every bird which uses these hedgerows, and lichens form a key part of the nests of chaffinches and long-tailed tits, two species which use these hedgerows. The functions may include camouflage, insulation and padding. Who knows, lichens having been used by people through history as a medical aid (for anything from cuts to rabies) could possibly have survival value for young animals in their nests.

Few lichens survive in a well-manicured arable landscape. It seems highly likely that the slow-growing lichens are on the wane, as more and more of the countryside gets pruned back and dried out. Since their value in indicating air pollution has been recognised, and their possible usefulness in medicine indicated by antibiotic research, lichenologists are concerned about local declines in lichen populations.

The decline in both moss and lichen growths in these hedgerows could be accounted for by the new, more drastic, cutting policy since the farmers have been using the flail, or by the measured increase in air pollution. Meanwhile, I find today, as on many other days, a piece of lichen dropped just here on the rabbit-run. Something is finding it useful.

EYE TO EYE

January 10. Snow gleams crystalline on the fields and banks, reflecting an eerie peach colour from the low winter sun, which barely appears over the hill these days. Tracks reveal where the blackbirds have marched down the edge of the lane hoping for a few bites from the locked-in hedges. As I walk in the early cold, a blackbird deep in the hedge plucks a rose hip and tosses it into the back of its throat, then stares at me.

In the cottage garden, all the birds are begging boldly for food. The robins come right up to the back door, and the garden is full of robin *clicks*. Wrens, chaffinches and dunnocks are coming up close, the wren flying desperately against the window-pane. Even a pair of carrion crows perch on the lower branches of the hedgerow oak, and eye the compost heap covetously.

Down the lane, a robin *clicks* at me from low down in the hedge, for a change, instead of singing from higher up. At the Chapel end, another robin sings tamely at me from a twig, and another down by the copse shows himself just as directly, staring at me through the large, round eye, the eye that helps give the robin its Christmas-card kitsch, but which is really designed to enable the bird to forage in the dim, early-dawn light. Sometimes the cottage robin follows me down the lane like a faithful dog.

It is a well-documented fact that birds grow tame in cold weather. The instinctive alarm and retreat are somehow inhibited or outweighted by the need for a kind of association with man based on food-and-shelter needs. Unfamiliar birds come closer, allowing themselves to be examined. A mistle thrush drops down on to the low hedge and looks around, a fieldfare raids the hips from the garden rose bush, redwings lurk nearby. The beggars near the door include a pied wagtail and a bullfinch. Even the usually shy dunnock stands unconcernedly on a twig just feet away from my field-glasses.

In the same way that the jackdaw perches on the sheep's back, the resident and visiting birds of the hedgerows have formed an association with the human species. In bird species as a whole, all gradations of relationship exist from brief tolerance through heavy dependence, from the occasional woodland visitor shyly

Tame robin

Staring now at a robin, his feathers fluffed out, his gaze steady, I find I can speak to him, and even move suddenly, without spooking him or causing him to flinch or blink. It is hard, watching him stare back at me, to accept the fact that birds are among the more instinct-dominated of animal species, and that almost every tiny component of their complex behaviour is programmed genetically at conception. Originally a wild, woodland bird, the robin has developed a genuine association with man. The progression out of the woods and into the farmland hedgerows, the gardens, parks and cities, has been relatively quick in evolutionary terms, so it is hard to eliminate the possibility of learning (in the sense of conditioned response) as an element in this association. The robin's well-known propensity for following the gardener as the spade turns over fat worms is a good example of learning — on a par with the tits and their milk-bottle tops. But there appears to be a deeper link here between man and bird, developed over the centuries, when individual birds which have attached themselves to the human settlement have survived on human leavings or cultivation

peeping out of the hedge, to the sparrow, blackbird or starling highly adapted to urban life, and to bird-tables. The hedgerow birds are halfway along. They tolerate us, and use us when they need us, but can they be said to be attached to us in any more than a casual embrace of occasional necessity?

The blackbird adapts

activities, and this attachment has been selected by their breeding success. Has it become programmed into the birds' genetic make-up?

It is not as if I set out deliberately to tame the robin, like Dr Niko Tinbergen and his greylag geese, or Len Howard, who had a wonderful wild-bird menagerie. These birds are being taught by experience, not by intentional human conditioning. Is it fanciful to wonder whether, indeed, this is the way truly symbiotic relationships are evolved? If humans go on destroying so much of their natural environment that they need to protect and feed the birds in their artificial ones in order to enjoy the colourful feathers and pleasing songs, then the means of survival they give in exchange for the aesthetic returns may some day become essential to the robin species — and to *homo urbis,* too.

There is one enormous catch in all this: cats. To benefit from human food, robins must run the gauntlet of one of our favourite domestic pets. In an investigation of 100 robin deaths, Dr David Lack found that no fewer than 44 were killed by cats, which do not even eat them. With such a heavy price to pay, the bond must already be fairly strong, and this could reflect the diminishing of the original habitat, those vanishing woodlands and copses. Man-made habitat, such as hedgerows and gardens, is becoming essential to the local populations of the species.

Even if this all sounds a bit speculative, the robins give much the most vivid impression of friendship among my hedgerow birds. The tits will alight briefly near one's window, or on the hedgetop, but they quickly look away and fly. The dunnock sits motionless enough, and lets me walk by close, but he does not follow, only tolerates. The blackbird usually *pinks* a protest or two, and then ignores my proximity. Chaffinches fly by and show off as they would to another chaffinch, but they are far happier returning to the high shrubbery, and the wren, well, the wren's feelings are expressed in his teetering knee-bends and furious click-scolds. He will not come close to be fed. The robin is certainly not treating me as a member of his own species. I have never seen one display at me, only at other birds.

Bird counts have shown that as woodland decreases, and the land becomes more and more bare, with trees spaced out, the small song-birds prosper because of the shortage of sparrow hawks and other predators. But kestrels have shown that predators, too, can adapt to city life. It seems a dubious tactic to allow, or force, the birds to flee from a treeless landscape, and invade the towns. Already, much is heard of the measures necessary to control flocking birds on public streets and buildings.

A Snowy Night

January 16. More snow falls early in the night, heavy and wet, coating the lane and the hedges with soft white. Later, the clouds rush on and allow a faint starlight through, and the mammals of the hedgerows venture out to do a little hopeful foraging. The temperature drops sharply.

Where the watercourse crosses the lane, and drains the fallow field, a brown rat emerges from the hedgerow, and descends into the culvert to drink and hunt. In a straight stretch of hedge under a stump, a shrew wakes up and quickly crosses the lane for a drink out of the not-quite-frozen gully. Out of a large hole in the rotten stump opposite the copse, a bank vole pokes its nose and takes the plunge, leaving an imprint of its tail as it slides down into the lane to search for the base of a thick grass clump to nibble. It comes across a fallen elder twig, and bites out the soft nutritious centre.

As the night wears on, the predators arrive, hungry. A stoat crosses near the copse, and leaves behind a tell-tale dropping to betray a new-caught victim. But the mice stay close under the hedge, and in their under-snow tunnels. The farm cat stalks through the field in the early hours of the morning, and is lucky enough to discover a roosting bird just before dawn.

The fox has been hunting in the fields above, and returns now with an empty belly. As it crosses the lane on a favourite mammal-crossing, a rabbit crouches terrified in the half-light under a thick piece of hedge. The fox passes on, upwind, to make a kill in the hedge where the mice congregate, and leaves a bloodied paw-print as it goes through the hedgebank on its way down to the beech woods.

As the dawn greys the landscape and sky,

blackbirds, *chooking* and *pinking*, stalk along the edge of the lane hoping for a winter insect or two in the shrubby leaves, then repair to the hawthorn bush to pluck the few last fruits. A part-severed earthworm lies on the snow where one bird hurried to shelter. Another rabbit braves the early light and investigates the lawns at the Hall but, finding very few leaves to graze on at the bases of the trees, makes a curved track back to the warren. Higher up in a deserted field, a party of rabbits come out of their warren and play in the snow, then return for the day.

As the sky turns a dirty pink, and the human observer appears in the lane, the quiet is thick and deep. Most birds leave their feeding efforts to a few hours before noon, and another similar period after the sun has passed the apex of its low parabola, but in the deep woods the tits and wrens are exploring every twig, pecking behind the ivy which crawls up the oaks, investigating crevices in the bark and ceaselessly searching for food to keep their small bodies going.

In the cottage garden, one bird has failed. A hen song thrush lies frozen on the path. Winter has left its grim message: adapt or die.

MATES

January 26. A subtle change is taking place in the bird life of the hedgerow community. A warm, thawing day after rain brings out early feeders and snatches of song. Wrens are singing more strongly, robins are behaving territorially and the other night the blackbird pair roosted together under the holly bush.

It is easy to forget how long before breeding the birds must start the complicated business of pairing and staking out territory. The day-length has changed perceptibly, and thus a warm day is the trigger for pairing activity, as distinct from courtship, which much later will lead to mating.

Robins have been pairing for weeks, although they have not yet established spring territories. The cottage pair settled the matter first in December with a minimum of singing. They have hardly been heard since as they go about their crucial business of staying alive in winter. This pair could be the same as last year's. At the copse, another male exhibiting a strange melanism which produces a streaky belly, is still looking for a mate judging from his persistent singing even on the dullest days.

The songthrush dies

Further along, near the Gweche, a third winter robin territory is unsettled, and I believe there is no pair there yet, only the odd one or two singing birds. At the Hall, at least one pair seem to have settled matters, as I see two flying together and hear no song. These differences in pairing habit could be explained by the fact that some robins migrate in winter, while others stay put. The cottage pair is resident, and the other males down the lane probably are too, but most females migrate, and so do some males. They may go only short distances, or as far away to an offshore island such as Skokolm, which is less than 100 miles from here.

The song is becoming territorial in the cottage birds' case (they both sing), and in the others' it is a plea for a mate from a species which has no visual indication of its sex. Male and female even sing the same tune.

Such liberationist relationships are not for the wrens. All winter, the males and females have fed and roosted together. But the females have had no status, and there is no certainty that their association is a genuine pairing. Repeat pairings from year to year are unusual, and wrens in a rich territory may be polygamous. The singing they are beginning now is a territorial song, and as such is distinctly related to pairing. The earlier wrens pair, the sooner they can get on with the breeding, and the more likely that they will succeed, provided the caterpillars arrive on time.

Blackbirds are more steadfast than robins or wrens, with repeated and life-long pairings the rule rather than the exception. But the blackbirds are too busy yet to devote any time to the complicated rituals of display and courtship, and their association is more a loose sharing of the territory than a genuine pairing. They are matey without being mates.

Their distant relatives, the mistle thrushes, have been paired since early last month. They are establishing a potential nest site somewhere in a copse uphill towards the farmhouse, from where they raid the hedge and the hedgerows that intersect the lane. I often see them in the vicinity of the Hall, where a small collection of trees could make an alternative nest site for them. These birds require a slightly higher tree than the smaller blackbirds, and a range much wider for their nesting and feeding purposes.

I have not seen a song thrush since the tragic incident during the recent snow, when a female song thrush's dead body appeared overnight in the cottage garden, while the male took refuge in our woodshed for four days. Whether this was a pair I cannot possibly confirm, but it seems likely.

For the rest of the hedgerow birds, tits, chaffinches, dunnocks, nuthatches, the matters of sex and nesting are a long way off as they concentrate on survival. The great tits seem to have changed their song, but it will be another month before they need to translate their territorial urges into any kind of overt breeding behaviour.

There is just one more rather delightful exception to this generality: the bullfinch pair that visit the hedgerows every week or so, are paired permanently (they often pair for life), stay together winter and summer, roosting, feeding, nesting and raising their brood together in an alarmingly anthropomorphic way. It is almost as if these foes of the human gardener are becoming more human than humans.

February-March

EVOLUTION OF A HEDGE

February 3. A warm interval, with spots of sun, interrupts the February gloom and frost. Ash-buds swell to black thumbs on the leader branches, and hazel catkins drop their yellow flowers overnight like window-blinds. These two species are more frequent in these hedges than in most. Plentiful hazel and ash could indicate great age in a hedge, along with a great variety of species. The time has come, with the swelling buds making identification easier and the structure of the huge, bent-down trunks clearly visible, to assess the age of the lane's double hedgerows, using both physical evidence and documentary research.

First, the count. Dr Max Hooper, the doyen of hedge researchers, studied them intensively in eastern England during the 1960s and 1970s, and formulated a rule of thumb (Pollard, Hooper and Moore, 1974). By comparing known ages of hedges with the counts of species of hedge shrub in 30-yard stretches along their lengths, he found a significant correlation between numbers of species of hedge plant and the age of the hedge. The theory is that older hedges are gradually colonised by different species of plant distributed in this rich habitat by wind and animal-dispersal. Ash and hazel are good examples of these two kinds of dispersal.

Dr Hooper's rule works out at about 100 years for each species, plus 30 years to allow for the time needed for dispersal to get started. I got someone else to choose six 30-yard sections in order to eliminate my own prejudicial knowledge of the hedges. The first section contained nine species, the second 12, the third six, the fourth (by now we have passed the Gweche, and are on more acid soil) nine again, the fifth

eight, and the sixth, near the Hall, 10 — not including a wild cherry which grows slap at the end of the stretch chosen.

There are also four other species of shrub in the hedge which fell through the sieve of my friend's random choices: birch, oak, alder and rowan. The average of these 30-yard counts comes to nine species. This count would bring the hedges back to the year 1055, about the time when the laws of Hywel Dda, the great Welsh king, decreed the uses of land down to such details as the value of each kind of tree as timber. (An oak was worth two cows, a beech, half as much.)

But Dr Hooper was the first to emphasise that his system of dating hedges was valid, as far as he knew, only in the east. More recent research, by Dr E. Pollard in Huntingdonshire, and by Dr R.A.D. Cameron in Shropshire, has shown that the relationship between species average and age can vary by a factor of 500 years (Cameron and Pannet, 1980). In some areas they found hedges with many species that were dated much later by documents. Both of these experts, and other recent researchers, have pointed out one reason: the hedge may have been made out of a woodland "assart" (an allotment for clearing handed out by lords of the manor or landowners). The new holder felled the allotment, ploughed up the field but left a string of saplings on the edge, which he then bent down and "laid" to make a hedge — a multi-species hedge from the start. The Hooper rule applies better to those later planted as single-species hedges, often at the time of the 19th-century enclosures, when common land was converted to farms and estates.

I find in my study hedges huge horizontal trunks, especially in the western end on the south side of the lane, and in the end near the

Hall. The species appearing in the hedge are similar all along the lane's half-mile, but the relative prominence of species varies enormously. There are hawthorn places, hazel places and holly districts, and the same with beech, oak and ash. The whole western end seems to be largely a two-species hedge, with hawthorn and hazel, while at the eastern end there is a more balanced mix of species in large swatches.

From the purely physical evidence, it looks as. if the eastern end was the result of woodland assarting, and the western half was a mixture of planted hedges and woodland relics. The reason is the balance of species. The hedge-counting system does not work well in Wales, but what one needs to do to establish the beginnings of a hedge is to find out when the local woodlands were cut down.

Alas, this kind of detective work is challenging and full of pitfalls. The documentary research proves sparse and confusing. I will do the unscientific thing and start with imagined scenarios of possible explanations, and then examine the meagre archive material. I believe this lane to be typical of the problems of dating these rich Welsh hedges, and I am reinforced in this belief by local historians.

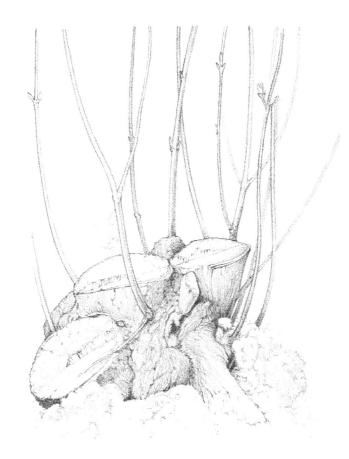

Rejecting the 11th century as being unlikely and, anyway, unverifiable, let us think about 1250, a time when many forests were cut. The Normans have colonised the coast of South Wales, and the estuaries of the west, and English kings have pushed into the forests of eastern Wales, where the Marcher lords are to be given land. But the Commote of Iscennen, where our hedges are located, is in constant dispute. At 300 feet above sea level, the lane itself and its immediate environs arc likely to have been part of the band of Welsh occupation at 300-to-1,000 feet. Here their settlements among the forests defy the invader, and provide bases for raids on the colonists.

These woodlands, probably not prehistoric but continuous relics of the ancient pedunculate oak forests, are being used as pastureland (pannage) for pigs, cattle and sheep among the trees. Their timbers are valued by law and custom as a continuous renewable resource not to be squandered. Charcoal-burners take chunks out of the forests, and ship-builders and castle-constructors are preying heavily on them, but much of it by coppicing and pollarding (cutting down to near the ground), rather than clear-felling to make fields. Underwood — the young trees that grow up where pollarding or glades permit — is subject to various forms of common rights allowing people to pick up sticks, cut brush, harvest acorns or otherwise use the resources, all of them renewable. Laws govern such matters as Smoke Silver (payment for firewood) and Woodhen (exchange of a hen for wood-gathering rights), and strict rules assure the continuity of trees. Twelve mature trees have to be left in each acre felled or coppiced, for instance (Linnard, 1982).

This lane could have been a fairly important trackway in those times, flanked by varying densities of woodland on either side. It was oakwoods with undergrowing ash for the most part, possibly with some beech-stands. At its far eastern end, a mile or so beyond the end of my study area, the lane points at an ancient religious site known as Capel Dewi, and beyond that lies the Mynydd Du, or Black (as in magic) Mountain, where other ancient paths and cairns criss-cross.

The castle is being built on the site of a previous Welsh fortress conspicuous on a 300-foot limestone crag at the head of the narrow valley. Princes and lords who occupied the castle before and after this time would have preserved forests in the environs for hunting as well as pannage. But during the 13th century, the invaders had a nasty habit of forcing the local inhabitants to cut great swathes through the forests as military roads, thereby goading the local princes into revolt from time to time.

On the whole, this was a period in these parts when agriculture and woodland were synonymous. A pastoral, knightly and warlike people were managing the land with all the skills that the landscape historian Oliver Rackham describes as "woodmanship" (Rackham, 1980). The arable open-field system of feudal England was virtually unknown. The lane was unlikely to be properly hedged, although it may have begun gradually to sink and collect surface water, forming ditches and banks.

If we now skip to the 16th century, we find the Marcher Lords in charge of the eastern lands as far as Brecknock Forest, not many miles to the east of the Black Mountain. The Act of Union in the mid-16th century has replaced Welsh laws with English, including the ancient law of gavelkind, which give way to the English primogeniture. This means that instead of requiring a man's land to be divided equally among his sons on his death, it all goes to the eldest son. Fragmentation of land is arrested, and now the way is clear for the building up of large estates. Monastic lands are added to this trend as the dissolutions proceed.

English lords are busy buying up bits and pieces of land from a Griffiths here, a Williams there. Welsh lords, like the nearby Dynevors (Rhys or Rice by family name), are building up their estates and constructing their grand houses. Titled Welsh ladies are attracting money to their estates by marrying English titles and wealth, and providing fields as dowries.

Fields along the lane are changing hands often these days while the Tudors reign. Leaseholds, sales and dowries turn up in the records of the family estates, along with references to nearby landowners. Stone houses have replaced the rude huts of the medieval charcoal-burners, who have now expanded their activities to serve the newly burgeoning iron, and other metal, industries. The new forge at Llandyfan two miles away from the lane, and the even-nearer lime kilns, take much wood as

the land is cleared gradually for more intensive grazing. The great Tudor expansion of agriculture, industry and trade has its impact even in these wild Welsh woods.

Another leap of imagination takes us to the 18th century. The fields along the lane are almost exactly as they are now — pasture-land for grazing cows and sheep, interspersed with cottages with one-to-four acres where the cottagers raise vegetables, chickens and pigs, brew beer and harvest the hedgerows for fruits and nuts and fodder. One or two of the cottages could have been built to establish squatters' rights during a time when the custom laid down that a man could occupy one acre of common land if he could build his house and have smoke coming out of the chimney within 24 hours. One cottage is probably some kind of country pub, another houses a blacksmith and his workshop. The lane is still traversed chiefly by man and horse, with just the occasional ox-cart squeezed into its narrow width to transport timber or hay. People are planting hazel and holly deliberately in the hedge to provide windbreaks for fruit trees, and to give the stock extra foraging. The landowner at the Hall is replanting whole stretches with shrubs bought from the newly established nurseries on the big estates.

By the early 19th century, the countryside here is well populated. Every farm has its labourers and "servants", milkmaids, shepherds, farriers and all. The Anabaptists in 1808 get permission to turn a field called Y Groft, at the western end of the lane, into a chapel and churchyard, along with a right of way to pass down the lane and perform baptisms in the Gweche (where a platform of rocks can still be seen). Processions of white-clad baptismal candidates between the blooming hedgerows are a frequent sight in these days of ardent nonconformism. During the latter part of the century, and well into the 20th, farmers are trying to make their hedges pay by grafting fruit on to the hedge-shrubs, but the animals over-eat and die, so these linear orchards are soon cut down. Meanwhile, the smithy becomes the Smith's Arms, and thrives until the Baptists object to the sight of rows of empty bottles so near the chapel and close the pub down.

During all these centuries, a variety of hedge management has been used by the different landholders, and a variety of plants have crept on to the banks from the woodland edges and filled the gaps in the hedges themselves. It is possible to read odd bits of the land-use history by studying the plants in the hedge: hops here point to home brewing, along with ground ivy (alehoof); nettles usually mean cow muck; dog's mercury and sanicle are survivors of the woodland-relic copses.

Documents take the lane quite clearly back to the 17th century, when estate maps of the Dynevor and Cawdor estates which owned most of the land can be pieced together to verify its existence as a lane between cultivated fields with, therefore, hedges. The 16th-century records of many fields in the area changing hands as dowries or leaseholds provide good evidence that the hedges go back at least that far. Earlier than this, we enter the mists of conjecture, as no specific documents exist — not in the libraries or archives, not in the family histories. But certain early maps, and a drawing found in the National Library of Wales, hint at likely possibilities.

Early 18th-century maps by Bowen and Kitchin indicate cleared heathland and pastureland for most of the area around the lane at that time, while sizeable forests are marked elsewhere. They also show a trackway going along a route that is decidely similar to the lane's. Maps of this period are extremely approximate, so this is not by any means concrete evidence, but the lane's deep banks and curving narrowness mark it as venerable, if not ancient. The lane also appears to have marked some administrative boundary within the commote. Saxton's 1578 map shows a similar trackway, and a similar lack of woodland cover, in that area, but accuracy was even less acute in those times.

A diligent historian, William Rees, in 1933 compiled a map of South Wales as he reckoned it to have been in the 14th century. He found that open-field systems were confined to the wider valleys, that it was a time of great changes, with tribal groups breaking up. But the Welsh system of mountain roads and bridle paths was, he says, very complete.

The Rees map, again, shows a trackway remarkably similar to the direction of the lane, connecting Capel Dewi and the Black Mountain to the town of Llandeilo, an important religious and commercial seat since the Dark Ages. The earliest road maps, published in 1675 and later, do not help, except in showing that land throughout the nearby Towy Valley area was by this time thoroughly assarted, made into fields or common grazing land.

From all these clues, the variety of species and presence of hawthorn and hazel, and from documentary evidence, I would date these hedges somewhere in the 16th century. The logic of earlier history points to the use of land by Welshmen for pasturing, pannaging, harvesting timber, burning charcoal and practicing all the medieval arts of woodmanship that made the timbers worth two cows. But the 16th-century leases indicate organised fields, and settled ownership, as parts of large estates or smaller farmholdings.

The fact may be that these hedges have evolved slowly, instead of being planted, or even assarted, all at once. A painting made for the Earl of Warwick in 1787 shows a view of the castle on its clifftop, "seen on the approach to it from Llandeilo Fawr". Though it is by no means identifiable as this particular lane (which is in any case out of the way from the castle to the town), this drawing does create an image of what the trackways and bridleways of the time probably looked like. On the left is a pollarded hedge of oak and beech, growing on top of a steep bank. A man on foot, and another on horseback, traverse the deep lane downhill. On the right, a beech wood borders the road with well-spaced, mature trees on ground which is again higher than the lane. The castle ruin looms mysteriously in the distance, just as it does today from the lane as I walk it every morning.

The creation of the hedge I am watching today was a matter of many centuries, I am sure. The key to its ecological richness is the fact that it emerged from primary woodland. Its inhabitants, both fauna and flora, are direct descendants of the woodland-edge species that thrived before the fields were made.

The snails may provide the clincher. Dr Cameron, who made the Shropshire hedge-dating survey, has also managed to correlate ages of hedges with species of snail in them (Cameron, Down and Pannet, 1980). Using three locations in Huntingdonshire, Worcestershire and Shropshire, and a sample of hedges whose dates and origins were known, he found first that woodland-relic hedges contained more species of snail than enclosure hedges, and that hedges along roads were richer in snail species than those separating fields. He also identified certain indicator species of snail which correlate with the ages of hedges. The hedges in my lane are inhabited by three of the indicator species: Aegopinella pura, Cepaea hortensis and Ena obscura, associated with woodland-relic hedges in other parts of the country. (And possibly by a fourth.) The number of species of snail in the hedge was found to be even more strongly associated with age. Dr Cameron found almost 10 species on average in his Saxon and medieval hedges in south Warwickshire, while later hedges ranged from 5-7 species (for 1500-1800) down to a mere 1.4 species for 20th-century hedges. Snails are convenient as indicators because they are slow to move. They thrive on a stable environment.

I have identified six species in my snail-counts, but there may be more to come when I do my spring counts. The case for my hedges being woodland relics of the 16th-century clearances is building gradually, and meanwhile, the absorbing reading of history in the plants and animals of the hedge goes on.

HIGH FLYERS

February 16. A terrific alarm-calling was going on early this morning among the hedgerow birds. After I went out, I could see why. A pair of buzzards was circling the hedgerows and the hanging wood below. These birds of the high ground and upper airs occasionally descend to prey on the well-stocked hedgerows, especially the lane and adjoining fields. One December day, I saw one alight in the Gweche beech, wipe its beak on the branch like a satisfied diner and fly off pursued by a rook.

Tawny owls haunt the western end of the lane, where they come and go from the woodland on the western flank of the limestone ridge. They hunt all night, as I have found when I go out late, but I hear them *kewicking* most often as they go to roost in the early morning. Their activities, as always, are most noticeable after heavy rain or melting snows, when small mammals are washed out of their holes.

One wintry morning, I was startled by a sparrow hawk silently jetting low down the lane in hopes of surprising prey on the banks. Birds of prey are rare hedgerow visitors, but they provide proof of the value of the hedgebanks to the small-mammal population. Another category, including rooks, jackdaws, starlings and magpies, could not be called strictly hedgerow birds, but all depend on them for food, shelter or structure at some time or another.

On a misty morning, the only sound is the scissoring of wings as the mixed flocks of starling, rooks and jackdaws flow over the field like waves, fly, land again, and soar off. I watch the way they use the hedgerow trees to pause in and scout the countryside. They always leave one or two behind as look-outs, and take advantage of the hedge shelter when they place their troops. A variety of tree and shrub layers, with alternating field and woodland scraps, is essential to the feeding patterns of these birds. Rooks now nest primarily in small groups in hedgerow trees, rather than in traditional large woodland rookeries. These birds enter into the life of the hedgerows by competing with the resident birds, who mob and alarm when they come.

Still closer to the hedgerow life are the huge

Tawny owl hunting along the hedge

Buzzard and Sparrowhawk.

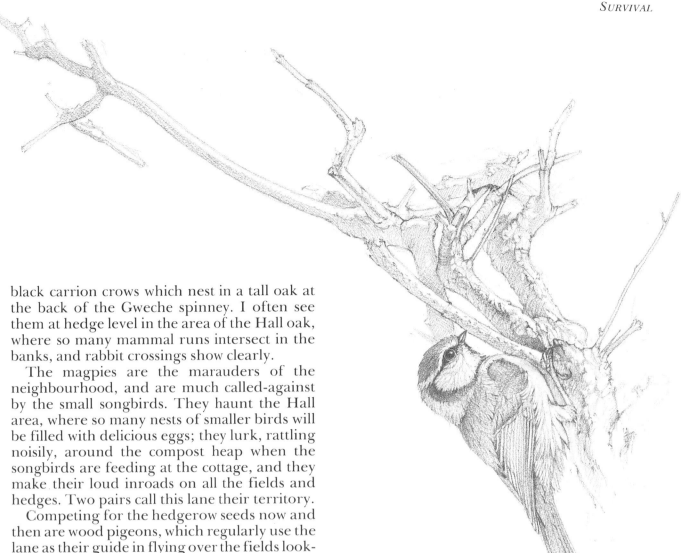

black carrion crows which nest in a tall oak at the back of the Gweche spinney. I often see them at hedge level in the area of the Hall oak, where so many mammal runs intersect in the banks, and rabbit crossings show clearly.

The magpies are the marauders of the neighbourhood, and are much called-against by the small songbirds. They haunt the Hall area, where so many nests of smaller birds will be filled with delicious eggs; they lurk, rattling noisily, around the compost heap when the songbirds are feeding at the cottage, and they make their loud inroads on all the fields and hedges. Two pairs call this lane their territory.

Competing for the hedgerow seeds now and then are wood pigeons, which regularly use the lane as their guide in flying over the fields looking for fruits and seeds. I enjoy encountering them in the lane, and seeing them respond by a sudden 90-degree turn, the better to eye me with their side-facing eyes.

SURVIVAL

February 20. A blue tit takes a birch catkin from the hedge, and flies to a branch to peck at it, holding the food plant in one claw. A couple of dunnocks go along the grassy side of the garden hedge methodically picking up leaves in their beaks, and throwing them aside to uncover any invertebrate life. A robin hammers on the softening ground at the edge of the cow pasture, under the ravaged copse's fragmented shelter.

The freeze has loosened today, and feeding strategies are adjusted. Birds that were deep in

the hedges and ditches yesterday now find other places to feed. Feeding times are adjusted to spells of warmth and dryness, while for some birds the temperature and pressure-changes signal a cue to move — from ditch to tree, copse to field, or to a different area altogether.

In a hundred ways, the birds of cultivated land respond to a complex combination of stimuli, which allows them to seize opportunities for keeping their small bodies from disastrous weight-loss in the hard parts of the British winter. The birds appear to have developed a set of built-in, or partly learned, survival strategies. The responses to cold, to wind, to the sight of twigs or trunks where food has been found before, to the feel of soft earth containing dormant seeds, to the sound of threats, the comfort of flocks; all are part of the intimate adaptations of birds and habitat.

Yesterday, a flock of six or seven blue tits flew out of the deep, rough ditch at the side of the cottage. This unusually low-down feeding station for blues can perhaps be explained by the sight today of a cloud of winter midges emerging from the damp below. But here are the blue tits now at the tall, mature trees further down the hedgerow, where twigs still harbour the occasional moth-egg or butterfly-egg, the cases in which larvae of flying insects pause for winter, galls full of grubs and the remains of spider nurseries. On the larger branches, the great tits are exploring the cracks for just such food, robins are tolerating each other in their zeal to feed on the ground under the trees and chaffinches fly down from the branches on to likely sites in the field.

Passing by the tall ash, I hear a rustling and fluttering revealing a blackbird presence among the leaves. Higher up, the robins are finding morsels behind the thick coating of ivy worn all over the trunk and lower branches of this tree. Ash keys are beginning to disappear now as the bullfinches range far and wide for their particular late-winter choice of seeds. Chaffinches ignore these, and go for an assortment of dried seeds in the hedges and meadow edges. Many birds take their turns at the ivy-covered richness of this spot.

In the field behind the Gweche oak, a pair of blackbirds, male and female, are feeding on molehills. Now and then an obliging half-eaten worm may emerge to be snatched up, a trick they have learned from the family feeding parties. Another winter attraction are cow-pats old and new. On the cold winter days, old pats still contain larvae and eggs of their many scavengers, and on the odd warmer days like this, a hatch of winging dung-flies may even appear. Sheep dung in the road, and horse droppings, also attract bird-feeding attention. The dunnocks and a couple of robins are picking out seeds from old droppings in the lane.

Although the last showers of nuts and berries on the lane have gone — all at once, as if at a signal — I still find small caches on the hedgebanks, or the occasional dropped rose hip, yew berry or hazel nut. The nuthatch is still hammering in the cottage oak, so it must have either found, or has hidden, a supply before it turns to insect food.

The bird community is more conspicious in its feeding today in the warmer air, but in recorded fact, birds feed for longer hours in cold weather, logically enough. To build up enough calories to survive the night a blue tit is known to spend as much as 90 per cent of the daylight time feeding. Wrens seldom let up, and other small birds are the more steady feeders. Early mornings are quiet in winter, not because the birds stay roosting late, but because they are feeding quietly behind the hedges, in the copses, on the edges of the woods, in the barn even. By 10 o'clock, when the sun warms things up slightly, they may allow a little time for singing; then back to work at the ceaseless task of keeping fed and warm.

Wrens are conspicuous by their absence in this part of the winter. During the freezes, they seem to disappear entirely. What is happening is that these small birds' large territory, held in winter as well as breeding time, is now coming into play. The thicker, lower levels of shrubbery and wet ground provide the kind of nourishment they must have each day. A rotten log full of woodlice, a clutch of caddis-fly larvae in their cases, the tiny pupae of flying insects, are exploited by the wrens' quiet pursuit. Short-winged and manoeuverable, the wrens disappear into the foliage of the deep ditch and the overgrown hedgerow running down to the woods. At night they roost in their old nests, packing many birds in together for warmth.

Others of the hedgerow regulars take up new positions in the deep winter. During the recent snowfalls, all the birds came into the garden for bird-table feeding. Magpies frequently left the fields and raided the compost heap. Sparrows, on the other hand, forsake the houses at the chapel end in cold weather, and fly down the hedgerow to pick up a stray seed or two.

Visitors who are not regular hedgerow or laneside inhabitants come by more frequently. The mistles *churr* harshly in the Hall garden before retiring to their already-chosen nesting site. The pair saw off marauding wood pigeons from the holly tree the other day. A goldcrest flashes by at the Hall end of the lane, returning towards the garn, a wooded crag where these birds regularly breed. A green woodpecker gives his laughing *yaffle* from the copse oak. Redwings and fieldfares often turn up to range across the fields and pick up the rose hips, or the last few dangling haws. A fieldfare plucked rose hips from the same bush at the cottage every day during the long week of snow. Flocking and moving about the countryside is a key part of the survival strategy of many farmland birds, but the functions of flocking are manifold. More pairs of eyes can see both food resources and predators, while young birds can learn from old. Predators may take one or two individuals of a large flock in a surprise move, but most will survive.

One of the most spectacular survival techniques in this lane has been hinted at by the large piles of snail shells which keep appearing on the banks. It looked at first as if some inhabitant of a hedgebank hole had done its spring cleaning, and turned out, in one pile, 26 empty shells, in another, a few feet away, 13 more. The odd part about these shells was that most were of old, long-dead snails, and few of them were cracked as a thrush would do by smashing them on an anvil stone, nor were they eaten into as if by mice.

Despite the lack of any anvil, or signs of thrush-smashing I have concluded that these were the leavings of a thorough song thrush. Desperate for good mollusc protein, the song thrush that frequents this part of the hedge and copse has been digging deep whenever the ground is soft enough, and pulling out old snail shells in the hope of finding a fresh one, then discarding them. Some of them might well have come from mammal holes, but the compact piles littering the roadside are bird's work. It must have been frustrating, judging from the number of well-worn shells, some packed with earth, a season or more old. The bird may have come to the end of a seasonal fruit harvest, and turned to the soil in desperation.

The use of the land by the farmland species for winter foraging is divided within species by territory. I saw a blackbird recently defend its favourite hawthorn bush from another blackbird, and there are other raucous squabbles between blackbirds. But when blackbirds, song thrushes and mistle thrushes share territories, they either manage to find different food-types, or use different kinds of places to find their food. The mistles stay in the tall trees,

A mysterious pile of snails

mostly, and specialise in certain fruits, the song thrushes go for the ground in copses or under the hedges, and the blackbirds, which eat a wide variety of animal and vegetable food from snails and worms to seeds and fruit, exploit the grassier places when they are not raiding their favourite hawthorn or rose bushes. If times are especially hard, it has been found, the larger members of the thrush family outlast such smaller species as redwings (Simms, 1978).

Tits are the classic illustration of related species using the same territory by specialising in different layers. The great tits in winter spend most of their feeding time on the ground, or on the main branches of big trees; the lighter, more acrobatic, blue tits choose to swing upside down and flit among the higher twigs, and the marsh tits go for the underwood shrubbery. I find these generalisations are borne out in this particular hedgerow habitat, but that does not mean I never see these birds sharing a twig or a branch. The other day, a cold one, two great tits and about four blue tits were deep in the stubble of a long stretch of low-clipped hedgerow, all clinging expertly to the hazel, ash, hawthorn and sycamore twigs and thoroughly cleaning up the bud-axils and cracks and crannies. Once or twice I have seen great tits displaying their bibs, and seeing off blue tits in a low-to-the-ground feeding position.

Dr David Lack, who has studied and written (1971) about the ecological isolation of bird species, has found that adaptations to the different feeding niches in the changing farmland countryside have emerged, and are still emerging, as sub-species become differentiated. The tits with short beaks have tended to go for food on leaves and twigs, while those with longer beaks feed in conifer woods. The agile blue tit is adapted to strip the bark off small canopy twigs, and find insects less than two millimetres long. Almost the only seeds it eats are the birch catkins. The great tit, on the other hand, can drill into the ground to extricate dormant seeds, or find insect items in deep cracks in tree-trunks.

Enormous exceptions arise among these ecological generalities. I saw for myself this year that when the beech-mast is abundant, as it is every three years or so, all the tit sub-species feed on it at the same time. At different times of year, and in different weathers, the birds spend a percentage of their feeding time on other levels of foliage.

Between November and April, for instance, Dr Lack found the great tits in an Oxford wood spent half their time feeding on the ground, 16. per cent at the branches, 14 in dead parts, five in twigs, four in leaves and buds and 21 elsewhere. The blue tits at the same time spent 34 per cent of feeding time in the twigs and buds, 32 elsewhere, 16 in dead parts, eight in branches, seven on the ground and three in leaves. All this (assuming that "elsewhere" would include that overgrown ditch) corresponds with the overlap seen here.

Finches are even more specialised in their adaptions to food and feeding stations. The chaffinch, most common bird in these hedgerows next to the blackbird, has a small beak for a finch, and must find many different kinds of weed-seeds, plus a few insects, to survive the season. It seems to find the right mix in the local hedgerow environment. The bullfinch needs to range more widely to find the kinds of seeds and buds that its strong beak and dexterous tongue can cope with nicely. I see bullfinches here only once or twice a week. The greenfinches and goldfinches which breed here regularly are to all intents absent now. Their winter needs for weedy places with spec-

ial seeds are seldom met by the hedgerows in winter. Now that the thistles and brambles are nearly gone, they are exploiting local waste ground, the many derelict quarries and ravines where their other winter-plant needs abound.

Birds of all kinds seem to use the hedges themselves more in bad seasons and weathers, reverting to the pastures and trees when the wind dies and the sun grows warmer, then falling back on the bird-table in snow. Aside from flocks which pass or pause, I frequently see as many as 27 birds using the hedgerows and copse in the space of about 45 minutes on a cold winter morning. The bird population, if anything, seems higher in this cruel, snow-and-frost-encrusted year — doubly cruel because last summer's sun and warmth, plus a damp autumn, good for invertebrates, resulted in a high breeding success and survival of young birds. Food supply, and the existence of suitable feeding structure, are fundamental to the sizes of bird populations, but strangely, the density of birds as counted by ornithologists over the years does not radically increase or decrease. Some species go in cycles, tits for instance, and others may move gradually into new ranges, as in the case of bramblings, but the excess of population or the failure of a food crop is taken care of by local or long-range migration more from than by excess deaths.

It appears that the final survival strategy for a bird to use is its wings.

SONG AND DANCE

February 27. The songbirds are starting to settle into their territories, their spring feeding routines and their pairings. Today, as rain and mist cleared before first light, I heard the first full dawn chorus. An occasional sunny day among the freeze-ups brings out an assortment of new music and distinct behaviour patterns.

Some, like the blackbirds, have long since occupied territories in which they will breed, but now they need to define them aggressively and defend them. Others, like the robins, have also occupied an autumn territory, and some of them have already paired. All the small song-birds are responding to hormone changes, temperature and day-length stimuli to behave territorially.

The first bird I encounter in the lane is, as always, the cottage wren. Surprisingly loud and full of confidence, the cock wren proclaims its presence — all three-and-a-half inches of it — with a new and beautiful liquidity of sound. Only yesterday, in freezing weather, this pair and other wrens were still crouching in a communal roost to keep warm. Now the cock is profligate in spending a good few grains of body-weight on the brilliant song designed to repel other males.

It is not the size of the bird, but the size of the territory, that determines the loudness of bird song. This bird is confirmed in its efforts by an answering song 100 yards up the hill from a hedgerow oak at the edge of the next wren territory. Winter has ruthlessly pruned the wren population.

The cottage wren always starts in the same place in an overgrown hedge at the back. It progresses to the side hedge under two giant beeches — the centre of this pair's territory, and their favourite lurking place. The cock may fly to the cottage roof, back to the hedge, on to an ornamental conifer and back again to the beeches, but higher up now. As it *clicks* in ever-increasing crescendo and pace, it does its knee-bending gesture of consummate, though miniature, arrogance. This outraged "teetering", as it is called, like an attempt to look taller, is a threat display. It soon gives way to flying and singing from post to post on hedge-shrubs, preceding me down the lane to the extent of its territory, about 250 yards away at the copse. It is positively exhausting to watch this busy bird

seeing to its domain, overseeing its mate, searching out and eating the vast amounts of food for its small frame and fast metabolism at the hungry edge of the bird year, and singing so intensely the while.

At the western end of the lane, two robins are proclaiming the boundaries. One holds the far end, with two tall oaks, some buildings and the chapel graveyard. The other uses the corner of the chapel-cottage boundary as its number one song post. The songs of these two birds have subsided recently, indicating that both males have paired, but they continue to join the dawn chorus, and there is still a good deal of border proclamation on a fine day like this.

Further east in the lane, the dunnocks appear. Here, where the hedges are thick and brambly, though cut short, and all the mature trees have long gone, the dunnocks are in charge, along with the resident wren. Today, one dunnock chooses a sycamore branch sticking up out of the hedge on the south side bordering the pasture, and sings, emerging gradually after each burst of song from the thicket of twigs. Its casual-sounding tune does not last long. Three or four dunnocks (I can never count these agitated birds properly) flutter down along the hedge, crossing the lane and back, then over to the field side of the cow pasture with a flourish of wings.

When I first saw this display habit, I thought it was some kind of distraction flight to lead intruders away from a potential nest site. But I did not know then about the colourful sex life and family arrangements of this conservative-looking brown-and-grey bird. Gilbert White, the great 18th-century cleric-naturalist, merely noted in 1774: "The hedge sparrows (dunnocks) have a remarkable flirt with their wings in breeding time."

It turns out that all their fluttering and chasing between pairs, trios, fours and more is part of an elaborate process lasting all spring whereby they choose not just a mate, but a marital set-up which can be monogamous (one of each sex), polygamous (one male, two or more females), polyandrous (one female, two or more males), or polygynandrous (more than one of both sexes).

At this time of year, before the breeding season gets going in earnest, they come out and practise their chase games. The hedges are their playground, their potential nest sites,

Dunnocks' spring flutters

their song posts, their shelter for feeding and their food: the be-all and end-all of their existence.

Towards the copse where the line of oaks leads up from the dark, north-facing depths of the valley, a congregation of birds has already assembled by 6.30am. This bird-roundabout is a place where non-hedgerow species, like starlings, rooks and woodpeckers meet the resident territorial birds which own the various feeding grounds. This calls for vigorous alarm calls from blackbirds especially.

Now, a flight of rooks and starlings takes off, leaving the chaffinches. I count 15 of these bright birds, the males' pink breasts and blue-grey mantles lighted up in the low-angled sunshine, between the copse and the Hall before nine o'clock. Most of the males are singing their hearts out, in their distinctive downward-pitched song, with its final flourish.

They are starting to play the chase games that go along with the establishment of territory. The migrants of the species which spent the winter elsewhere are beginning to show up now, and make the disputes more exciting. To the untutored eye, their aggressive chases appear like World War I aerial dog-fights: tight circles of two birds trying to gain ascendency, with dashes here and there by one bird flying directly at another. Less conspicuous, but just as important to the chaffinch, is an aggressive posture, when a male sleeks its head-and-neck feathers, spreads out its red breast and sways from side to side, also showing off the white wing-flashes.

They carry on like this day after day, endlessly patrolling and disputing the boundaries of their territories. If you watched long and carefully enough, you could draw the lines precisely. As it is, I have identified certain centres of chaffinch activity on the half-mile of the lane. One day I encountered a total of 19 chaffinches: a pair in the cottage hedge, three in the fallow-field hedge, one behaving like a sentry among the copse's fallen branches, two in the hedge opposite the copse, one in the bushy holly tree between the copse and the Gweche, four in the spinney, six more flying from hedge to hedge at the Hall in that dipping chaffinch flight. This was at 10am on a cold February day. Over the next few weeks, this area will be carved up between some of these birds, and others will move on. The chaffinch count-down to breeding is under way.

A little later I listened while robins sang at the copse. A loud song at the east corner was answered by a short burst from an invader opposite. This bird then flew to the ground, then away, in typical submissive response to the song of a territory-holder. Another loud singer performed at the west corner. Perhaps they will make two territories out of the reduced copse, and parts of the hedges, this year. These birds seem louder now that the cottage robins have paired.

The song thrush has started singing lately, and today it has chosen the copse for running through its amazing repertoire of short melodies, each repeated two or three times. It sounds, in its vehemence, like a whole aviary of different species. I have been hearing another at the Hall, where well-spaced trees and lawns provide a superb feeding ground for the thrush family.

Blackbirds are carrying on their raucous *pinks* and *chooks*, but they are not in full breed-ing-song yet. They are getting angry at the younger members of the family flocks who stayed together for much of the winter. The back of the copse is a focus for blackbird activ-ity, and I have seen birds squaring off aggres-sively at each other. The sloping pasture under the Gweche oak is another. Blackbirds have a way of looking angry: they face each other, ruff out their rumps and spread the tails fan-wise, calling in high-pitched voices.

By nine o'clock, the tits have joined the hedgerow bird community. Great tits and blue tits establish themselves in the Gweche oak most days, after some flitting down the hedge-rows. There have been perceptible changes in the songs of these versatile vocalisers for many weeks now, but their summer *tee-too, tee-too* is still rare and faint.

The pair of mistle thrushes are already nest-ing. They have established themselves in a shaggy hedge that intersects the lane just below the Hall. Brash and protective, they defend this territory against other species, as well as any invaders of their own kind. Their buzz saw call is not so frequent now, but I hear them singing in the spinney behind the Hall most mornings.

Just before the light begins to fade in the afternoons, a short reprise of the morning song comes together. From the same positions as the dawn chorus, but without the chasing and posturing, the birds remind competitors and potential mates of their existence. The blackbird is the last to sing, having stayed late, plunging its beak into the hedge bottom for invertebrates released by the new warmth. With a loud "good night" of *chooking* and *pink-ing*, it goes to roost under the holly, now joined sometimes by the female. The wrens are hid-den in the foliage of the deep ditch, tits and chaffinches are in their woodland roosts, and dunnocks among the overgrown hedges and stumps. The lane's bird community is ready for the night's hazards.

The Song

March 3. Heavy, cold rains after harsh frosts have washed the colour out of hedges and fields. Snows and torrents seem to have drained the energy from the land, and the long winter pause is breathless. But the pale sun spends more time above the horizon each day, and small spells of subtle warmth between gales are evoking responses in time-evolved ways. The song thrush has chosen today to perform a chorale, a symphony, an opera of a territorial song. He has, as Thomas Hardy put it, "chosen thus to fling his soul upon the growing gloom".

And what is soul it is! Perched on a forlorn piece of overgrown hedge behind the cottage, this bird sings at least 32 different short melodies. At that point human memory fails, as the thrush pours out ever-changing phrases before coming round to a reprise of its impro-visations. It incorporates every conceivable twitter and peep, warble and whistle, in its twice or thrice-repeated snatches. It vaguely mimics all kinds of birds, from the local warblers to distant sea birds. (The thrush authority Eric Simms has identified songs and calls of everyday species, like blackbirds, and exotic ones, like nightingales and stone cur-lews, in a suburban song thrush.)

For two solid hours, this bird stands upright in its characteristic, perching posture, and sings without pause. Then, for another two hours, it faces the other direction, uphill, and carries on. I hear it again, later, at the copse, where it has been doing most of its singing until

A songthrush's marathon concert

today. It started singing there about 10 days ago, and its song has increased gradually like the day-length which cues it.

This bird performs in the chilly mornings and the lowering evenings, stopping only for feeding and preening in the middle of the day. Two hours at a go is usual for a song thrush, but this one favours four or five. What can possible call for such persistence? Is it merely territorial overkill? Is it trying to sound like flocks of different species, and thus claim a larger piece of *lebensraum?* Or is there some reason for the depth of this bird's mating need?

Mimicry is one of the delightful mysteries of the bird world. It is hard to imagine what combinations of new genetic patterns and imitative learning techniques have evolved into such an elaborate song structure. How could these farmland birds learn to echo the seashore or lakeside inhabitants? Thrushes' territories are larger than those of blackbirds, and much larger than robins. With their habitat changing rapidly during the last 4,000 years, one can only speculate that their territorial needs have developed special qualities as the woodlands have disappeared and been replaced by gardens and parks. In these newer habitats, full of delectable insects and snails, their territories are smaller.

The significance of the song may in this case be less related to territory, anyway, than to mating. The bird has long since occupied a definable territory and defended it. Now is the time to lure a female into it. The grand old man of animal behaviour, Dr Konrad Lorenz, was one of those to document the fact that birds sing longer and louder when they are unmated. (With some exceptions, as the blackbirds go on singing long after pairing.) Birds also become especially passionate singers if they are bored and lonely, still more so if they are in wilder places where contact with the hens may be more difficult.

A female song thrush died in the cottage garden during a four-day cold-and-snow period in January. A male at that time took refuge in our woodshed, where I fed it until the snow started melting. If it is the same bird, this familiarity might account for its using such a nearby song-post for its marathon effort during a dreary day, with 50-mile-an-hour gusts blowing. It could even be possible that this bird had already begun the pairing procedure with the dead hen when that January snow came.

It appears that our resident song thrush has every reason to startle the cold March air with his epic song, whether the trigger is the lack of mate or the size of territory. By evening, when gloom increases and the bird takes up its song again, one agrees with the poet:

> "That I could think there trembled through his happy good night air
> some blessed Hope whereof he knew
> And I was not aware"

TIMETABLES

March 15. Lumps of icy snow are lying on the ground in patches. Wind and dark, scudding clouds alternate with sun and spells of warmth, then hail and later more snow. The late winter is full of deceits and illusions. Lesser celandine, already starting to bloom, has frozen in an open position. This earliest of spring flowers, with its shiny yellow starbursts, has successfully adapted to the stress of wintry spells. The petals, which normally close in response to a lack of light, in evenings or on rainy days, get curled backwards by freezing, yet when the thaw comes the flowers appear none-the worse. The structure of these common hedgerow flowers is somehow so flexible that the continual tension and relaxing of the ice crystals can be absorbed without damage to tissues.

Young plant-growth has been creeping along at an increasing pace in the last few snowy weeks. Cuckoo pint has been shooting up overnight. I counted 100 new plants in the space of 10 yards, already four inches high. Strawberry leaves, and the related Potentilla sterilis, are multiplying fast, but in miniature. Dog's mercury is making an appearance, leaves one day, buds the next, through the mossy, north-facing bank, and hundreds of tiny, two-leafed seedlings are growing in the bare spaces left by the straying ewes. Wild gooseberry and honeysuckle leaves are bursting on their woody stems in the hedge, and winter buds are unfolding in their pre-ordained sequences.

Some early plants are triggered into growth by daylight alone, some by a combination of daylight and the occasional warm period. Nothing demonstrates the robust character of the hedgerow community as neatly as this continual renewal of plant life, changing, but always repeating the processes of growth and maturity, whether by renewing and replication from underground and ground-level storage organs, or by germination of over-wintering seeds. As always, it is the diversity that keeps the hedgebanks so well stocked. While grasses and summer weeds are pausing and dying back, another set of populations colonises the empty spaces, snatches up the early sunlight and winter moisture, then subsides. The timetables of these diverse plant communities will prove crucial before long to the chain of herbivores, from pollinating insects and leaf-eating snails to the birds and spiders that prey on the plant-eaters.

These earliest growths are of several different kinds. The celandine is a renewal from underground fleshy tubers, although there may also be a few which are the results of earlier seeding. There is a distinct band of lesser celandine along these banks, soon to turn into a yellow ribbon among April's violets.

Cuckoo pint sends up its numerous leaves from a tuber, a large, poisonous organ once used to make starch for Elizabethan ruffs, and earlier to act as aphrodisiac once the poison alkaloids were boiled out. They are growing in many different parts of the bank, high and low, but not many will grow on to bloom in their phallic way in May.

Dog's mercury may look boring, but it is a plant of relic woodlands, and traces the woodland origins of these hedges. Great swatches of it are developing, again, on both sides, but more abundantly on the sunnier side. The strawberry and potentilla have been plodding on all winter as die-back of other plants allows. These creeping plants have edged into the bare spaces left by the sheep and machinery that

Dog's mercury

have scraped patches of the banks clean, while most of the other plants with runners are on stop.

But the most prodigious growth in all this snow and ice and hail is the seedling phenomenon. Garlic mustard and nipple wort are the two plants whose seeds seem to get there first with the most. Both are opportunists which shower the banks with small seed in summer, ready for just such a chance seed-bed as the sheep-gropings provide. I counted 400 two-leafed seedlings of garlic mustard in one four-square-foot patch near the cottage. If only a tiny fraction of these survive, that is still a pretty successful regeneration. No wonder they are called Jack-by-the-hedge in some places.

Oddly enough, some of the most successful early germinators will be less flourishing by late spring, and others that play for time will take over. Studies have shown that early success sometimes leads to overcrowding, and the plant's own density causes a whole small colony to die, or nearly do so. Plant-eaters grazing on a colony of young plants can be beneficial to the species as a whole by reducing the density of

lesser celandine

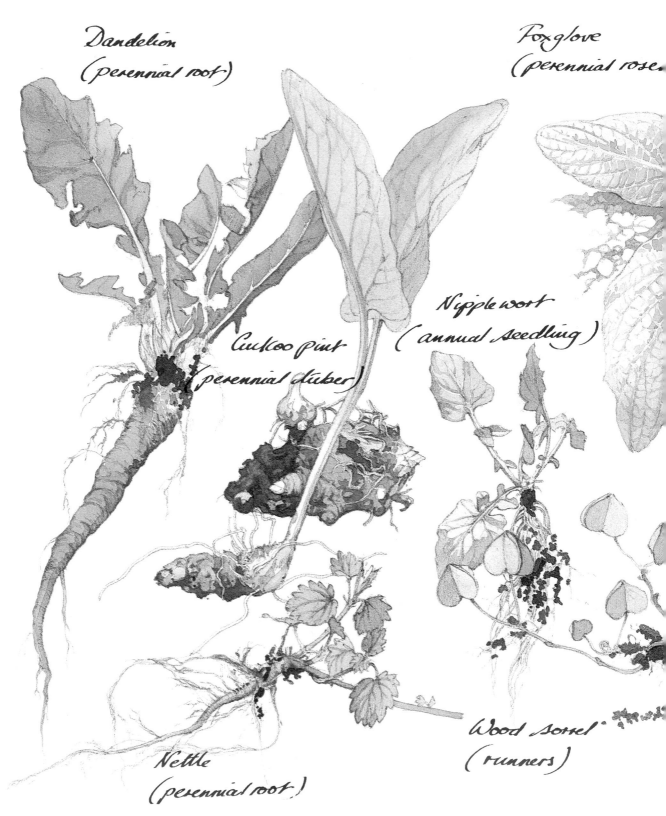

Dandelion
(perennial root)

Foxglove
(perennial rose.

Cuckoo pint
(perennial tuber)

Nipplewort
(annual seedling)

Nettle
(perennial root)

Wood sorrel
(runners)

Celandine
(perennial rhizome)

Strawberry
(runners)

leaf growth at a crucial time for the strengthening of the plants under leaf-shade. Quite a few of the present seedlings, for instance, will give way later to the clever climbing goosegrass, which also now presents two tiny leaves to the weak sun.

Most of the hedgebank herbs are still marking time. The ability of early growers and the everlasting plants to survive the alternating freezes and thaws, dry periods of icing-up and moist meltings, is linked to their metabolism. When the light, warmth and moisture are inadequate, the plant only takes in enough energy for its daily survival. The cuckoo pint, for instance, has been measured for carbon-dioxide consumption and respiration. If the light is inadequate, the plant takes in only the same amount as it gives out, failing to store energy or to grow until the light conditions improve.

Other plants in the hedgebanks are making slower, less measurable, growth. Dandelions are visibly more frequent now; rosettes of foxglove are just perceptibly larger, thriving towards the eastern end of the lane, where the soil has less lime, and the banks are steep, partly shaded and less competitive.

A middle section of the lane has been fairly drastically undercut by machines working on a neighbour's new house. Seeds here have not been able to land on vertical banks scraped down to bare, slippery clay. But the stop-go frost and thaw is doing good work here. Today I can see several places where frost has loosened and crumbled the earth, and made it fall towards the ditch, changing the profile back to the more gentle slopes that have supported centuries of plant growths. The dormant seeds, the nearby runners and rootlets, will now have a friable, hospitable soil to colonise. The changing day-length, warmth and rains will do the rest.

The hedges themselves are joining the relentless march towards spring. The winter buds are racing to maturity, with the early swelling of ash and beech buds being overtaken by the showy hazel catkins, revealed as perfectly formed flowers now under a 10x lens. But the obscure red buds of the hawthorn will be the first leaves to burst.

Birds, too, are changing. Between hailstorms, seven greenfinches arrived in the cottage garden to sweep up the remaining weed-

seeds and size it up for a summer breeding centre. Wrens and robins burst into antiphonal territorial song as the clouds break briefly. Even the dunnocks, shy, sly birds, are singing openly now. But where has the song thrush gone? That hope whereof he knew has been fulfilled, and the pair are searching for nest sites in the woodland glades. The seasons chunter on through the weather like a slow train.

THE HUNGRY GAP

March 21. Hips and haws are gone. Holly berries have been cleaned off the lane, and only a few reddening acorns lie scattered on the paving. Most of the hibernating insects still have a month or two of pause in this long winter before they emerge from holes, hidden foliage or cocoons to feed the hungry nestlings. As the day warms in a pink light after a wet snow overnight, what can the birds and mammals be finding during this hungry gap?

A great flush of bracket fungi has broken out on one of the old stumps in the lane. The day it first appeared, I noticed a cluster of millipedes clinging to the underside of the fruiting-body. Breaking it in two, I found half-a-dozen mites. By next morning, the tops of the remaining fungi were heavily pocked and grooved, the edges nibbled. Before long, they looked like derelict umbrellas with most of the flesh eaten away, leathery as it is. One of the Trametes species (versicolor), these fungi were providing a temporary food for invertebrates like snails and slugs, mammals (chiefly mice) and birds.

(Distinct bird marks appear on the upper surface, along with shallow depressions probably made by a snail.) Another small, brown fungus fruiting-body has sprung up at the Hall end of the lane, and been colonised by mites.

In the woodsy part of the lane, where dead branches collect at the bases of the hedges, a piece falls out of a rotting oak to reveal the usual diverse array of wildlife, including two kinds of millipede, a ladybird, spiders and their egg-cases, a small hibernating snail, a tiny beetle, several minute white larvae, four of those ubiquitous woodlice, a tan-coloured larva with black eyes and small antennae, and numerous almost microscopic bugs. On a hawthorn branch, tiny incrustations could be eggs of wintering moths, or some kind of tiny fungi. Near the same spot, a hatch of tiny, moth-like insects with white spots on their wings fly briefly, then disappear. Small brown pupae of varying shapes turn up in the detritus whenever I grab a handful of dead leaves and soil.

The hedgerows are providing a tenuous life-saving bridge into spring for all kinds of hungry animals. New birds come; a pair of long-

Bracket fungus

tailed tits are including the hedge, and the Gweche spinney, in their newly marked breeding territory. Willow warblers turned up at the demolished copse the other day, and today a pair of treecreepers fly out of the thick shrubbery to explore the cracks in the old oak tree opposite the copse.

The other end of the hungry gap is just hinted at, as small things begin to crawl off branches and out of holes. A new generation of slugs is emerging from the soil in thawing intervals, to be snapped up by a busy shrew or starling. A cluster of large garden snails arrives today inside the entrance of a large mammal hole, clasped in a slimy embrace.

In the nights, a few orb webs are thinly spun over the mouths of the mammal holes, where warmth inside the runs might form air currents to propel an awakening insect into the spider's trap.

Meanwhile, the bank voles have been filling their empty stomachs with the centres of elder sticks, leaving two or three lying tooth-marked on the bank near the copse, where an old stump is riddled with mammal holes. Clumps of couch grass are dropped on the banks from time to time, showing a sharp bite taken out of the rhizome by vole, rabbit or squirrel. Snowdrop bulbs are dropped half-eaten, too.

It is the lucky combination of sheltered feeding sites for herbivores, the fact that so many different kinds of foods are concentrated here, and the high concentration of invertebrates, that makes these particular hedgerows especially attractive to all these animals right now.

The hedgerow plant species are fundamental to this rich ecology. A classic study of a predominately hawthorn hedge in Hampshire (Elton, 1966) found that late-winter and early-spring inhabitants of the dead ends of hawthorn branches included one beetle species making galleries; a hibernating beetle which specialises in crucifer plants (cabbage family); a

mould-eating species of beetle; springtails; mites; young spiders and woodlice, all in among the lichens and algae which cling to the hawthorn; several ladybirds and a hibernating weevil. The interesting part of this collection is that it represents species from four different habitats centred on the hawthorn branch.

Before long, the full spectrum of insects and other invertebrates will hatch, wake, emerge from the ground, walk off these versatile winter twigs and make the hedgerows teem with food for nesting birds and breeding animals. The ability of the hedgerows to fill the hungry gap is one of the keys to the survival in farmland of so many species up and down the complex, interrelated, food chains.

Spider web above hole

Hedgehog

March 24. A complicated mixture of hormones and temperature cues is working deep in the hedge litter. A hedgehog slowly unrolls in its untidy refuge at the intersection of the lane hedge and an overgrown side hedge. Now a process of trial and error begins. It snuffles out on a warm evening to start building up its depleted body-weight.

The laneside hedges are full of the food of hedgehogs — invertebrates. Last autumn this particular animal regularly left its droppings in a gap in the cottage hedge while it passed between its daytime burrow in the thick hedge, and its nightly prowlings and circlings in the garden and field behind.

Now, however, it does not venture out from the thick cover of the hedges, but after a brief exploration which uses little energy, the wintering instinct returns as the night temperature drops. Back it goes to its pile of rubbish, lumber and old pipes left in this corner. It cools down almost to the air temperature, slows its breathing and heart-rate and waits for a better day in this cruel false spring.

April-May

Flowers And Bees

April 6. The first dog violet bloomed a few days ago in the midst of a howling gale, and today ribbons of yellow stars have surrounded the pale dog violets. Lesser celandine, with its five shiny yellow petals, obstinately announces the season through the cold. All over the banks, liberal sprinklings of strawberry and potentilla flowers fill in the spaces. The spring display of flowers progresses in defiance of the cold spring.

Leaves are not much good yet even in the hedgerows, which generally precede tall woodland trees into leaf by several weeks. The first tiny hawthorn leaf appeared four days ago, and tasted delicious (they call them "bread, cheese and beer" around here). Only hazel and willow and dog's mercury have flowered before this, apart from the winter blooms of snowdrops escaped from the Hall gardens. Now the inconspicuous little pale green petals of the dog's mercury are blooming on both male and female flowers.

It is easy to see that day-length is the main trigger for these early hedgerow blooms, rather than warmth. My records for previous years show that variation in the dates of first blooms is slight — later in some years when the spring has seemed more advanced to human senses. Both calendar and climate must be involved, however, because in a winding hedgerow you can see that where shade, moisture and aspect to the sun vary, so does the timing of plant-growth. Violets, celandines, dog's mercury and others bloom in sequence as the ground and air warm up in their particular niches, flowering distinctly later on the north-facing bank. Soil moisture, and the timing of summer and autumn cuts, enter into the formula.

These early flowers have good reason for their timeliness. Plants of woodland origin hang on to their early flowering habits, derived by natural selection from the need to grab the daylight and sunshine before the leaves of the forest canopy blot them out. They are adapted to ignore the bitter stop-go temperatures of a British April. Frozen violets simply glitter and sparkle in the sunshine, droop a little as they thaw and carry on blooming. Lesser celandine recovers its original shiny properties. Dog's mercury lies under the hedge, where its demand for just so much a proportion of the light is met, and where its early flowers are protected from the worst of April's gales.

Other herbs on the banks are putting out blankets of leaves: cuckoo pint, nettles, garlic mustard, wood sorrel, wood anemone, speedwell and ground ivy most noticeably. But the majority of the shrubs in the hedge itself are merely exhibiting swollen buds and half-emerging leaves, as if caught in a film freeze-frame.

It is enough, this paltry half-frozen beginning, to set off the chain of interactions that makes these hedgerows, and others like them, such a rich repository of wild life. Already a flight of bees has investigated the celandine, and midges have hatched out to smell the dog's mercury flowers. Micro-moths are on the wing again, and today the first bumble bees appear. A flower bug and some kind of hoverfly visit the lesser celandine.

Old farmland and woodland once harboured a wide variety of flowering plants. Since neolithic times, and mostly since the 13th century, woodlands in Britain have declined from more than 50 per cent of the countryside to less than 10 per cent, much of it conifers, which have restricted herbal ground layers. This means fewer glades and woodland edges. More recently meadows, with their profusion of wild flowers, have been ploughed up for cereal crops or, around here, for the planting of grass leys, using only four or five species of grass, for intensive grazing. Thus hedgerows and gardens are the main places to find woodland plants in most districts, while the same, plus waste spaces like quarries, railway embankments and roadsides, applies to meadow flowers and weeds. Gardens and hedgerows are the only places where early-flying insects are likely to find the food and shelter they demand.

Of the 19 species of bumble bee that appear in hedgerows in summer, the buff-tailed Bombus terrestris is the first to catch my eye. The queen, with its hairy, multi-coloured abdomen, leaves hibernation in the bank, and flies along the row, taking pollen here and there, and searching in and out of mouseholes. The queen will not choose quickly, but will collect a bit of moss and grass together, then, perhaps four days after it has emerged, load up on pollen and nectar, form it into a slab of "bread", as it is called, and choose a nest-hole. There it will lay eggs on the bread, form a chamber out of wax, roofed and walled, and build a honeypot. The early flowers are essential to the earliest bumble bees for the start of their cycle of egg-laying and development.

Later comes a succession of bumble bee species, queens then workers, as the nectar and pollen in the hedgerows increase. I have counted four different Bombus species here, and two or three of the cuckoo bees that come along later, imitating the bumble bees and stealing their bread.

When the early Bombus eggs mature, and the workers hatch, later hedgerow flowers benefit from a large number of efficient pol-

Queen bumblebee

linators. This is only one of many ways that the diversity of hedgerow life — the early flowers and the late — promotes further richness.

Apis mellifera, the honey bee, is out again today, too, but only a few are braving the April rigours. One large bee is trying to take off from a lesser celandine cup with pollen bags on its back legs so full it can hardly stagger into flight. There are local hives, but I suspect there is also

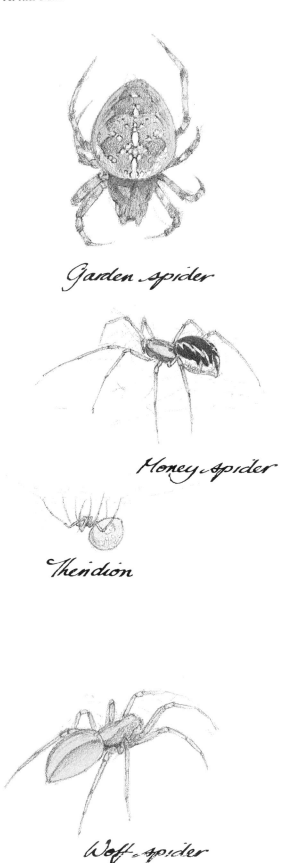

Garden spider

Money Spider

Theridion

Wolf spider

a wild colony somewhere in the south-facing hedgebank. In late February, when an unseasonal blast of sunshine woke all kinds of slumbering fauna, a flight of bees appeared from this spot three or four days running, having a go at garden flowers such as aubretia and winter heather.

More lowly insects than the royal bee families play important roles in the foundations of the hedgerow ecology. Those wintering eggs and larvae that have survived the prying of the tits and chaffinches are on the move. Out of the dormant sticks and burgeoning leaf-buds crawls a host of six and eight-legged summer invertebrates. A good shake of one of the budding hawthorn branches inevitably produces a shower of small spiders, a collection of barely visible winged thrips and a beetle or two, small, black and fat. This is only the merest beginning of that plant's insect bounty. Another rich source of unfolding invertebrate life is the ivy-covered holly, where spiders of several colours and sizes are among the livening-up inhabitants right now.

Spiders are good examples of the complex interactions of different hedgerow animals. Conspicuously active in autumn, but present all year round, they come in many sizes and species. They eat huge quantities of insects in the hedgerows, unquestionably playing a part in keeping population balances under control, possibly saving some plant-forms from exhaustion, if not extinction.

The sheer number of spiders is striking. On the grassy bank on the north side of the hedge, on the edge of the cottage garden where there is a good deal of cultivated soil, I find shoals of wolf spiders in April, male and female. These lone hunters appear in crowds out of their wintering shelter in the hedgerow litter (leading to the false assumption that they hunt in packs like wolves). Their longer back legs give them away as members of the Pardosa species, which like to sunbathe on hedgerow leaves. Voracious eaters, they are sharp-eyed, and can make short work of even such minute and agile prey as the springtails that share their litter bed.

When you add up the list of their own predators, it seems impossible that so many spiders could survive the long winter of hungry birds, shrews, moles, hedgehogs and spiders that frequent these hedgerows. Blue tits working on a stretch of hazel and hawthorn today are getting mouthfuls which I safely assume to include kin to the spiders I knocked out of one of those branches earlier.

The moth is another plentiful hedgerow invertebrate which relies on diverse plant life. A rather boring small brown moth has been flying among hawthorn for several months. This is appropriately called the early moth, with a female wingless form that lives down in the litter. A small white pyralid moth comes to the hedgerows as soon as the grass starts growing, and seems to stay all summer. Another tiny moth is displaying a striking white spot on its wings.

Both flowers and leaves are already being systematically demolished by a range of petal-chewing and leaf-eating insects. Garlic-mustard and cuckoo-pint leaves show bits taken out of them today, and not by snails. Petal-eaters may do a bit of pollination later on, but it is too soon for that now.

New summer species of midge are beginning to hatch. The various members of the fly order, to which midges belong, arrive in sequence, some of them staying only briefly in association with one plant, others hanging about, sampling foods, and producing repeated crops of offspring.

The dog's mercury now blooming pallidly on both banks is a good example of reproductive overkill. Like many hedgerow plants, dog's mercury may sometimes be cross-pollinated by early midges, but it does not depend on this one fragile reproductive thread. Wind-pollination between male and female plants is the rule, and to increase the odds, each male plant is estimated to manufacture as many as 1,300 million pollen grains. Even so, the main way of reproducing for dog's mercury is by underground, asexual, increase. They say it moves along the hedgerow at the rate of about eight inches a year, other things being equal.

The contrast with lesser celandine is great: bright celandine uses colour to attract pollinating insects, dog's mercury a fetid smell; celandine lures many different types of insect, dog's mercury uses the wind; celandine has large hermaphrodite flowers, dog's mercury is small and insignificant-looking, and produces male and female flower-forms. Both, in the final analysis, hedge their bets by producing strong vegetative growth. One can speculate that these woodland plants could be in a kind of evolutionary backwater here in the hedgerows. Sexual reproduction from flowers is a mechanism that supports change, smoothing over the effects of sudden mutations so they are more adaptive, while clonal-root increase is a survival mechanism suited to a restrictive, competitive habitat. In a less crowded environment they might rely more on seed production, and evolve in that direction.

Later in the day, I notice new blooms forced out by the lengthening hours of daylight. The pale lavender petals of ladies' smock show up near the watery ditches; more violets and strawberry flowers have unfolded during the day. A lone starling rattles its voice in the copse, and a blackbird sings on a post near the stream, boasting of its rich territorial rights.

MINDER

April 9. Every morning and evening for the past few weeks, weather permitting, the rabbits have been grazing passionately near the old rabbit warren in the hedge behind the lane opposite the Hall oak. About 15 yards from the lane hedge, where I can watch through a convenient gap made partly by the rabbit crossing, the family takes up the same position nearly every time. The big, mature rabbit, which I take to be the buck from its size and behaviour, is usually nearest to the hedge, where the grass may not be so thick, but where the height of the bank gives the animal a good sweep of vision. The smaller adult, and a young rabbit, graze in line, forming a triangle with the buck and the hedge.

My presence does not put them off much (the wind is right today). After a brief freeze by the guard rabbit at the hedge, with ears forward, they continue nibbling the newly growing grass just beginning to provide spring nutrition. Their eating movements are fast, swinging in arcs right and left around their bodies.

But this morning a dog comes down the lane, and the rabbits know. At a signal — the guard thumps the ground with its hind legs — the young one runs straight for the hedge, then runs along under it to the hole. The third rabbit runs towards the buck, and past it into what

I know to be the main burrow entrance on this side of the hedge. Only then does the big buck take shelter, lolloping into the hole.

It appears to be a sentry system which puts the oldest and strongest member of the band nearest to the refuge, but in fact this rabbit is also in the best vantage point for sentry duty on the rise of the hedgebank. Rabbits' adaptive behaviour is generally fairly simplified. The young rabbit appears to have one response — make for nearest cover, while the doe, as I assume the other adult to be, heads for the hole entrance, which she knows from experience. The big rabbit's actions are a more complex combination of genetic programming (the thump) and experience (the dog is a serious threat).

It is a small family (not counting any new young which may be below in the nest), and the old warren is certainly under-populated, possibly a reflection of the number of predators: foxes, buzzards, hounds and farmers. This particular set of tunnels has been there for a long time, and is an ideal location, under a thick hedge, to keep the soil of the raised bank fairly dry and friable. The land slopes down to a youngish beech wood on the side away from the lane. The main entrances are on that side, where droppings are nearly always visible among the herbiage and brambles. But the lane-side is best for morning and evening grazing in the sunshine. The rich paddocks at the Hall are accessible from this side, too, and the animals make clearly visible runs going through the lane hedge daily. They also have made at least one temporary "squat" in the lane hedgebank where they can hole-up for a while, or mark their territory against other rabbits.

Since the myxomatosis virus, carried by fleas, killed off nearly all the rabbits in the middle of this century, these animals lay-up in smaller numbers, even as the general rabbit population fluctuates upwards from time to time. Observant farmers here and elsewhere have noticed that the post-myxo rabbits live more in the open, move around more often. Conclusions have been drawn that this change of behaviour is an adaptation to the virus, but recent opinions have knocked down this theory. Rabbit populations appear to be kept low by the fact that whenever they become denser, the fleas, the virus and the farmers

Buck rabbit oversees his family

move in. This means, purely and simply, that there are never enough rabbits to maintain an elaborate system of burrows. Hence the small, single burrows in the hedgebank, and the wider roaming over their less densely populated territories.

The grazing is getting richer now, and the rabbits that were kept under cover and nibbling the hedge shrubs and bark, or the root-swellings of the grass, are gradually spreading out. It is easy to watch them as long as you stand still. The rabbit's eye, adapted for wide-angled vision at dawn and dusk, is not too good at pinpointing shapes that do not move. After grazing, they play, preen and ruminate during the day, and if they get hungry before the dusk grazing period they can always use that interesting rabbit technique of ingesting special pellets evacuated from the anus.

Later in the summer, they go even further afield, probably up a nearby crag where there is a larger rabbit colony, as the fields here get heavily grazed by cattle, and harvested by machinery. Right now, the rabbit population is in a state of happy stability, and enjoying it, too.

AGGRESSION AND SEX

April 19. Spring is felt today, not through any one sense, neither sight nor sound alone, but all joined together. The feel of warmer wind blends with the sight of buds bursting on the ash branches, and the froth of blossom on the blackthorn. The ribbons of yellow lesser celandine, now in the lower hedgebanks, multiply the liquid song of the blackbird raising its orange beak to the blue sky. And above all, there are the new smells of damp earth and softer air driving off the sea, being dried now by the reflecting sun off the land. There is, too, just a little buzzing sound.

The chaffinches' descending notes, the great tits' *tee-too-tee-too*, are so tied up with spring and summer memories that they actually make the listener feel warmer. Even more evocative, in a way, is the fact that the hedges and trees are busy with birds displaying, flying in a special way, posturing as they sing and call and generally behaving in a sexy and aggressive manner.

The long process of choosing and delineating a territory, pairing, courtship and breed-

Agression display

Chaffinch pairing display

ing, started for some species a month or two ago, and now each has reached the nesting climax in its own particular way.

Most conspicuous in their sex and aggression are the chaffinches, who treat the lane hedges and copses as an arena for their macho exhibitions. It takes an extremely sophisticated eye to distinguish between the fighting of two males, and the aggressive sex chases of a pair. I can pinpoint two main focuses of chaffinch territory by now in the lane's aegis, but they fly some distance during the day, feeding and preening and displaying. The tattered copse has been the centre of a chaffinch pair's breeding life for some years, and it still holds an attraction for them, despite the felling of all the mature trees but two. The other favourite centre is at the Gweche, where a narrow line of trees and shrubs follows the stream to the north and south of the lane.

Today at the copse, a large male is showing off his red breast and belly by tilting to one side, flipping his wings to show the white flash, with his head held up and beak pointing upwards at a high angle. The female is invisible, low down in the shrubbery, but she issues a low *tupe, tupe, seep* now and then to demonstrate her submissiveness. The male flies from perch to perch among the thin, bare saplings and coppiced stumps. Yesterday I saw a male doing the so-called "moth flight" display at the chapel oak, to a female which flew down to the ground, then off towards the upper wood, spurning him.

Over the last few weeks, the pairs have been chasing each other through the foliage for as long as 10 or 15 minutes non-stop, and I have seen displays that could have been the typical crouching posture that leads to pairing. The female is gradually gaining confidence in the territory, and in the male which holds it, before she turns to nest-building, and finally, becomes the dominant matriarch of the pair. As far as I can piece it together, it appears that an old chaffinch, probably last year's territory-holder at the copse, claimed it again in late February, early March, when I heard it singing there. With pauses when the weather froze, or snow came, it sang there, and chased other chaffinches. Now aggression is giving way to sex, as the male approaches, then lures to its territory, subdues and finally courts and mates the chosen female.

At the Gweche, another male has been gradually assuming command of the linear wilderness. I saw it fly at rivals after *pinking* loudly, and displaying, on several occasions. When the first true dawn choruses started at the end of February, they began to sing antiphonally, one going as far as the first small holly between the copse and the Gweche, and the other claiming the larger one opposite. A third resident bird was singing in the unclipped hedge and trees at the Hall oak and ash.

Threat and chases continued until the end of March, broken by spells of frozen weather. Then the females appeared to have joined them in the chases, and the two kinds of behaviour blurred.

One day in early April, the ritual of carving out the boundaries and pairing was dramatically interrupted by the arrival of a small flock of young, rather thin, migratory chaffinches. I saw them at 7am, bright and lively in the cottage garden, where they appeared from the wood below. Down the lane they flitted, swooping as they always do, chasing and feeding here and there with a soft sub-song. The copse attracted them, and I watched them fly among the small trees there, almost caressing them with their wings. When exploring a new territory, the birds ritually investigate the crotches in small trees as possible nest sites.

After that, I began to see more deadly earnest fights. A female sat high in the copse oak, while the resident male threatened another. Tight circles of fighting, bee-line dashes and loud calling followed, with one bird chasing the other into the thick fallen undergrowth, where the fight continued. Oddly enough, this fight was remarkably similar to the rapes which follow later in the breeding cycle.

Down at the Gweche, the story was the same: resident birds ousting the migrants with bullet-flights, threats and chases, in this case resulting in a division of the territory, with one bird taking the streamside trees south of the lane, and the other holding the large beech tree and the growth running north. Chaffinches often do use a man-made boundary as their own.

In this late, cold spring, the kiss-chase continues as the frozen violets, strawberry flowers and pale ladies' smock arrive. The birds are not inclined to get on with the copulation and clutch-laying. The leaves are not out on the oak trees, so the nestlings' food, the caterpillars,

Robin displays at bullfinch

will not be there. These timings are crucial to survival, and the birds adjust their breeding schedule to the cues of weather and plant-development.

Robins go about things a little differently. They have held a more settled territory since December or January, but are still being called upon to defend it from invaders, and to advertise their presence to potential mates. They do it with song, chiefly, going quiet during the cold spells when food is all-important. The full breeding song has been echoing from hedge to hedge for many weeks now, most often sung from the same specific song-posts, at corners.

The red breast is the key to the robin's aggression. I first had a good sight of the display in March, when an intruder appeared at the cottage hedge. The resident took up a commanding position on the lane-hedge boundary of his territory, clicked and sang, then showed his red breast by stretching up and back, presenting as much red as possible to the bird opposite. The interloper took the hint, as they usually do, and flew down to the ground, then

away. Robins appear to have evolved a policy of establishing dominance without actually fighting. When they do fight, observers have found, they are likely to sing all the way through the mêlée.

Occasionally, robins in the lane will tolerate a stranger. One day by the Gweche oak, a pair and another male were feeding side by side under the great tree on a cold frosty morning, when ice crystals coated the leaves shaggy white, and the fields stood pale between the black hedges. The outsider pecked on the ground for some time before it flew to the hedge and away without a note or a gesture from the resident bird.

Other times, antiphonal songs proclaim the boundaries between two resident birds. At the copse recently, two males and a female were sorting out a boundary dispute. The resident bird, the one I recognised as the autumn territory-holder because of its streaky melanistic colouring, saw off one intruder, but another bird was allowed to sing at the far western end of the copse, perched jauntily on the gatepost.

This was evidently becoming the outpost of another territory. That makes five pairs altogether whose territories impinge on the half-mile length of lane.

The oddest display of robin aggression I have seen was by that particular bird which holds the fallow-field hedge in its territory. One day I found him displaying his red breast madly at a bullfinch which alighted to pick off a hawthorn bud or two. The male bullfinch's red colour acted as a false stimulus to the resident robin's aggressive response. Since the bullfinch went on eating for some little time, the robin became agitated but did not try to fight. Species with no red feathers have no such effect on robins. Researchers have found that robins will even display aggressively at a scrap of red cloth.

For the last few weeks, some of the robins have gone quiet except for a short song at dawn, and I have seen them carrying nesting materials along the forlorn, wintry hedgerows. The cottage pair went silent first, indicating they were paired, then the pair at the Hall and finally the two copse pairs and the pair at the chapel end. Earlier glimpses of birds carrying material (the first as long ago as February 28) could have indicated trial nests. The female at the copse flew into a rotten stump, low along the lane, carrying a bit of grassy material, but later I found no nest there.

Dunnocks are even further behind in their courting and mating. Their lively sex-chases are continuing in many parts of the lane, and if they have managed to settle their pairings or trios or quartets, I have not been able to see it. One clear-cut territory is indicated by their constant fluttering games in the hedges of the fallow field, the cottage garden and the overgrown hedge behind. I catch them lurking in the depths of the lane hedge here, or hear them singing, gradually emerging from the foliage as the song is repeated. Often, they appear as a pair first, and then are joined by one, two or three more birds for the typical "flirt" up and over the hedge. I have also heard them singing antiphonally at the hedge which intersects the lane at the cottage. The same day another pair was making this territorial declaration at the Gweche oak. The dunnock story is a continuing serial.

Blackbirds order their affairs monogamously, if noisily. To human ears, their song has gradually become more sexy over the last six to eight weeks, but this is an illusion, because blackbirds' song is almost exclusively territorial, developing long after pairing, and continuing after courtship. There was an aggressive period in March when they did much chooking, rattling and screaming at each other. Now I see the resident birds in certain key places, chiefly where shaggy hedges intersect, squaring off and chasing potential intruders. One pair is centred round the cottage boundary with the derelict field next door, one pair at the back of the copse, one at the Hall ash, where the hedge running back to the mistle thrush nest intersects the lane. A few times I have seen another at the far eastern end of the lane near the Hall, where I suspect the garden forms another territory. Their aggressive lowering of the head and direct-chase flights are indications that the females are near to nesting.

In the last few days, the pair by the Hall ash have gone very quiet after the dawn chorus. Serious nesting could be the reason. A wren's nest is in the making in the deep part of the bank in the same area near the Hall oak. Every time I pass by, the pair get excited, and I see them flying repeatedly in and out of a hollow made by an overhanging bent-down trunk there. The season of territory and aggression is finally and distinctly giving way to brooding.

The function of all this sorting out of territory is not simple. The spacing out of the species is closely connected to breeding, which in turn is connected to both the acquiring of mates and the availability of food for the young. In the case of the chaffinch, Dr Peter Marler (Behaviour, 1956) believes they also need a place where they can display and mate without disturbance from other chaffinches. If one bird catches a pair copulating, it will violently attack them. The function of blackbird territory, according to Dr D.W. Snow (1958), is likely to be the spacing out of nests so that food supplies are enough; a pair with a territory can feed efficiently, and also find ways to avoid predators. In robins, Dr David Lack (1965) found that the territory helps with the acquiring of a mate foremost, and with the food supply second. Like most modern experts, he rejects the impression of Gilbert White that "such a jealousy prevails between the male birds that they can hardly bear to be together in the same hedge or field". Robins simply cannot

breed unless they have an established territory.

The important part played by the various kinds of hedgerow shrubs and trees, the banks and ditches, single trees and tangled brambly places in ritualised breeding behaviour, is self-evident. Birds need branches of different heights to play their dominant and submissive roles. They need song-posts to declare their possession, tall and smaller trees as look-outs for intruders, food and mates, certain kinds of trees for special display flights, sanctuaries to take refuge in and all kinds of very specific structures for their nesting.

The lane-hedges do not form a territory in itself for any bird. The dawn chorus illustrates this. The first sounds come from the blackbirds up on the hill, and down in the hanging woods. Wrens and robins join in loudly from the back overgrown hedges, moving on to the lane hedges fairly quickly. Fragments of song thrush and dunnock's song come next, and by seven o'clock the full sound of these, plus chaffinches, blue and great tits, makes a chorus of it, augmented by various songs from the woods and adjacent scrub.

The April climax of sound rings across the fields just as the settling of territory turns into the more secret business of raising a brood. As Richard Jeffries, the 19th-century writer-observer, described in The Hills and the Vale (1980): "Grass blade comes up by grass blade till the meadows are freshly green; leaf comes forth by leaf till the trees are covered; and like the leaves, the birds gently take their places, till the hedges are imperceptibly filled."

ARRIVALS AND DEPARTURES

April 23. Where is the lizard? By coincidence, I have noticed for about five years that on or about this date a lizard makes itself known in a part of the hedgerow near the cottage gate where piles of stone (or is it a tumbledown wall?) provide nooks and crannies for this kind of reptilian resident. I remember the date because it is Shakespeare's birthday, and the banks are usually blazing with spring flowers. And so they are, right on time: violets and lesser celandine, white daisy-like stitchwort and faded lilac-white ladies' smock, blue speedwell and ground ivy, along with wood sorrel and wood anemone, with their fragile blooms drooping in the grey winds.

Some animals come like flowers on a day-length schedule. Birds adjust their breeding to the good and bad years, but do much of their pairing, territorial behaviour, courtship, mating and nesting on cue, whether the time is right or not. Lizards are acutely sensitive to temperatures. If the sunny air above is warmer than the nest below, it will emerge and take advantage of it. Usually that happens about

now, but evidently this year's cruel April winds have given it pause.

Hedgerows also make homes for snakes, toads and slow-worms, but these creatures seem to diminish every year. I saw only two slow-worms last summer, and have not seen a grass snake for two or three years. A toad used to live and breed under a stone in the cottage garden, but no longer.

It would take a much wider study to establish the prevalence of these animals in the hedgebanks. Neighbouring naturalists have found slow-worms in thick habitats with plenty of stones or corrugated tin lying about for the creatures to crawl under. Older inhabitants recall all of these reptiles and amphibians as being more plentiful, but that is merely anecdotal evidence.

Glow-worms and stoats are two other increasingly rare inhabitants of these hedgerows. I used to see glow-worms at least once a summer, but they have been absent for about six years. Stoats are now once-or-twice-a-year walk-ons in the hedgerow scene, whereas a few years ago a neighbour's son, who was good at finding them, hunted stoats with his ferret.

Some of these species are near the edge of their range, being animals of warmer climates; others, like the stoat, have responded to fluctuation in population of their prey, rabbits. All of them, when they do arrive, head straight for the hedge banks.

A Nesting Diary

May 7. Another nest takes shape in the sparse, behind-times foliage of the lane hedges. Walking close to the fallow field hedge, I suddenly made out a perfect round shape fastened to a gnarled, multi-forked beech shrub. Made of moss and lichen woven together with spider's webbing, the chaffinch's nest is carefully wedged in a fork behind the only thick part of the hedge where a few of last year's beech leaves cling drily. A pair nearly always nest in the copse, but it would not be the first time they have chosen the lane hedge. So skilful is the camouflage, that if I step back as little as three feet, it vanishes from sight.

But the nesting along the lane has been a sad story this year so far. First broods are something of a gamble, rather like choosing the right moment to jump on a moving carousel, remembering that birds are cued not by rational decisions, but by pre-programmed instincts and conditioning. There is a high premium on hatching the first broods just as the larvae, feeding on the rich spring growth of the leaves, provide the necessary food for the nestlings. A brief diary of the last two weeks nesting in the lane tells the story:

April 16. Blackthorn buds are only just starting to burst, but the cottage robins are consorting in the ditch. He courts by presenting food, and she allows him to feed her directly. They retire deep into the foliage behind the chapel graveyard, as they have been doing regularly for a few days now. The nest, in an old mammal hole on the north-facing bank opposite the cottage-chapel boundary, is finished. It frames the hole with a mossy, grassy entrance-way, overhung slightly by fern foliage, but dangerously exposed to passing traffic of a four-legged kind. Just four feet off the ground, the hole is lined with leaves, moss and hair, protruding like a lip from the floor of the hole. East of the copse, another pair are carrying building materials to the bank opposite a big stump.

Nuthatches are flying into a hole in the tall ash at the copse. About 20 feet up, the hole has been made (probably by other birds) where a branch fell, or was removed. They are bringing bits of bark

Few robin nestlings survive

and leaves to it. Public as this location is, the food supply is handy, with a huge oak opposite, and a line of scrub oaks running back from that. The ash itself is thickly coated with ivy, behind which lurks a feast of invertebrate life.

April 18. The cottage robin is laying, but the pair still flit about, not yet incubating. The east-copse pair come out of the nest-site one after the other, and fly nervously up the hedge on the other side of the lane, where growth is high, if not thick. They too are starting to lay.

In the deep part of the lane near the Hall copse, the cock wren of the territory has constructed a football-sized nest around the hole formed by a huge mossy, bent-down trunk at the top of the hedgebank. The hole is so well concealed that the birds seem simply to disappear.

Another nest is being made in that same bank only a few yards away. A female blackbird has chosen this unusual site (blackbirds prefer tall shrubs and thick hedges), possibly cued by the height of the hedgebank, and put off other sites this year by the lack of foliage.

April 21. A third robin pair has started vanishing into a hole opposite the Hall oak, building. The other two pairs are sitting now.

April 23. The blackbird hen is sitting on her clutch in the Hall hedgebank. She tilts her head up, showing her spotted throat and eyeing the intruder nervously.

The nuthatch has plastered the hole in the ash with mud so that it is just exactly nuthatch-sized in diameter, and no woodpecker or squirrel can squeeze inside. They are still busy poking things into the hole.

The east-copse robin and cottage-robin hens are still sitting. Hall robins have completed nests in the deep hole only three feet off the ground opposite the all-embracing oak tree.

April 25. Tremendous nesting activity is going on all around the hedgerows.

Everywhere, birds are carrying bits of moss, grass, fluff, hair or food. A song thrush dabbles in the mud of the chapel-end ditch, then flies into the cottage-garden hedge with a beakful of building materials. Another robin is building at the chapel end, probably in the graveyard where stone walls make nestholes, and the wren which holds the large territory ranging from the cottage to the copse has started building in the fallow field hedge there.

Nest predators are about. At first light, the vixen cries in the overgrown field, and magpies are noisily disputing the lane territory.

The blackbird hen leaves the nest on the deep bank long enough to feed and preen, alarm-calling as I approach, then returns to sit. Bare banks are beginning to show bloom — stitchwort, violet, speedwell, celandine — but not many leaves.

April 26. Sitting robins nervously crouch, fluffing out feathers while cocks feed.

The arrival of many new birds, summer visitors, adds to the activity, especially at the copse, where willow warblers and garden warblers are flying and calling. Chaffinch sex-games are getting more serious. A rape is attempted at the copse today.

April 28. Hall robins have finished building, and started sitting in their deeply hidden nest under an overhanging branch. Pied wagtails are carrying nesting material to a shrub near the Gweche. Carrion crows are sitting on a huge nest at the back of the spinney there.

May 2. Three small beaks are gaping in the cottage robin's nest. Both parents are feeding intensely. Blackbirds at the Hall appear to be hatching, too, but other hedgebank birds are still incubating. Mistles appear for the first time in weeks. I wonder if they have fledged their first brood.

May 3. The grim realities of hedgerow life are played out. As I round the corner to the blackbirds' nest, I can see from a distance that disaster has visited in the night. A tangle of nesting material, moss and growth from the hedgebank and pawed-up earth is scattered in the lane. A few drops of blood are smeared on the paving, and a faint, smudged paw-print can just be made out in the mud of the ditch. Judging from the height, and from the force used to pull down so much earth and growth, it was a big animal — fox or dog. Since it happened in the night, when the dogs are kept inside, and the paw-print looks suspiciously elongated, rather than rounded like a dog's pad, I nominate the fox to help me with my enquiries.

May 4. Found the cottage robins' nest empty. All chicks were gone, and the robin pair were singing again in a tall hedge nearby. I suspect cats here, as there are many within range at this more populated end of the lane.

May 6. All three robins' nests are now emptied. The Hall-end nest, opposite and about 15 yards away from the blackbirds' tragedy, was also pulled down, but not so forcefully. It could have been a magpie attack, especially as the robins were probably not hatched yet, and those notorious egg-fanciers have been active in that territory. The east-copse pair were the last to fail, the nest untouched but empty. Only the nuthatch, safe and high, and the invisible wrens, escape.

A bare, well-flailed hedge, and a somewhat subdued hedgebank during a poor, late spring, are not the best places for rearing a brood. When the time comes for the second brood, the foliage will be out, and the birds will choose sites that are better concealed and protected from predators and winds. Most years, the robins would have got a small first brood from the hedgebank, and the blackbirds would probably have chosen a better site.

Of more than 20 species of birds which regularly nest in the hedgerow shrubs and banks, most will choose more thickly grown hedges. The lane-hedgebanks lured those robins because of their useful mammal holes, and

more so in a year when bare spring shrubs are providing little shelter from winds. The deep part of the lane, where the blackbirds nested, is a popular crossroads for large mammals, judging by their packed-down runs crossing the lane. Foxes, and possibly stoats, come along here to follow the rabbits down to their warren, or to the beechwoods. In the more travelled sections, clipped and suburbanised, there are the cats.

These woodland birds have adapted well to a changing countryside, and hedges may be only a poor substitute for woodland, but they are all they have. The more untidy, less "productive", the land, the better for breeding songbirds.

WILDWOOD FLOWERS

May 10. Bluebells are flowering in a small-scale wildwood right inside the hedge near the Hall ash. They flourish here in a part of the hedge where the lane drops a good eight feet from the height of the pasture behind. Aside from a few straggly individuals, they flower nowhere else along the lane. In eight or 10 yards of thin hazel and ash, the dappled shade, and the moist, leaf-covered soil with perfect drainage off the steep bank, combine to give these choosy bulbs their ideal growing place. This year they are more profuse than ever, as the close cutting of the hedge allows more light into their miniature woodland glade.

Nearer to the copse, another woodland echo sprinkles the bank densely with delicate white cups faintly bruised with reddish purple. The six star-points of wood anemone are opening now after early-morning rain had turned them into drooping white handkerchiefs.

To complete the woodland illusion, another ghost of the ancient forests has been sending out smaller, even more fragile, white flowers with a tracery of purple veins leading down-wards to the nectaries. Wood sorrel grows in three or four places along the lane, but only here, opposite the copse and beside it, does it gain a massive foothold, as it does in woodland glades.

The appearance of these three beauties — bluebell, wood anemone and wood sorrel — in a hedgerow has more than casual aesthetic significance. All three plants indicate that these hedgerows have provided a refuge for the species of ancient woodlands, and all three appear to have a precarious future.

Bluebells reproduce almost entirely underground, from their bulbs. A mother bulb, if it receives enough energy from the spring sunshine through the leaves of the plant before the trees above come into leaf, produces small daughter bulbs to fill the spaces between plants, and create those crowded drifts. Like other bulbs, they depend on vigorous leaf-growth in a short spring period for their year-round growth and reproduction.

The flowers are pollinated, too. Bumble bees, hover-flies and other insects probe their bells to suck nectar from the ovary walls of the flower stigmas. A fruit forms, and duly drops

to the hedgebank. Single flowers here and there along the banks may indicate bulb-eating voles, or seed-loving mice, as transporters of seed. Why then do they not increase and spread all along the banks? Bluebells never seem to appear in newly planted woodlands, either. They do not even really prefer the shade of a deep forest — they simply take over there because they can tolerate a shade that other plants cannot.

The answer is that their seeds seldom land in the right place. Bluebells have a strict need for much moisture, but good drainage. They must be damp, but not waterlogged. Where the general drainage is poor, bluebells sometimes grow on a mound or bank; where conditions are dry, they seek out a hollow where moisture gathers temporarily. If they are growing in a moist part of the world, like west Wales, they need to be in a shady bank where they will not be dried out by sun or wind, but where the water drains away after torrents of rain.

Here they are, and here they will stay, as long as conditions are right. And bluebells are stayers: their pollen has been found in neolithic peat in Suffolk. These plants I see today are probably descendants of the wild oakwood, just as the hedge shrubs are probably descended from the old woodland trees, cut down, coppiced, pollarded and re-grown over the centuries.

Wood anemones have a similar habit of shooting out magically in early April, carpeting their chosen pitch, flowering briefly while their leaves soak up the energy for next year, then falling back to their underground existence. A thick, horizontal rhizome accounts for the creeping progress of this plant. It sends dark green, deeply-cut leaves straight up from the runners, then a taller stem for the flowers, with a single whorl of leaves about halfway up the stem.

A selection of early flies is attracted to the heavy crop of pollen in wood-anemone flowers, and a bumble bee gives it a try, but there is no nectar in these flowers — the petals are actually sepals (the usually green outer structures of a flower). The large numbers of stamens give the illusion of prolific seeders, but as in so many hedgerow plants, the work of increasing is nearly all done underground. Wood anemone makes seeding even more difficult by preventing self-pollination. The pollen tubes simply will not grow properly in the stigmas of the same flower.

The rhizomes keep this plant coming back in a thick, persistent carpet each year, but it has little hope of spreading in an aggressive environment such as a hedgerow. It cannot spread west because the copse would shade it too much and too early; it cannot spread east because too many greedy weeds, like bracken and hogweed, hold the territory there. Wood anemone is destined to stay put.

Wood sorrel has a similar problem. This burgeoning trefoil, with the small pretty flowers admired by poets, and bitterish leaves often picked for salads, grows from thin runners. Like anemone, it folds its petals when rain threatens, and it too thrives in the early spring before the rest of the vegetative crowd comes along to steal the light.

Low-growing wood sorrel makes three tries at reproduction. In spring, its flowers are arranged so the stamens can shed pollen on the same flower's ovaries. Yet the fine tracery of lines on the petals are there to guide insects, and promote cross-pollination. In autumn, the wood sorrel, like the violet, sends up a cleistogamous flower which never completely opens, self-pollinates and forms seed inside the bud. The seeds of both spring and autumn flowers are explosive, spreading the plant a little way.

In the hedgerows, as usual, wood sorrel increases almost entirely by runners, although it does a little better than bluebells or wood anemone. It also lasts slightly longer, and sends out new leaves and runners in the autumn, dying back again in winter to start all over again. The small trefoil leaves need more time, it seems, to extract enough energy and store it up in the runners.

Curiously, wood sorrel is a member of a large family of mainly tropical plants (Oxalidiceae). The tropical members of the family go to great lengths to rule out self-fertilization by bearing long styles and short stamens or vice versa. The British acetosella has only one array of male and female organs, and these are of nearly equal length, adapted for self-pollination. The mystery is why there are nectar-guides on the petals, an adaptation to insect cross-pollination. The answer is lost in evolutionary history.

There is something about a woodland glade, or an old hedgerow, that suits these three plants. They are still plentiful in parts of the country where there are enough old scrub-lands, woodlands and hedgerows. But what they all lack is the ability, through successful seeding, to leap over poor, unsuitable ground to find their niche. Their origins are historical, and if their special soil, light and moisture conditions should be changed, they would vanish from the local scene.

SUMMER RESIDENCES

May 18. Warm, insect-laden airs, and ripening flowers, are attracting more summer bird visitors to the hedgerows. Some of the strangers are just making a short, local shift in their territory as seeds or insects come into season; others are migrating from a distance. Some have come to nest and raise a brood or two, relying on the rich ecology of the woodland edge, spaced out as it is over the fields and hedges, gardens and wood relics. Others are just passing wanderers, feeding on their way to more appropriate potential nest-sites.

There is always something exotic about the newcomer: a flash of colour, an odd call or an unusual flight-pattern to mark its newness. Today's arrival was a complete stranger to me, a small brown bird. I saw it on a piece of fencing just east of the copse, where weak foliage had been broken open repeatedly by cows, and the owner had put up a few feet of post-and-rail. The bird was perching there as I approached, and from a distance I might have thought it was a young robin. It took off, not in retreat but to attack a passing insect in the air. Then it gave a strange, buzz-like call, and disappeared to the other side of the copse. It was a spotted fly-catcher. The woodland-edge or glade habitat, mimicked by the hedgerows, is just what these birds are after when they finish the long journey from tropical Africa to breed in green, wet Britain.

Other passing birds include two that arrived on the same day back in April. A tree pipit gave its song-flight from the fallow-field hedge, flying up in the air, then singing as it came down on to the grass and weeds. It soon went off to the north.

A whitethroat allowed a glimpse of itself later that day near the Gweche spinney. These birds used to be heard, if not often seen, with some predictability here, but they have become

Greenfinches and Goldfinches arrive

seriously scarce. Hedgerow loss affects them more than it does most species, but their present sharp decline is the result of the drought in the African Sahel, their winter habitat. The local Conservation Trust has reported a general drop in whitethroat population, but with an occasional small surge in certain years (1982, for example).

Greenfinches and goldfinches have been around since March and April — not migrants, but birds shifting their territory for the breeding period. The greenfinches first arrived along the lane in a small flock at the end of March, and pecked on the ground in the various gardens where old seeds have been embedded in the earth since autumn. Since then they have never been far away, but I only hear their *zzwee* calls in the copse, flying over the fields, or at the cottage garden, sporadically.

Goldfinches are forming breeding territories, notably in the Hall garden and the cottage garden. On days when they are in residence, their twit-ups seem to fill the place, especially when the lawn-mower brings down the dandelion heads.

These birds illustrate the radical difference in the way the two kinds of finches organise their breeding territory. The chaffinches and bullfinches that I have been seeing all winter and spring establish a fairly large breeding territory early, in the chaffinch's case, before pairing. They feed in the same territory they defend, spacing their species out over the countryside in confident expectation of finding food within their established territory.

The greenfinches and goldfinches breed communally, tolerating other males within a few yards of their own nesting sites. They only defend a small territory from other males, not their large feeding grounds. All the time they are laying, incubating and feeding their nestlings, they range wherever the seeds are plentiful, as far away as two miles. Their different territorial habits are related to their different foods: seeds ripen in sequence, and are likely to be bunched in widely dispersed locations, whereas in the chaffinches' case, the caterpillars fed to the young are contained within the territory, in the hedgerow, copse or oak tree.

Warblers started arriving in April, first the chatty garden warbler, then the small, velvety, pale willow warbler, with its melodious falling-note song. These two species behave more like the resident birds, establish territories with a guaranteed insect-food supply and defend them, but they seem to breed more gregariously than our defensive year-round residents.

The garden warblers are nesting in a line of scrub oaks behind the cottage, where they emit loud alarms, and agitated flutterings. But their soft, prolonged warbling just as often comes from the copse, clearly within their feeding range. Willow warblers follow the lines of shrubbery all over the lane's immediate environment, singing and calling tamely at me as I walk, sometimes even flying directly at me before taking last-minute evasive action.

I saw the swallows first at the east end of the lane this year, behaving as usual like an air circus. These birds establish themselves every April at each end of the half-mile, where there are buildings. The martins come to the cottage, where they play out their argumentative family dramas under the eaves. Here are two classic examples of species which share the same territory (the air above the farmland) amicably. And neither competes with the resident birds, or other migrants, for food. Their high-flying, wide-ranging habits only occasionally impinge on the insect life of the hedgerow. When they do, the sight of the smart swallows swooping low over the hedges means that weather conditions are just right to keep the insects low. Other days, they fly at enormous heights or wider ranges. They seem to use the hedgerows as a focus, as do many other migrating birds and temporary passers-by, like wood pigeons.

Then there is the cuckoo. Every year we hear a cuckoo call from a wood that scrambles down the limestone ridge, south and west of the lane, and I have watched it work the hedgerow for nests of other birds.

This year it came on May 2. I heard it call, and snatched up a low-powered pair of glasses to see it flying over the trees down in the hanging wood by the river. I got it into focus as it paused on a stag-headed oak. To my astonishment, two smaller birds landed a few feet away on the same tree. The cuckoo flew off, and the small pursuers followed, not attacking or mobbing the cuckoo, but shadowing it, for all as if they knew it was up to no good. They kept their eyes on it for about 20 minutes as I watched them fly from tree to tree while the cuckoo investigated the woodland remnant for roosting and feeding sites. It must have thought bet-

The cuckoo flies to the wood

ter of it, because it moved on, and has not been heard since. This is the first year in an aged neighbour's memory that there has been no cuckoo based on the woodland near the lane.

Other migrating birds have arrived in nearby woods. Across the valley is a chiff-chaff territory, and this bird often comes within earshot with his eponymous tune and barely audible little subsong. Blackcaps go by from time to time, pausing at the copse, but I have never heard one defending a territory in the immediate area. A pied flycatcher flew off the hedge, and down towards the river, one day in late April, but never came again.

Water birds are near. A mallard has chosen to nest in the hanging wood near the river, but it is unlikely to raise a brood with the foxes' earth not so far away. Herons were dispossessed of their heronry when the hanging wood was plundered by the timber merchant four years ago, but a few hang about now on the other side of the river in a woodland patch further east.

The various visitors blend well with the residents by reason of their different foods (the finches), or by finding it in different niches (the flycatchers or swallows, which feed in the air). Farmland, with a mixture of structures and plant life, can support a wider variety of bird species than monotonous landscapes, wider even than plant-rich gardens. Taking all the residents, winter and summer visitors, and allowing for my undoubted deficiencies in patient observation, the environs of this lane seem to hold an average selection of species of songbird. The larks are slightly to the east, and one lapwing to the west, and we lack some of the other birds of more open countryside.

SEXUAL TECHNOLOGY

May 20. There is one plant which is both utterly typical of the hedgebank, yet consummately individual. Both familiar and mysterious, it deserves to be watched with more attention than the generalist can afford. All along the banks today stand the dried, wilted spathes of cuckoo pint, every one facing backwards into the hedges.

Even the names it has been given in the past and present point up the extraordinary qualities of this plant, which crept out of the woodlands into the hedgebanks as long ago as Anglo-Saxon times. Then, it was used as an aphrodisiac, but the roots or leaves would have to be boiled to get rid of their poisonous alkaloids, saponins and hydrocyanic acid. At this stage it was called cucu pint — translatable as "lively penis" — or wake pintle or wake robin; same meaning. It was already a common sight in the woodlands, which were the main habitat of man and his domestic animals in this part of the world.

Later the roots, from which arrowroot starch comes, were used to starch Elizabethan ruffs and collars, but the "proper" name, lords and ladies, did not even appear in the 17th-century herbals. Geoffrey Grigson, in the Englishman's Flora, notes 103 local names ranging from Kitty-come-down-the-lane-and-kiss-me (Kent) to Jack-in-the-pulpit (Cornwall, Somerset, Lincolnshire — and the USA). Here in Wales it is called sheep's cock.

Whatever the name, this is manifestly a sexy plant, and the drooping spathes today are the sign of what could be called metaphorical exhaustion. In achieving cross-pollination, the cuckoo pint uses an array of devices that would do credit to Heath Robinson. It also illustrates the interlocking evolution of single plant species in tandem with a single insect species.

First it uses colour, smell and the mechanical device of a tall, green, leaf-like spathe which holds the purple or yellow spadix in a niche-like "pulpit". A small hairy owl-midge, also called a moth-fly, a member of the Psychoda family of flies, is attracted to the plant and, sooner or later, lands on the spathe. The colour contrast between the purple or yellow spear of the spadix, and the pale green background spathe, is thought to help the midge identify its nectar-producing food plant. The smell, helped by a temperature increase of as much as 15 degrees centigrade generated in the spadix, lures in the fly. It descends, crawling or slipping to the heart of the flower, passing by a fringe of bristles growing out of the male flower and encrusted on the central spadix. The heat increase is timed for around 5pm, when the midges are out in flight in large numbers.

Twenty or 30 flies may crawl into any one flower at this stage (4,000 have been recorded), but the curve of the spathe and the presence of those bristles keeps them from flying out again for the time being.

The female stigmas in the lower part of the structure are receptive and now, if any of the flies have visited a previous flower, they pollinate the stigmas with pollen stuck to their hairy backs and wings. The stigmas shrivel up as soon as they are pollinated, and that signals the

Cuckoopint

male stamens above to break open and shed new pollen all over the hairy flies. The final step the plant takes to assure cross-pollination in the future is to produce a drop of nectar from the stigma, rewarding the fly. After that, the bristles fall off, and out goes the fly to find another plant. The fertilised cuckoo pint withers fast, collapsing over the spadix, and fruits begin to form in the ovaries.

It sounds like evolutionary overkill to some scientists, but it works well enough to keep plant population plentiful although,

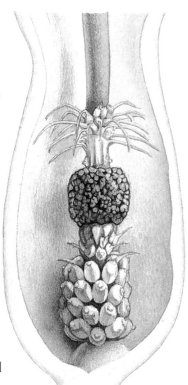

Cross section of Cuckoo pint

like so many hedgerow plants, the cuckoo pint also reproduces from its underground roots. In fact, the seeds take a year to germinate, and only about a third of them do so; then the plant will not begin to flower until five or seven years later.

This elaborate sex machine is designed to avoid self-pollination. Cecil Prime, who has written an enormously readable book about Lords and Ladies finds it easy to tell whether a particular colony has spread from roots or seed. The clonal, asexual offspring will have far less variation of leaf-spots and colour.

There are advantages to both methods for a plant's future. Sexual reproduction steadies down the influences of sudden evolutionary change, while shuffling the various gene characteristics around. In a plant like the dandelion, which reproduces asexually only, there exists a variety of species, but no variety within the species. This kind of evolution is hit or miss, whereas sexually reproduced plants are continually modifying their adaptations through a mixture of genes and further selection. The advantage of root propagation is its persistent

reliability (Huxley, 1978).

There remains the question of why the cuckoo pints in these hedgerows have turned themselves inward towards the hedges, even before they were fertilized and fell over. The reason is that it is a plant that needs much water — it dies back if it dries. So it can only thrive in damp shady woods, hedgerows, copses and scrub. Nor will it grow at southerly latitudes. By the beginning of June here, it will haved died back, and other plants will usurp its favoured part of the hedgebank in late summer.

This has been a dry spring. The complex pollinating mechanism of the cuckoo pint uses up quantities of starches and sugars, and water to transport them through the plant's tissues. The heat of the fly-trap may evaporate some of the plant's water through speeded-up transpiration. As one more clever twist, to conserve water for all this, the plants turn themselves towards the shade.

HAWTHORN

May 30. The slow greening of the hedges and trees is joined, now, by a crusting of white. The soft May blossom has been lightening the hedgerows, but only where they have been allowed to wax untidy. Hawthorn blooms on old wood, which explains why so many hawthorn hedges are flowerless. In the lane, several white sections show where the flail could not get close enough to destroy the flowerbuds. Twining round a huge stump in the fallow section is a glowing and buzzing hawthorn intertwined with ivy, encrusted with lichens and moss. It buzzes because, of all the hedgerow shrubs, the hawthorn attracts the most interesting, diverse and plentiful insect and arthropod life.

It takes only a few minutes to clock up a list of 15 to 20 species attached to this hawthorn on a morning like this. Not only the blossom, but those delicious red leaf-shoots that delight the human predator, also attract six-legged or eight-legged species. A dazzlingly bright green spider no more than two millimetres across its round abdomen, is busy spinning a web on one of these apices. It hangs below, waiting for winged visitors to tap and tug on the wires. Sharing the same tender leaf are half-a-dozen aphids, one of the greenfly species, which have already sucked the leaf and formed short threads of wax, which they deposit behind them. Hover-fly larvae, attracted by the plant, have arrived in time to harvest the aphids, leaving the wax behind. Another leaf has the empty strands of a recently vacated white cocoon.

A small black beetle, prevalent in these hedges all summer long, lies curled among the bright pink and blackening stamens of a blossom. Another beetle, large and mahogany-coloured, crawls among the yellow stigmas of another flower. A black weevil with a long, thin snout and a reddish underbelly, crawls into the same flower.

On a white petal higher up, a horse-fly sucks nectar from the moist tissues — it has to be a male because the female of this species sucks only blood. Two other fly species, an ordinary house-fly and a red-headed fly, are fighting over the feast on another bloom where pollen is ripe. A bumble bee arrives, and the two flies see it off together.

A whole range of small spiders drops out of a jostled branch — tiny round bodies, yellow, pale green, speckled like a bird's egg, black and a long-legged white one. A bee drops by a little later, and several more species of bumble bee.

I have counted capsid buds, flower-beetles, leaf-hoppers, weevils, sawflies and moths. The plant-eating insects arrive for the nectar, then a whole sequence of predators comes to prey on the herbivores. By the time the petals drop in a few weeks, the hawthorn will have nourished scores of different species, just as during the winter it sheltered a different range of invertebrates and fed a selection of birds. And in the autumn, its berries gave sustenance to yet another selection of birds and mammals, insects and molluscs.

Some of today's inhabitants will be adult forms of those that wintered there as eggs or immatures; others of the winter crop crawl off to pollinate, and lay eggs in other hedgerow or garden plants. New predators are provided by the rest of the hedgerow-and-field habitat, notably from cow-pats or grass-roots.

Researchers have counted 86 species of moth and butterfly which feed and shelter, as caterpillars or adults, on hawthorn. Twelve of these feed only on hawthorn, while the others interact with other hedgerow specialities, such as the later-blooming roses. The hawthorn seems to specialise in the smallest fauna of the hedgerow, or perhaps it is that the invertebrates which appear at May-blossom time happen to be small.

This ubiquitous shrub is not the champion among insect habitats. It comes just after the mature oaks, hazel and birch in the league table, and just before roses and wayfaring trees among the shrub layer plants. But hawthorn is one of the most plentiful shrubs, a prime inhabitant of woodland edges, thriving on the hedgerow treatment, and providing food and shelter for the very species that interact with the other hedgerow plants.

For example, a common flower-bug (Anthocoris nemorum) winters in the hedgerow's hawthorns and other shrubs, emerges to feed, in turn, on willow, blackthorn and hawthorn, taking a little plant food, but mainly preying on the many other insects brought out by the fragrant blossom. A distinctively patterned capsid bug (Liocoris tripustulans) lives chiefly on nettle, eating the leaves and laying its eggs in the leaf-stalks, but it is a wide-feeding insect in these hedgerows, and I see it on hawthorn just as often.

On the other hand, three kinds of weevil are specific to hawthorn, living their whole lives on or near it. One, a bright blue weevil with a long snout (Rhynchites caeruleus) lays its eggs in the shoots, then nips them off so that they fall to the ground, and when the larvae hatch they feed there deep in the grass.

It has to be said that the hawthorn does shield some pests to farmers and gardeners. A carrot aphid likes to winter in egg-form on hawthorn twigs, and when it hatches in early spring, it multiplies asexually like mad, producing several generations of wingless females, as so many aphids do. Then, just as the carrots come up in the neighbouring gardens, it produces a winged generation to plunder them. Fortunately, so few carrots have been grown here recently that this pest has not emerged.

This habit of hedgerow shrubs of harbouring pests, has been the subject of long debate and study. It boils down to the aphid-ladybird equation, much like the chicken-egg question. The aphids feed large numbers of ladybird larvae, which are also housed by the friendly shelter of the hedgerows. The ladybirds fight a good many garden and farm pests, so the effect may be neutral.

The multiplicity of insects and spiders, larvae and lepidoptera that are attracted to hawthorn is partly a function of its long history as a woodland-glade plant. Long-established plants have more species of predators and shelterers than recent introductions. The woodland-edge shrubs, which now populate hedges, tend to have more flowers, more berries, more predators — insect, bird and mammal — than the trees of the deep forest, and far more than the conifers of recent forestry plantations. The berries, in turn, are what helped to bring the hawthorn, rose and brambles out of the deep woods into the hedgerows, by bird dispersal.

A shrub population like this moves outwards from the woodland edge, including hedges. It is like other edge habitats: the seashore, the pond's margin, the streamside.

They are busier, more varied than broad heaths, bogs and deep woods. Hedgerows like this one, whose various shrubs just grew gradually out of boundaries, laneside planting and woodland edges, are the richest in their plant-animal interactions, whether to the advantage or detriment of man's cultivations.

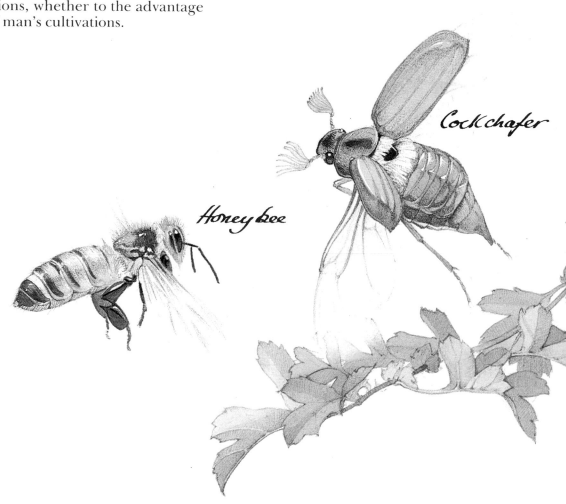

Cockchafer

Honeybee

Capsid bug

Flower bug

Garden chafer

Horsefly

Hoverfly

Hawthorn shieldbug

Bumble bee (worker)

Seven spot lady bird

128

June – July

BREEDING PLACES

June 2. A field vole crossed the lane from the best cow pasture to the fallow field today, vanishing into a hole at the base of the hedge, near an old stump. An intricate set of mammal-runs honeycombs the bank here, as in all parts of the lane where stumps and roots or bent-down trunks make interesting tunnelling territory.

Most of the voles in this hedgebank are bank voles, woodland animals which like the copse better than the hedgebanks, and stick to close cover. They are hard to see, but the main vole-run I have been able to identify goes down the north-facing bank nearly opposite the Gweche oak in a leafy place. I have seen two voles, on separate occasions, crossing the lane here, hustling into the field, and probably down along the hedge there, into the well-covered streamside. They have been breeding since April, starting in the hedgebank hole, but moving into the copse to make their mossy nests under fallen logs. These animals generally have four or five pregnancies a season — they always look pregnant to me. The number of offspring is usually four in each litter, but the total population is probably not very high in this area, which probably indicates a high rate of predation by owls. (I heard one fly off *kewicking* this morning.)

A few days ago at dusk, passing the place where bluebells bloomed in the hedge earlier, I was startled by a congregation of wood mice; at least six of them were scrabbling in the leaves. (They apparently like to eat bluebell flowers, too.)

I have been catching breeding females for several months now. They start coming into breeding condition in March, and are easily distinguished by their nipples and "perforate" vaginal openings. The mice I saw recently, however, were probably a young generation preparing to migrate to the fields for summer. The intersecting hedge behind this point, a little to the east, makes it a popular crossroads for wandering mouse populations.

Trapping of wood mice in fields and hedges has revealed that this most populous of hedge mammals wanders freely in and out of hedges and fields at all times of year, but spreads out far more into the fields in high summer, screened now by long grass and shaggy field boundaries. The original Greek name of this animal, Apodemus sylvaticus, refers to its habit of moving from one place to another. The home range of the wood mouse is more than 2,000 square metres, with much greater movement in summer. The bank vole's wanderings fluctuate more widely, between about 500 square metres in winter to over 5,000 in summer. Right now, after about two months of breeding, the mouse population is well on the way to its summer maximum. A female mouse has an average of four pregnancies a year, with around five in each litter after a 25-or-26-day gestation period.

Another mammal which seems to have completed its summer move out of the hedges and into the fields is the mole. These hedgebank fortress-builders have spread out in a series of untidy, but highly visible, zig-zag runs dotted with mole-hills, choosing especially the second-best cow pasture sloping down towards the woods. Some of their runs can stretch as long as 150 metres. Moles prosper in their entirely underground lives, making for the hedge-banks when the fields are hardened by winter again, to make still more of those annoying (to humans) hills while trapping the rich invertebrate life of the pasturelands. Moles breed more slowly than the other small mammals, despite their evident success as a farmland

species: usually only a single litter each year produces about three young.

One of the unsolved mysteries of this hedgerow year is the nesting place of the animal that takes its name from the hedges. Once hibernation is finished, the hedgehogs vastly prefer the gardens, with their juicy, close-cropped grass, accessible insects, worms, slugs and millipedes for their evening rounds. I have not seen a single one this year. They seldom forage in the hedgebanks in the summer's glut, and they must find plenty of grassy places for their daytime rests and breeding places. An animal that is easy enough to lure to the back door to feed, the hedgehog is one of the most elusive in the field. This does not mean it is scarce because, alas, there are many traffic casualties along the busier roads at both ends of the lane.

HUNGRY NESTLINGS

June 3. The nuthatches are flying in and out of the nest at the copse ash every 59 seconds for as long as an hour at a time. They alternate, one working from the huge oak opposite, the other exploring the ivy-covered ash itself. They find caterpillars, beetles and a wide variety of other arthropods.

All around the lane, other parent birds are hard at it. A chaffinch pauses with its mouth full of some kind of worm-like creature as I pass the copse, and the streaky robin flies back and forth between the hedges there, hoping I will go away before it reveals where the nest is located. The blackbirds are making air corridors between the developing invertebrate life of the pastures, and the nest hidden in the rough back-part of the copse hedgebank. Wrens are so speedy at exploiting the undersides of the hedges' leaves, where all manner of caterpillars are hiding and munching, that I seldom see them. The only evidence the mistles have given of their busy first and second brooding has been the frequent mobbing of the buzzards which threaten their fledglings.

The timings and placing of the breeding birds' nest this year are all mixed up because of the late spring and heavy predation of the early nests. The robins got to work again right away and, although I can only identify three nest-sites this time (as opposed to four which failed in the naked hedgebanks), I believe they will raise a full brood each in their second try. This time they have chosen well-concealed sites, back from the lane itself, but near enough to use the hedgerow bounty for the heavy feeding schedule.

Two blackbird nests are identifiable: the one at the back of the copse, and another in the Hall area. The wrens that built that intriguing nest in the hedgebank earlier seem to have abandoned it, but I think their preferred nest at that territory is on the edge of the small copse that runs back from hedgerow there. The other wren's nest is in the fallow-field hedge, sheltered further by a derelict vehicle rotting away beside the hedge. I am not sure whether they have laid in this nest yet or not — it is still early for a second brood.

The song-thrush pair, after all that singing in the lane, have retired well behind these hedgerows into the edge of the woods down towards the river. I see the male feeding in the lane area sometimes, but they have gone very quiet for some time now. The other thrush territory that meets the lane near the Hall must contain a nest well back in the copse there.

The chaffinch nest that appeared so beautifully wrought in the hedge near the copse on May 7, has been abandoned without a brood being raised in it. I have a theory that the pair made that nest because the copse, centre of their territory, had been cut down. There is plenty of cover in the copse, but much of it is dead wood, not suitable for nests, partly because the branches do not sway in the wind, partly because they are not very high. The nest they finally chose was somewhere in the overgrown hedge running down to the hanging wood — well placed for the oak's caterpillar crop. I suspect there is another chaffinch nest in tall shrubbery at the Gweche, but it is well hidden from prying eyes, and they are not feeding as yet.

Garden warblers are making a racket just behind the cottage garden in the row of stag-headed oaks running downhill. They are nesting in the thick shrubs along the ditch there,

Dunbar

Green oak tortrix

Buff tip

Lackey

Magpie

Silver Y

Early moth

Six spot burnet

Yellow shell

Moths provide hedgerow food

feeding frequently as far as the copse, 150 yards away, and carrying food to the nestlings.

The two gardens along the lane have become finch paradises. The cottage-garden air is full of goldfinches twitting and flying about with the typical purposiveness of a breeding pair feeding young. There is more than one pair at work within a small area, nesting in the evergreens.

Greenfinches and bullfinches are also nesting in the protection of the hedgerows, choosing the taller hedges in the field boundaries, from which they can exploit the wide area needed to find their successions of seeds. Dunnocks are a bit of a mystery this year. They do not usually bother to hide their nests very secretively. There is one territory behind the cottage, but the birds are keeping a low profile, seldom flying out of the taller hedges. Another pair fly in the stretch of open hedge between the Gweche and the Hall, but they have not chosen the exposed lane-hedges this year. It seems their preference illustrates the value to birds of letting the hedges go for several years, and then laying them instead of continually flailing them.

The tits are mostly nesting in the woods. They emerge to do their acrobatic feeding exploits in the oaks, along the hedges where hops and bramble and nettle attract caterpillars and occasionally in the gardens. One pair of blue tits have nested in the chapel-graveyard wall. Great tits seldom emerge from the woods. It is a secretive business, this nesting. Each species has a time when the pairs are making themselves visible and audible, then they fall silent incubating and finally allow the odd glimpse of themselves during the frantic period of compulsive feeding of nestlings.

Some 23 birds are breeding in the immediate area intersected by the lane, and regularly using the lane's hedges and trees to feed nestlings. The first broods of three species were in the lane hedgebanks, where there was more foliage and shelter than in the field boundaries at that time. All but one of these failed. All the second broods, and many of the first attempts, have been in the hedges, trees and walls further back. Two further pairs, long-tailed tits and pied wagtails, have nested within 25 yards of the lane, along the Gweche.

The timing was delayed by the cold spring and resulting lack of invertebrate food coming along. The oak-leaves did not burst until near the end of May, always a bad portent for the summer. Nobody knows exactly what cues trigger off the final nesting activities of most species. They obviously do not just wait and see if the leaves come, and then the caterpillars. A classic study of great and blue tits in an Oxfordshire wood has established that there is a timing mechanism. Every year the first broods were in the nest at the same stage in the caterpillar cycle, even though the date varied by as much as five weeks. This coincidence was not as neat or beneficial as first appears. The hatching of the broods was spread over two or three weeks, indicating some lack of precision. The same research also concluded that the broods that fell right in the middle of the caterpillar period were not necessarily the most successful — the earlier broods had more surviving chicks whether the caterpillars were at their peak or not (Lack, 1966).

The conclusion now held is that birds time their nesting and egg-laying by day-length first of all, and then by weather conditions in March and April, perhaps even as early as February, when the hens' hormonal systems are preparing them for egg-formation. The same conditions that affect the birds also affect the leaves and the caterpillars.

Thrush-family pairs do adjust their starting dates to the weather. Eric Simms (1978) found that blackbirds were affected by wet weather, and also took longer to start their second broods in different conditions. The first broods were affected by the availability of earthworms, the second by the caterpillar supply. But again, it is the weather that gives them the cue.

Clutch-size is also adjusted to the food supply in some species, but this is a complex relationship. In the best of summers, and the worst, the fact is that parent birds — blackbirds, wrens, robins, song thrushes, tits, chaffinches, goldfinches and greenfinches especially — are kept desperately on the go satisfying the demands of their hungry nestlings.

Blue tits have been found to increase body-weight for egg-laying by as much as 50 per cent, then drop down below their winter weight during the effort of feeding the larger fledglings. At the beginning of breeding, they visit the nestlings with food once or twice in 15 minutes; by the time the birds are nearly ready to leave the nest, the parents may make as many as 14 to 16 visits every 15 minutes (Perrins, 1979). Like many species, they adapt their foraging expeditions to the changing populations of invertebrates. For a few days, the hedgerow oaks are full of tits, then the birds move somewhere else.

The number of birds nesting in the approximately 20 acres I have been watching along the lane coincides with average numbers found in Wales generally, and the western parts of England. Old hedgerows have been found to be especially attractive to nesting birds because of the wide variety of insect life in them. The other side of that coin is the peril from predators in a shrubby, mixed landscape. Buzzards come regularly from the open country just east of the lane, and magpies are working the hedgerows methodically. Two pairs are disputing the Hall end of the lane, where nests are now full of fledglings. Each year I find evidence of predators on young birds: a blackbird still in spotty plumage lies panting and bleeding on the lane as the magpie takes flight noisily; a small thrush nestling is dead on the bank.

The hedges, in fact, are the last resort of nesting birds. Nearly all the birds I see are originally woodland species, and most choose first a woodland glade, or the untidy edge of a wood, for their nest-site. Furthermore, the breeding density of birds is greater in parks and gardens, and a generally well-populated suburban landscape is the richest of all. These songbirds thrived on man-made agricultural and residential landscapes for 3,000 years or more, even prospering where the woodland predators like sparrow hawks have declined. What they cannot do is adapt to large expanses of open, treeless, hedgeless landscape, and not all of them can move into towns. Wrens refuse.

One pair of breeding birds can be expected for every 100 yards of hedgerow. But that does not mean that every 100 yards grubbed out kills two birds. As long as there is enough scrub and woodland, wetland fragments, scruffy ditches, unpointed walls and odd out-buildings, the particular birds will survive. The point at which the bird population drops drastically, as it has done in places with very large fields, sneaks up gradually and irreversibly. Hedgerows are only so valuable because the mixed woodlands have declined so sharply. What the birds really want is a human population of untidy smallholders fond of trees and soft fruits.

WATER

June 12. When a long, dry period is followed by weeks of heavy rain, the drainage system of farmland is severely tested. Soil mechanics dictate that a dry soil quickly becomes compacted by rain, resisting absorption of water and increasing the run-off into ditches. Last spring was the driest anyone here can remember. (Or is that a cliche of the countryman?). Just as the plants, trees especially, needed water for their spring growth, a succession of highs brought cool, dry air over a habitat geared for wet Aprils. Now the rains have started in earnest, at a time when delicate pollens, fragile butterfly wings, exposed birds' nests and sun-seeking blooms want them least.

Watching this morning as the hedgebanks pour water into the ditches out of the pipe-like holes made by mammals, it is easy to see that hedgerows play a crucial part in the water balance of the fields, at least in a moderately hilly district. The ditches have been deepened in the fields surrounding the lane, and most of the sloping pastures have been fitted with drainage pipes to guide excess water into these man-made watercourses. Where cattle are grazed intensively, the lack of standing water or boggy places is an essential of good husbandry. One of the farmers here grazes a superb herd of dairy cattle in a density exceeding one milch cow for every two acres.

Today, the ditches around all the cow pastures are tinkling and splashing. The lane ditches are muddily swirling into the drains, but the holes that spout water into the lane are running clear, with water filtered through the stony, root-entwined loam of the hedgebanks. After a period of rain like this, the water keeps on running off for days and days, even after the topsoil seems to have dried out completely. With so many plants operating their root-systems at full tilt, rain at this time of year is soaked up relatively quickly on the hedgebanks, then released gradually. The soil under the hedge, meanwhile, is still dry and crumbly.

What is happening at the lane is only a small and partial example of some of the complex principles of water run-off and soil mechanics. Textbook examples abound to show that vegetation prevents soil erosion by water as well as by wind. (There is not much wind erosion in wet west Wales.) Well-tended grassland does not suffer much water erosion either, except along fast-flowing ditches where the momentum picks up.

What can happen (and is happening in some places where drainage is super efficient, and a high fertilizer-input is used) is a rise in the leaching of minerals from the soil. Muddy ditches point to a loss of mineral content running away to the sea. When rains come in long, steady spells, leaching can be a problem. Hedgerows help to keep the water back, especially when they cross the hill-slopes horizontally. On the other hand, the shading of the field-margins also probably slows down water evaporation and inhibits growth. As far as shelter goes, studies have found that hedgerows have a bad effect on the strip of pasture just next to them, but a good effect on the next 13 feet inwards.

All the pros and cons of hedges: the expense of managing time, the effects of shade, the harbouring of pests, versus the long-term efficiency of a living fence, the good effects of shelter on crops and animals, the harbouring of beneficial insects and birds, have been studied and argued about for several decades. Scientifically controlled tests on some of the advantages and disadvantages have proved inconclusive, partly because the scale of more conclusive experiments would need to be too large to be practicable, and take so long that by the time the answer came, the hedgerows could all be gone, and a good measure of soil nutrients with them.

Farmers in a dairy-and-sheep country like this are, on the whole, friendly or neutral to hedgerows and copses. Many have just not bothered to try to eke out a little more pasture here and there, because it would not pay. After all, they live among the hedges, and have made their living in the gavelkind tradition of small fields and moderate yields of grass crops. There are always a few in every countryside who appear to get a kick out of proving their power over the land by ripping out hedges and performing surgery with machinery. An added threat to the untidy, fragmented landscape in the recent past has been the state grants available for measures to promote farming efficiency. In most cases it is only when the farmer is pushed and pulled by economic manipulation of markets, subsidies, grants and quotas that he is tempted to alter his environment in the interest of short-term profit.

The most important lesson writ large from my compilations of minutiae of hedgerow life is that variety of structure, fragmentation of habitat and a small scale is essential to a balanced, stable, fruitful wildlife of the kind that has managed to survive for more than a thousand years in agricultural Britain and parts of Europe.

The ripping out of a few yards of hedge, or the clear-felling and removal of a small copse, may do no more than displace one chaffinch breeding pair, a handful of snails, a few thousand insects and a couple of dozen voles and shrews. Britain's wildlife has suffered a gradual impoverishment as agriculture has become more and more industrialised. A few badgers disappear one year, the otters the next — this is the insidious danger. The one certain outcome in farming change is the poverty of

the monoculture where an industrial view of agriculture has inflicted an extensive one-crop economy on to the landscape. This poverty is not only aesthetic, but could be harmful in the end to both farming and wildlife.

The irony is that only in the periods of history when the countryside has been well populated with people using up the renewable resources of the woodlands and farmlands to their own profit, have they taken care to conserve it. A well-managed woodlot that produces an economic crop of firewood, timber and small sticks for many purposes, can go on for ever. A depopulated countryside dominated by machinery quickly turns bare and quiet, or lends itself to new species of predator. Hedgerows and mixed woodlands are man-made artifacts. By chance as well as design, they have become one of the happiest blends in all history of human engineering, with answers to the needs of the remaining other species. Since the Bronze Age, men have adapted their activities to the earth's ways. It would be a pity to let economic determinism spoil such a salubrious relationship.

VILLAINS

June 17. The hedgerows are great, leafy banks now — shaggy and curly, flower-spangled and draped with climbers. Patches of waving, broad-leafed grass alternate with swatches of aggressive weeds like dock and hogweed. A lovely woodland scene is made in the deep stretch of lane near the Hall by red campion and rust-tipped wood melick waving in the dappled light. Nettles are taking over in places where animals or drainage from fertilized fields have enriched the soil, and hop is thriving on the cottage hedgetops. Parachutes of dandelion float along the lane among the glittering abseil threads of spiders. The hedges themselves are growing fast, with hawthorn's red-tipped shoots high up, and sycamore and ash twigs rampant. It takes a bit of prying to find the flower-blooms among all this foliage.

The growth-spurt of early summer is complete, and insects are taking advantage of the high nutrient content of leaves, flowers and pollen at this time of year. Wave after wave of new species crawl and fly over the hedgerows, applying their specially adapted mouth-parts to the juiciness in the greenery.

Conspicuous results are achieved by the leaf miners, tiny larvae that hatched out, starting a few weeks ago, and the sawflies that followed, turning all the broad, green dock leaves into lacework. Mining insects have performed a variety of abstract artwork on hazel leaves, beech leaves and brambles.

The mining insects are nearly all small moths which insert their eggs insidiously between the layers of leaf cells, so that the hatching-and-growing larvae can tunnel along, feeding as they go on the inner layers of the leaf packed with carbohydrates. In the case of the dock leaves, which had exploding populations on both sides of the lane, but especially on the north-facing banks where other plants grow less easily, the sawfly larvae engineered a sudden crash. It seems that a highly successful "weed" species which forms a small-scale monoculture in a section of the habitat is likely to get its come-uppance from predators which have adapted to it. (Hogweed is also susceptible to many leaf and flower herbivores.)

Most of these plant-destroyers specialise in one plant, the moth or other insect having evolved at the same geological period as the plant. Bramble has its own miner, a moth which makes a characteristic squiggle on the leaves, starting out narrow, as the young larva hatches, and widening as it grows fatter. A moth larva like this can be spotted by the frass, or excreta, which is left in blobs or streaks in the mined leaf. It is hard to catch them at it, because the whole process of hatching and eating its way through the leaf takes only a day or a few hours.

Hazel leaves are mined by a fly larva which leaves blotches on the leaves, and those holes in beech leaves were probably made by a moth larva that makes a case out of the bits of leaf to hide itself while it eats neat holes.

Watching a caterpillar eat its way through a leaf is possible with the daytime species, and the speed of consumption is impressive. Grasping the leaf edgewise between its forelegs, and balancing with its hind pro-legs, a caterpillar can cut a fast sequence of crescents out of a leaf, and eat its way to the ribs, in no time at all.

Other types have mouth-parts adapted to

and other brassicas, demolishing them in relays until it hibernates in October. The magpie moth, so pretty on the hogweed today, is laying its eggs just around the corner from the currants and raspberries.

But the five or six kinds of caterpillars that I see this morning, munching away in the hedge, are a small selection compared with the large numbers that come out at night. The green tortrix, which plague the oak and feed the nestlings, the early moth on the hawthorn, the winter moth everywhere, the yellow shell, the snout and the Dunbar, are some of the many Noctuids and Geometers that inhabit these particular hedgerows, and feed mostly at night, even in this excessively rainy summer. Added to this are one or two sawfly larvae, whose parent hymenoptera have inserted their eggs into the plant stems and buds so that these caterpillars (with more pro-legs on their abdomens than the butterflies and moths) will have their food plant at hand when they hatch.

More subtle leaf-and-flower-chewing insects include bugs and beetles families. A pretty yel-

Mined Bramble leaf

peeling off the outer cuticle first, then sucking up the soft centre of the leaf. Damage can be catastrophic in terms of one plant, or a clump of food plants, but it is usually the plentiful weeds that attract the more destructive larvae. A few plants are susceptible to many different species of moth and butterfly caterpillars: nettle is one, with some 23 known predators of this kind; hawthorn, too, has many, as do the older trees of Britain. Bird's foot trefoil, a low-growing plant which thrives here on the barer parts of the hedgebank, attracts three species of butterfly larvae — the orange tip, the green-veined white and the small white.

Where there is more than one host plant, it can be a serious problem for humans. Those white butterflies are happy in the hedgerows in their adult stages, but they repeatedly fly behind the hedge to lay their eggs on the cabbages in the smallholder's garden. Turnip-fly is another hedgerow baddie, flying about in June, then laying its eggs on the roots of turnip

hogweed leaf

low-and-black capsid-bug has been inhabiting many different flowers in recent weeks, including honeysuckle. It does not do much visible damage, but has a habit of chewing key parts of a plant — stems, buds, flowers and fruits. By now the females have already reproduced, but they live on while the new generation, turning various shades of patterned orange, brown and yellow, eat their way to adulthood.

Shieldbugs also reach vulnerable plant parts. We have two notorious sapsuckers, hawthorn shieldbugs and squashbugs in these hedges. The first destroy a few leaves while waiting for the hawthorn berries to start forming as the flowers fall. The squashbug has a liking for the Rumex species, those docks and sorrels, but I have also seen it basking on flowers, such as lesser celandine.

Froghoppers are hiding in their creatively manufactured bubbles (made by blowing air through a fluid excreted from the anus), and sucking the sap of the host roses and other plants of that family. In addition to the cuckoo-spit froghopper, there has been a black tree-hopper in the hedges.

Far and away the most conspicuous plant-eating beetles under my lens are the weevils, with their long "rostrums", or beaks, adapted to penetrate specific flower parts or other structures for eating or laying eggs. I have been seeing bright green weevils on many different kinds of flowering plants, including nettle and hawthorn. A mottled grey, brown and black weevil appeared recently (the nettle weevil this time).

Two similar weevils were copulating on fig-wort, their food plant, the other day in the north-facing hedge, and today an electric-green flying weevil surprised me in the lane. Many weevils eat holes in leaves, but more damage is done by the larvae, which hatch from eggs inserted into flowers, buds and fruits. The hazel weevil is one which leaves evidence in these hedgerows later in the year as tiny holes in the shells of ravaged nuts.

Another type of insect that goes for the plant's important tissues is the flea-beetle, and one of them found its way to the nectar of a columbine flower by boring through the base of the trumpet, instead of going in at the front as the bees do. Thrips are destructive flower-infesters in the hedgerows, too, small as they are.

One of the most gluttonous beetles, one that reminds me of the notorious Japanese beetle of many years ago which plagued North American and European gardens, is the bracken clock (*coch a bonddu* in Welsh) which I saw on meadow sweet lately. A mahogany red-brown scarab beetle, this attractive insect attacks both flowers and leaves of young trees, especially enjoying the fruit trees. It flourishes near water, and is a popular bait for brown trout in these parts. Its larvae, white grubs, are fond of the roots of a variety of tender, useful plants.

But when it comes to villainy in the hedgerows, just as in the garden, the various aphids top the league table. The black-bean aphids have colonised those pretty campion flowers, and successive generations of green aphids have come to prey on hawthorn, rose, wild gooseberry, dock, hogweed and nearly everything else.

Once a biting insect has damaged the outer cuticle of the leaves of a plant, the whole leaf-structure tends to collapse, and the leaf curls. When this happens, an earwig often crawls in to have its daytime rest. The need of these insects for a cosy place to feel enclosed is the habit that gives it the somewhat unjustified name for crawling into people's ears. As to damage, it is more likely to harm the ground-level structures of a plant than to eat its leaves.

Leaf-eaters are undoubtedly important in the hedgerow's intricate food chains. Herbivorous insects make up a small part of the total ecology, but they provide some food themselves for an astonishing number of predators. The aphids are the livestock of the hedgerow economy, with a host of fauna depending on them. Ladybird larvae have colonised the very hogweed plants where aphids sucked dry every leaf yesterday, and have swept them clean today; hover-fly larvae, whose parent insects are now busily pollinating the hedgerow's flowers, will soon clean up the later generations of the ever-multiplying aphididae to see that next year's balance is kept within reason.

In fact, nearly every one of these leaf-eaters has its own enemies nearby in the hedgerows. Some of the caterpillars are inflicted with eggs of the ichneumon fly, and so are the sawflies, which many meals out of weevils, chafers, aphids and other beetles. Mammals of the carnivorous kind, shrews and moles, also keep the beetles down. As to caterpillars, they do well to survive the nesting season in these hedgerows without vanishing into the gapes of the fledglings. Even the micromoths, whose caterpillars mine leaves, can easily get caught in the hedgerows' many spider-webs.

Even if they survive all this, leaf-eaters do not always have it their way. Temperatures may be crucial, as the sun dries out the top leaves of tall plants. High winds and hard resins make for less leaf-predation — those outer cuticles are tough, and the insect must cling to the slippery leaf to get started.

Some plants have evolved defence mechanisms, even as the insects evolved their attacking devices. Hairs help to keep some predators at bay — leafhoppers are discouraged by them, and their young grow less well on a diet of hairy leaves. Some plants have developed toxins or bad tastes, like potatoes and cabbages. But one insect (the Colorado beetle, fortunately rare in Britain) has evolved an antidote for the potato poison, and the cabbage whites have counteracted the pungent taste of brassicas' distinctive mustard oils.

As to the plant victims of all this munching and drilling, the hedgerow community finds a robust stability in spite of it. The hogweed damage, the dock predation and the nettle's popularity with insects could mean that other, perhaps rarer, plants can come out of the shade of those aggressive plants, and have a chance at the summer sunshine and moisture. Diversity means that the more villains come, the more they are preyed upon.

SLIMY SUICIDE

June 25. Slugs, those nerds of the hedgerow, are behaving a little like lemmings these nights. The hedgerow contains many slugs, but probably not as many as the gardens, and certainly not as many as the woodlands, which are supposed to house up to 40 species of slug and snail. Here in the lane hedges slugs are mostly Arion species, which come in a wide variety of colours from black to grotesque orange.

They spend the nights munching on the rotting debris in the litter under the hedgerow shrubs. But lately, and this morning is a perfect example, they have taken to venturing on to the hard road in large numbers — 10 or more at a time. The result when a car comes along is horrible to contemplate, but may be useful in keeping the balance of power in the gardens. Slug innards are spread in large patches near the cottage garden and further towards the west end. Apparently they are more common near the gardens, although I do see them elsewhere in the lane. Why they decide to cross the road is a mystery. Their diet of fungi, rotting leaves, lichens and mosses is well supplied on both sides. The other night I saw one of them demonstrating a form of near-cannibalism, eating the remains of a dead snail.

Their sexual habits are no more attractive. I have seen them curled round each other in the hedge leafage, with a thick platform of slime between them, performing their strange rite of entwining and mutual copulation. The young slugs will come along just in time for the autumn crop of garden brassicas. Perhaps this is a classic case of the hedge providing pests with a home in their larder.

Aside from the busy shrews and the occasional hedgehogs, hardly anything preys on these watery sources of protein. This may be a rare example of the motor-car being a blessing to wildlife — or at least to the gardener.

THE POLLINATORS

July 6. Mist and sun, cool drizzle and steamy warmth alternate in this wet British summer. Among the leaves of the hedgerows, new blooms, new shapes, new scents come in successive waves, and along with these delights masses of insect opportunists. Sucking and sipping, sunbathing and copulating, chewing on pollen and petals, or even murdering and consuming each other, the insects of the hedgerows are performing a vast repertoire of acts of pollination.

Today the foxglove's tall spikes of brilliant trumpets bloom at the eastern, less calciferous, end of the lane. Shielding its pollen from the rains, this plant entices long-tongued bees into its secret depths by exhibiting a pattern of spots on its lower lip. A bumble bee disappears into one of the deep chambers, then into another, reappearing with a coat of pollen on its hairs.

Not quite so successful is the columbine flower a little further up the hill, where a beetle has chewed its way through the base of the dark purple flower-spur to get at the sweet nectars and not bothering to pay its duty as a pollinator. Other times, beetles manage to both pollinate and prey on the same blossom.

Another bumble bee is hard at work on a purple vetch blossom, working at closer quarters than in either foxglove or columbine. The vetch must only give a mere droplet of nectar, because this insect is working by numbers — in, suck, out, fly to the next bloom, in, suck, out; in a matter of fractions of seconds. The result is that the insect is forced to fly from flower to flower, and cross-pollinate the different plants.

Less hidden acts of flower conception are going on up and down the lane. Rose (two species) and brambles attract an enormous variety of visitors, from small black flies to beetles, from carnivorous flower-flies to hungry butterflies. Never mind that nectar is absent in these broad cups of pink-or-white flowers, the convenient resting place, petals and central disc both, the faint scent, the petal juices and, most of all, the exposed, brightly coloured pollen, are alluring enough to ensure consummation. The clientele of the cup-shaped flowers seems to be constantly changing as aggressive competitors chase away the first lot. This happens to mean better cross-pollination for this kind of flower. Roses even feed the mouths that bite them, and persuade predators like chafers to give some pollination in return for the juicy petals.

Cross-pollination is the name of the game for flowering plants, which depend on insects for a productive mix of genes. It is all well and good for plants like nettles, now blooming in large clumps, to nod and bend in the wind so that male flowers deposit a fraction of their pollen on the nearby female blooms in the same nettlebed. A large category of hermaphrodite plants are pollinated by insects, and it is necessary for them to find a way of avoiding mere self-pollination. Most of the hedgerow plants reproduce vegetatively from their roots, and self-pollination is redundant.

Remembering that all these mechanisms with apparent purposive intents are actually selections made by centuries of chance mutations and adaptation, the ways of pollinating are ingenious, and staggeringly varied.

In this one half-mile there are enough variations in flower-structure, colour, scent, timing and growth habit, as well as in the array of pollinators, to fill a whole book of botany, and a lifetime of study. Take the business of nectar production and scent. Two prevalent hedgerow plants here are honeysuckle and meadow sweet. Their fragrance is overpowering as I walk in a warm late-summer afternoon. Honeysuckle times its flower openings to save its nectar for the night-flying moths, especially the Silver Y, which I have seen once or twice in this lane. The scent that floats on the evening air indicates a nutritious, sugary meal for a moth-pollinator.

Columbine

Foxglove

Germander
speedwell

Red Campion

Stitchwort

Honeysuckle also has an arrangement whereby the stamens (carrying the male pollen) protrude in the first stage of development, while the stigmas (female receptors) are hidden. When the stigmas reach a more accessible state, the stamens bend down and allow the moths that have collected pollen from another flower at the first stage to rub it off on the stigma. Bumble bees, and predatory insects like capsid bugs, as well as schoolchildren, suck sweet honeysuckle by day, but none of these species does any successful pollination.

Meadow sweet, on the other hand, is a bit of a con artist, because the heavy scent belies the fact that there is no nectar. But the pollen of this plant is so plentiful and blatantly revealed, with those long, frothy-looking stamens in large clusters, that a huge number of visitors calls on these creamy flowers.

Today I see two kinds of fly on one of them: a large black-bodied member of the Musca family, and a yellow-bodied insect. Clouds of midges often browse over these flowers, and I have caught sight of a beetle or two, possibly accidental pollinators. In contrast to the precautions taken by honeysuckle against self-pollination, meadow sweet's tiny flowers have both stigmas and stamens ready and exposed simultaneously, and they are frequently self-pollinated.

It takes all kinds to make up a diverse community like the one in a hedgerow. Two plants that also have clusters of white flowers, the umbellifers, hogweed and cow parsley, offer a different kind of reward for the pollinator. Their clusters of umbels, with tiny-petalled flowers, provide convenient flat platforms for all kinds of insect activity, and they give both pollen and nectar. An assortment of bees, wasps, bugs, thrips, hover-flies and beetles dally there and pollinate the flowers.

Another group of insects come along to prey on the pollinators, often pollinating, too, as they attack. On hogweed, I have seen three kinds of cantharidae (soldier beetles and others), and a dung-fly methodically piercing the neck of a fruit-fly and turning it round with its forelegs to suck dry each part in turn. Cow-parsley positively encourages chance visitors by providing larger flowers at the edges of each umbel as landing platforms.

Hogweed has another timing mechanism to discourage self-pollination by this jungle of fauna. All the outer umbels open first, and all the small florets in each umbel open together. The floret goes through a programmed sequence: the stamens curve inward to hide stigma, then stand up and open to release pollen, in succession. The female stigma only matures after all the stamens have wilted in turn.

Another popular white hedgerow plant, greater stitchwort, which sprinkles the banks all summer long, has an even more precise way of encouraging pollination by the many bees and hover-flies that visit its partly concealed nectar. Rows of five stamens ripen in sequence, the inner row staying folded over the female parts while the outer row is ripe. Only when the inner row of stamens open outward and shed their pollen, is the stigma revealed to the pollinator. Bees fly from plant to plant as the flowers of each plant open consecutively. In the last stages, when all efforts at cross-pollination are finished, the flower can still fall back on self-pollination.

Many other flowers do as stitchwort does in opening up flowers in succession on each stem, so that plant-to-plant movement is encouraged. The hedgerow insects oblige by coming in large waves of hatches — insects such as midges, fever-flies and stable-flies. Some of them, like the St Mark's flies that came in April and stayed through May, arrive in plague-like proportions, but in the course of their activities they do much pollination for the lucky plants in bloom during their flying period.

To the hedge-watcher, the most interesting plant-insect relationships are the various deep and narrow trumpets being visited by long-tongued insects.

My records of the past few weeks — and of other years — show a rich mixture of bees, wasps and hover-flies. The colour, and striking behaviour, of hover-flies single them out in the crowd. Volucella bombylans, which mimics bumble bees, Rhingia campestris, with long, Hoover-like mouth-part, for sucking deep into flowers, and its red tail, and Bombylius major, another fly that mimics a hairy bee, are frequent visitors to such flowers as red campion, with its narrow entrance, Dame's violet, with its blue-lavender tunnels, and the gaudy thin tubes of hedge woundwort.

The sucking apparatus of these insects is made of their labelli (lips), not their mandibles (jaws). They are adapted to suck up exposed fluids, not to pierce and tunnel into flowers. Yet they insert their soft, flexible apparatus into these secretive flowers to perform their pollinating duties with great efficiency. The Bombylius I saw the other day was putting its narrow, tube-like drinking straw into a tight thistle floret. This pollinator is important for other tightly clustered flowers like devil's-bit scabious and clover, as well as some with less constriction such as ladies' smock.

The hover-flies are especially connected to some of the woodland plants in the hedgerows. Rhingia, and another one that turns up here, the wasp-like Syrphus ribesii, are often seen on enchanter's nightshade and germander speedwell, although I have seen only a smaller one at work there myself.

GRASS AND HERBS

July 14. Grasses are frothing and speckling with an assortment of flowering paraphernalia, hardly visible to the naked eye, but springing to life under the lens. Feathery meadow grasses, and drooping false broom, show up in the appropriate places of sun and shade. Cocksfoot, one of the mainstays of the grazing turfs because of its toughness underfoot, escapes into the hedgebank freely. Broad-leaved fescues grow in great tufts along the western end by the cottages, and false oat grass flourishes near the copse, while the wood melick near the Hall is turning rosier, and bending more gracefully as the seeds ripen.

The grasses of the hedgebanks are among the most-taken-for-granted of wild flowers on a laneside, displaying all the qualities of the successful weed: pollinating in waves of wind-blown grains as they bend and blow; seeding successfully into whatever open spaces the abundant opportunist can land on; growing even more prolifically from underground stolons, bulbils, rhizomes and clumps. Because there are so many grasses, it is easy to ignore the extraordinary talents which have made them the foundation of civilization, the basis for economic power and clout, or the curse of the grain mountain. The leaves which grow up from the base of the plant, sheathing the stem,

can constantly renew themselves after cutting, and their seeds contain a rich endosperm full of protein, carbohydrate and vitamins needed by animals. These unique abilities, and the readiness to grow in cultivated ground, are what encouraged men to grow grass for grains, and use it to pasture domesticated herds. When men grew grains they settled, and when they settled and prospered on the grains, they had time to afford arts, architecture and slaves.

False oat grass, examined under the glass, reveals a complex flower-structure equal to any more colourful flowering herb. The double spikelet on the flower-head has two kinds of floret. The upper one is bisexual, with three dark, hanging stamens ready to burst open and fling pollen grains to the wind. From that same part of the flower emerges a feathery, barely visible, branched stigma designed to receive the pollen in the join of its "feathers". The other floret has a long awn, an extension of its covering (lemma), and contains only the male parts, opening out later in a last bid for cross-pollination. If the female part is successfully fertilized, either from its own pollen or from another plant, a seed will ripen within the coverings of the present flower, which will become the husk. These oat grasses are also perennial, and will grow again from their bulbous tufts at ground level. This particular grass makes good hay, but is too fragile to stand up to the heavy treading of grazing cattle. Another oat grass in this same hedge, downy oat grass, is a different species, and not used for pasture.

Among the 20-odd different species of grass that grow in these two hedgebanks, some with variations of strains or hybrids, are two or three that have been deliberately planted in meadows, some of them no longer thought desirable in the changing fashion of pasture-seeding. Others are survivors, perhaps, from the old wild grasslands. Growing among them are white-and-purple clovers in a part of the bank no longer shaded by a hedge where the grass simply extends from the pasture. Here also grow wild flowers reminiscent of an old meadow: bird's foot trefoil, devil's bit scabious, betony, self-heal, some colourful hawkbits, thyme-leafed speedwell and (until a few years ago) early purple orchid.

The willingness of the graminae species to cross-breed and adapt selectively, to hybridise and develop strains, is the key to their success

Creeping bent   Common bent   Cocksfoot   Sheep's fescue   False brome

St John's wort   Silver weed   Hedge wound wort   Self heal

as the supporters of human populations. Those millions of square miles of waving wheat and corn in the North American grasslands, those vast steppes, those rice-paddy terraces, the great golden expanses of East Anglia and Wiltshire, along with the tiny, rich dairy pastures of Carmarthenshire, all stem, by nature or design, from the family of graminae. From oats to rye, from bamboo to sugar cane, they underpin the economic prosperity of Western society. Some people even say it is grass which distinguishes the prosperous north of the globe from the hard-up, root-eating south.

I had an interesting conversation about grass with a local dairy-farmer the other day. The types of grass used in grazing and hay and silage pastures, are changing all the time. A grass like cocksfoot, which went through a period of disfavour, is coming back into fashion because of its ability to survive trampling in wet pastures. White clover is regaining popularity because it can fix nitrogen, saving on the fertilizer bill. "We seem to go around in circles," said the farmer.

Grasses, especially grains, are being continually bred for this or that attribute, and without these green revolutions our superabundant, super-developed planet would not support us. Grasses lend themselves to extremes of artificial breeding by their readiness to form new genetic strains, and they exhibit qualities needed by agriculture — high yields, and resistance to trampling, disease or fungi. Every so often, a new quality fails, or becomes less desirable because of environmental changes, forcing plant scientists to change again, often re-crossing with older wild strains, some of which had better resistance to disease.

The need for conserving old strains has been recognised for many years now, and seed banks are being kept in many parts of the world. But seed-bank specialists themselves have expressed doubts about this conservation on its own. A plant stored as seed for any length of time may not be the same as a continuously growing plant in wild or domestic cultivation. The growing plant is subject to changes in climate, disease and other environmental influences. Wild refuges like hedgerows and waste spaces may one day provide the necessary gene pools for plant-breeders. There is universal awareness of the need to conserve wild plants that may not seem like anything but your friendly neighbourhood weed, but whose genes could be useful one day.

The hedgebank is full of other plants, among its hundreds, which were used in the past, and may yet be recycled into use. The fuzzy, yellow-stamened flowers of St John's wort, now lighting up the hedgebanks, were taken to America by the Pilgrim Fathers, who used the leaves to bind up their wounds. Hedge woundwort, self-heal — plants whose names reveal their past use in medicine — are admittedly part of a pharmacopoepia of superstition. Herb Robert's red colour was said to cure the blood, according to the doctrine of signatures (a plant that looks like your afflicted part will cure it), just as the roots of figwort, with their knobbled tubers, were thought to be good for piles and VD.

More modern herbalists, with a scientific background, find that some of the old cures had a basis in fact. Foxglove is a highly dangerous plant, but it also provides the basis for digitalis, a heart medicine; smelly hedge woundwort is thought to have volatile oils with antiseptic properties, and a large number of hedgerow plants are full of vitamin C. Betony will not cure everything from a sore head to a gouty foot as the herbalist Gerard said it would, but it makes a soothing tea, or a comforting poultice.

Other uses for hedgerow plants have come and gone in fashion over the centuries as the plants escaped into gardens, then out again into the hedgebanks. Ground elder is cooked in butter to eat, and its leaves used as a compress for aching feet. (Almost anything in the hedgebank put into hot-enough water, then cooled, will cure this condition.) Even the detested horse-tails that grow plentifully here on the edge of the coal measures have their uses, either as pot-scourers on account of their silica content, or (boiled up) as a spray against black spot in roses.

Hedgerows provide food too. Six different dandelions include one that is excellent in salads, along with garlic mustard, wood sorrel, ladies' smock and young hawthorn shoots (I add a dressing and some crumbled bacon for more flavour). Wood avens and elder flowers are supposed to keep the flies away, and dried hops in a pillow will put you to sleep almost as quickly as a lunchtime pint of beer.

Fruits, nuts and flowers of the hedgerows make a variety of pops, wines, puddings, savouries and snacks. One strives for the image of Laurie Lee's grandmother, who brought in "the gleanings of days and a dozen pastures, stripping of lanes and hedges — she bore them home to her flag-tiled kitchen. . . built up her fires and loaded her pots".

There are not many pastures, or other places, where fruitful wild plants are plentiful. Whether it is a simple grass that may yet be brought into the breeding station, pretty flowers like speedwell, bedstraw or tutsan, or a penny-saving dandelion leaf, the plants in a hedgerow are valuable in themselves, aside from their interlocking with animal species. In the midst of a dwindling natural habitat, the edges of an old lane, because of their history and the regular cutting down of rampant growth, have been made into a linear wild garden.

When the speedwells first appear in the hedge in June, they are like small, dark-blue eyes staring out of the herbage. The striking effect of the long stamens springing out of the white "eye" attracts the fly. The stamens are hinged near their base at a weak point. When the fly lands on one, the stamen drops down to the centre of the flower, so that the stigma touches the underside of the insect's body. The anthers also touch it, so the insect must either pick up or deposit pollen.

Enchanter's nightshade also spectacularly exposes its stamens in its miniature way, and drops the insect into the business part of the flower as quickly as possible. These woodland plants are fertilised by bees when they grow in a park or a hedgerow, but their original, and still faithful, pollinators are the hover-flies of the woodland floor, also now displaced to the hedgerow. Plants which attract hover-flies, though, like those which get pollinated by beetles, must sacrifice quite a lot of pollen in the process. The appetite of Rhingia, for instance, is satisfied by a clever mechanism for biting off pollen, rubbing the individual grains free, floating them in saliva and propelling them back into the mouth — a bit like a wet-dry vacuum cleaner.

The amateur naturalist is urged towards caution, however, in interpreting the evolutionary significance of all these insect-plant adaptations for pollination. As the authors of Pollination of Flowers, Michael Proctor and Peter Yeo (1973), explain in their comprehensive review of this complex subject (now, alas, out of print), some of the pollination by adapted mouth-parts and flower-parts may be accidental. Although there is a demonstrable association between highly evolved mouth-parts, and plants whose nectaries are less accessible, there is considerable overlap: as plants evolved more secretive habits to go along with specialised insects, short-tongued visitors continued, but the percentage of long-tongued insects probably increased gradually.

Other factors like social behaviour, colour and even the kind of sugars in the nectar, enter into the evolutionary processes. Wasps, for instance, with short but efficient mouth-parts, have a strong need for the sugars from flowering plants to feed their larvae. This may be one reason they go for many different flower-shapes. I saw one systematically disappearing into each dark purple-brown flower of a fig-wort in the north-facing hedgebank the other day. Butterflies, which have those very long, curled-up, highly-adapted tongues for sipping nectar, also sometimes prefer to scoop up the pollen from shallow cups like those of bramble flowers, or not-so-deep sources such as herb Robert, where I found a green-veined white today.

Bees certainly appear to have adapted methodically to different flower-structures (and/or vice versa), with the primitive species like Prosopia and Andrena having shorter, flatter tongues than the highly evolved honey bees with their longer, slenderer tongues.

Bees are the last word in pollination here in hedges, as in gardens or orchards. They are not only highly motivated, with all those cells waiting to be filled and their social programming to be obeyed — they are adapted in behaviour as well as sight and smell. They do not mind in the least if a flower like comfrey is dangled, swinging, so that they have to perch upside down to suck out the nectar. Crawling into the tunnels of foxglove or columbine is easy, and forcing their way into the strong-smelling hedge woundwort, or the tiny betony, is positively desirable.

The best feats of plant adaptation for pollination are subtle, and unfortunately invisible for most of us. The bee in the common spotted orchid looks, on the hedgebanks, as if it were making a simple in-and-out pollen transfer. But it really goes like this, according to research done in greenhouse labs: the bee, attracted by the design of purple-and-pink spots on the tiny orchid lower lip, crawls into the flower and inserts its long tongue into the spur, where the sweet fluid is concealed in the walls. It bumps its head into a swelling at the base of the stigma, breaking it open and revealing two sticky discs, one or both of which stick to the insect's head. The discs are attached to a cluster of pollen grains by an elastic thread. As the insect finishes drinking and flies away, the disc dries out and the individual pollen grains adhering to the bee's head are directed straight forward, so that when it reaches a flower with its stigma ready and sticky, the pollen grains are pointing right at the female part of the flower, instead of upwards at the pollen discs.

Such ingenuity somehow deserves more success than is enjoyed by these rather delicate and choosy flowers in such a competitive environment as a hedgerow. If you add up all the sippers and suckers of nectar, and eaters and storers of pollen, the casual rubbing-off by hairy predators which come to the busy flowers for prey, the fiercely chewing wasps and the short-lived, long-tongued butterflies, you can tot up 74 species of flower-visitors in one short, rainy summer of mostly daytime observations. Almost 100 different species of plants have flowered so far since spring, not counting some of the grasses, or any of the trees that do not usually bloom in the hedges themselves.

That such a variety encourages variety in insect life is unarguable. Insect species which only go for one, or a few, plants could easily

depend on hedgerows for their survival, and these could include some beneficial or delightful insects like bumble bees and butterflies. Equally there are plants like sanicle, whose white star-burst blossoms came into focus under my glass today. Four different insects species are enjoying these open or wilting florets, each at a different stage of development. A beetle crawls in the depths, and a flower-beetle, an aphid and a fly are all crawling on one tiny, complex structure of pollen-bearing florets. Such an attractive plant, now increasingly rare as a woodland relic, deserves to win the struggle for its historic niche.

ALL CHANGE

July 18. The bird world is quiet now among the leafage. A few odd calls from a willow warbler, and a robin's click, are all that a morning can muster. The relaxed atmosphere among the glut of hedgerow foods is an illusion. Just as the birds have finished raising their demanding broods, just as the summer's food is dropping from the pods, or flying along the hedges in quantities, the birds are going through yet another trying time, and they are doing it so secretly that it takes a patient watcher to catch them at it.

Every year, when breeding finishes, they start the moulting process. Robins are lurking in the hedge with no red breasts, chaffinches fly across fields, drab. The other day a mistle family took a bath in the Gweche, and preened together, combing their wings with their beaks and meticulously oiling their feathers from the preen-gland near their tails.

As the family parties of blackbirds assemble to learn how to exploit the bounty on the ground, the parent birds call softly from the hedges with a subdued subsong, the females looking as ragged as the first-year male young. The energy for moulting has to be supplied, and so the heavy feeding routine goes on, almost as it did during breeding.

The birds consume more oxygen during moulting, need large quantities of protein (the feathers are make of keratin, which contains certain amino acids), and their temperature rises because the feather manufacture requires its own blood supply. Finches were found to make an average of 27 milligrams of feathers a day during the moult. Any break in the food supply results in faulty feathers, with incomplete barbs or barbules — the vital mechanisms that make feathers work properly.

The hormone changes that signal the end of breeding also get the process of moulting going while the food supply is plentiful. Among the wonders of these adaptions is the fact that the migrant species, like the willow warblers I saw today looking bedraggled and splodgy as they lined up their young on a hawthorn branch, moult quickly to get it finished during the two months or so left before migration. Bullfinches and blackbirds go on losing feathers, and making new ones, for three or more months, while the gaudy tits take as long as four months or more to make their colourful winter yellows, whites, blues and blacks.

PRETTY PARASITES

July 30. Of all the strange relationships between the orders of plant and animal life, that typified by the collection of structures now beginning to swell on some of the hedge-plants is the most curious. Small flying insects of two families, some of them barely visible as they hover over their chosen plants, are boring holes in leaves, flower-buds and stems, and depositing their eggs. But they do not let go at that: these gall wasps and chalcids have a way of persuading the plants to alter their tissues and build small palaces with plenty of juicy vegetable foods for their offspring.

The gall wasps have been at work on the meadow sweet, the ground ivy and the hawthorn. Each species injects its eggs into the host plant in such a way that when the tiny larvae hatch, their presence sets the plants' cells growing and diversifying into various shapes. The meadow sweet's leaves have strange triangular pinkish galls going right through the leaves like a nail. The ground ivy's galls mimic the hairy leaf-surface, but in the shape of round excrescences. Sycamore is dotted with tiny red lumps. Later in the year will come successions of oak apples, spangle galls, marble galls, woody galls and, in the autumn, those spectacular galls on roses that look like some kind of brilliant crimson sea urchin, known as robin's pincushion or bedeguar galls.

When I opened up one of the pale spangle

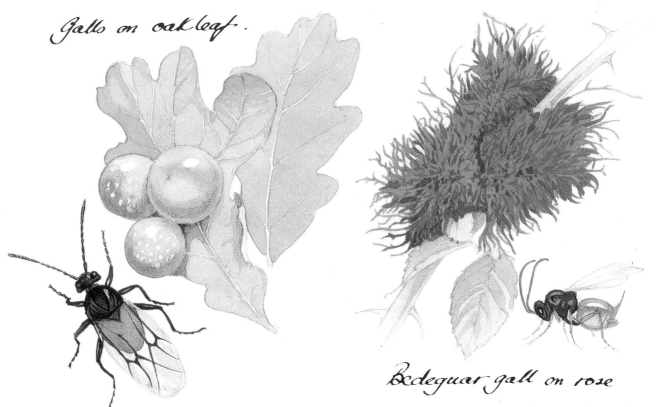

Galls on oak leaf.

Bedeguar gall on rose

galls on a rose-leaf — it was green, with brown blotches and a hollow centre — I found live larvae in the case inside, small green grubs with transparent bodies and dark heads. But some of the gall cells were empty. The Diplolepis nervosa, a relative of the robin's pincushion insect, had been parasitized by another parasite. This is typical. Ichneumon wasps, and other parasitic wasps, have a habit of drilling into the galls already formed by a gall species, and inserting their own cuckoos to eat up the juicy gall-tissues, starving out the original manufacturers. Galls may have three or more different species of occupants.

As the summer ends, and through the autumn, more parasites and gall-formers will come to the hedges to find their favoured plants. Some, like the robin's pincushion gall wasp, or the three oak-gall species, stick to one host plant — the rose or the oak. Others have a remarkable ability to induce many different kinds of leaves and buds to make out of their own tissue a specific structure dictated by the parasitic larvae.

The oaks here are regularly used by the marble gall wasp, the oak-apple gall wasp and the spangle gall wasp. The last two have the astonishing versatility to make two different kinds of gall each. In summer, the larvae produced by the males and females of the adult Neuroterus, an elusive little thing with clearish wings and a wasp-waist, induce flat, round spangle-galls on the leaves. These hatch out in early spring, and form a generation of asexual females which lay eggs parthenogenetically (without male fertilization) in the oak-buds. When the catkins form, they display small, round, currant galls. The adult males and females hatch in May and June, and start the whole elaborate process over again.

The chalcid gall-insects are rather pretty little fly-types, with shiny blue or green bodies. I have seen at least two kinds in the hedgerows. They pierce the galls of other species, and lay their eggs inside the already-prepared feeding chamber.

A place like a hedgerow, with its many attractions for insects, is especially good for these complex parasitic exploits. In the cut and thrust of insect survival, species of parasitic insect are likely to find the host plants and the other species of gall-makers they want. Every wasp and bumble bee I see seems to have its mimic coming along, some of which enter the nest of the species they mimic and put their own cuckoos in the cells — hence the term cuckoo bee for one family of these predators. Another manages to look rather like a harmless ant (Mutilla europaea), but attacks the bumble bee's nest. These are fairly common in the hedgerows, where bumble bees prosper among the nectar-producing flowers.

In fact, looking back over the records of the insect population of the last six weeks, I find that some of the most colourful-looking insects (bar the two dragonflies that strayed up from the stream) are those that have these awkward inter-species habits. The ruby-tailed wasp is a prize example. I have seen more than one of this species of parasitic wasps in the hedges since June, shiny bright green-and-red thorax and abdomen, or blue and red, flying among the hedgebank flowers on a sunny day like small, bright parrots. These insects are parasites of various wasps that are plentiful among the holes and rotting wood of the hedgebanks.

Walking at dusk today, I can see clouds of flying insects rising off the heavy, damp-leafed

hedges. The swallows know where to come, and perform jet manoeuvres up and down the lane to catch this aerial plankton on the wing.

Still another specialist plant-eater makes an extraordinary construction on a large clump of hogweed. A mass of caterpillars of a small moth, Depressaria pastinacella, has spun together the flowers and growing seeds of the hogweeds, and formed cosy tent-chambers among them to feed in. Only a day or two is needed to fatten these fast-growing tubes within their spotted skins, whereupon they open up their temporary homes, flee to the ground and pupate.

It takes all kinds to fulfil the never-ending destinies of the hedgerow fauna. A species of wasp may well prevent the moth caterpillars of a plant-eater from becoming too prosperous — and thus disastrous. A caterpillar can, in turn, see to it that one kind of rampant weed does not take over the whole territory. For the law of the jungle to operate successfully there must, indeed, be a jungle of varied species.

FULL GLORY

July 31. Roses and brambles are tumbling, pink, white and pale lavender, over the hedges. Here and there, the two-tone trumpets of honeysuckle hang along the tops, and hop vines are heavy with those straw-coloured, thumb-sized pineapples full of sleepy fragrance. Brilliant blue vetch flowers and their wispy tendrils decorate the high hedges along the copse to the Gweche region, and the startling purple foxglove spikes turn to red in the lowering light of the afternoon.

The final battles for *lebensraum* among the plant inhabitants of the hedgebanks are won by the stayers — the plants whose evolution has equipped them with habits and properties to outlast the competitive shrubbery, or seize opportunities when they arise. These are also the plants that depend on, and thrive in, the structure and management of a hedgerow: ditch, bank and frequently-cropped linear shrubland. Many of them are climbers and ramblers, and from 80 to 100 per cent of the populations of these plants are found in hedgerows.

Ruby tailed wasp

Velvet ant

White bryony and Bindweed

Roses and brambles, for instance, are woodland plants in origin, but they grow better in the sunny banks and hedges than in the deep woodlands; they always did edge out of the woods on to the heaths and fields. Like hawthorn, they positively enjoy being cut down every year, or every three to six years, sending out new shoots, blooming and fruiting under the stimulus of billhook and flail, to the delight of a cloud of flying insects, including today the brown butterflies of high summer. The brambles arch, Triffid-like, towards the ground, where they aim to take root, their hook-like thorns latching on to the shrubbery. Each arching branch holds clusters of flowers, all in different stages of development — some wide and inviting cups with masses of shaggy stamens to attract the pollen-feeders, some gone over to the pale beginning of blackberry fruits, stamens withered.

There are just two species of rose in these hedges, dog rose and field rose, but the brambles are another matter altogether: like dandelions and hawkweeds, brambles have adopted an asexual kind of reproduction, "apomixy". Seeds develop without any fertilization. In this kind of plant, variation is achieved, not by the mixing of genes from two parent plants, but by the evolution over a long period of time of a huge variety of species within the plant genus (in this case, Rubus). It is almost impossible to tell the difference in some cases — we call all the members of one sub-genus bramble.

Plants like hops and white bryony are married to hedges for a different reason — support. The hops send twisting shoots upwards to twine round other plants, and shoot upwards above the hedge, while the fruits and the broad leaves are attracting a buzzing of flies and a busy collection of feeding and pupating caterpillars. Many of these plants have escaped into hedges from the gardens of smallholders.

White bryony is less restricted to hedges than most of these specialists, but it appears here in the middle section of the lane, thrusting out small, counter-clockwise-twisting tendrils, and displaying creamy blossoms. Not much bindweed grows in these hedges, but there are a few of the all-white trumpets of hedge-bindweed blooming now, poised to invade the cottage garden.

The most hedgebound of all these hedge specialists, which blooms at the time the poet

John Clare called "full glory in the hedges", is the sinister-looking black bryony (no relation to the white). Back in May, huge purple stems burst out of the hedgebanks in several places. Thick and ridged, these queer stems waved and turned until they found something to rest on, defying the laws of gravity and plant-hydraulics in their ability to climb without hooks or tendrils or claspers. As tall as six feet they went, groping and bending, but still able to pump nourishment into the developing, but folded, leaves.

Black bryony

By now, in steamy summer, the moisture-loving black bryony has prospered best in the north-facing hedge just east of the copse, where it drapes and hugs the supporting shrubs in a shroud of dark-green shiny leaves. The flowers of this plant (Tamus communis) are not all that important to it. They grow on stalks springing out of the leaf-axils in small white clusters. Those clever stems have twined around some hogweeds, brackens and honeysuckle. Berries are beginning to form on some of them, full of poison.

Strangely, this plant produces clusters of red-and-yellow berries designed, one would think, to ensure dispersal. Because of the poison, the bright berries are the only colour hanging in the hedgerow through the late autumn and into winter. Then, the poisonous saponins which prevent them from being eaten wear off and, sure enough, the birds come along and oblige. The design has a function, if not a purpose: the berries keep the bryony seeds moist, for if they dry they die. In deepest winter, all the hips and haws and holly berries will be gone, and bryony berries will be ready for dispersal when the birds are at their hungriest. This is one of the hedgerow's typical examples of interlocking needs and timings.

But the reason the whole flower-and-berry sequence is not all that vital to the plant is the familiar hedgerow habit of vegetative growth from the roots. A huge root which ancient herbalists found reminiscent of the mandrake (another poisoner), absorbs July's solar energy, and stores up enough in its starchy interior for those eerie stems to grow on next year and perform their elaborate twistings. Typical of the successful plant in a competitive environment, the black bryony is a stayer, a thruster. Its nearest relatives, not surprisingly, are tropical yams; its method of arrival or survival in a temperate island is lost in the mists of evolution and history.

As a rule, hedgerow plants are much more likely to resemble the plants growing in nearby woodland than those in the neighbouring meadows and gardens (despite escapees like hops, stonecrops, dame's violets and snowdrops). But, like every rule, this one has many exceptions. A host of opportunists has been peeping out of the bare spaces of the banks in places where animals and machines have scraped off old growth and topsoil. One such space cultivated by sheep last winter has exhibited a succession of plants over the year. Garlic mustard and goose grass rushed in first with hundreds of two-leafed seedlings. Then creeping jennies and broad-leaved cuckoo pints overshadowed many of these, stealing nourishment from below, or sun from above. Now, one of the most successful plants in this same area of about three square yards is nipplewort. A weedy-looking plant with forking stems and rather boring yellow flowers, its stems and seed-pods now turn a deep, reddish purple as it invades every spare cranny, and peers over the graveyard wall.

Another bare space near the stream, where the bank has been carved down to clay, boasts one lone yellow loosestrife blooming late. A place near some house-building works has burgeoned with a brilliant display of bright red-purple great willowherb, from alien seeds brought no doubt on lorry wheels. Nearby, a single wild turnip's tiny yellow flower brightens the bleak clay of the lower bank. These banks are roadsides, as well as woodland, meadows, garden colonies and herbal collections. When there is disturbance, seedlings move in.

More often, the hedgebank is claimed by its ancestral root-producers, the tangle of reproductive plant-material stored in the depths of its soils, thriving in a richly mulched, sheltered, well-drained, sun-and-shadow habitat. If one wanted to manufacture a place where sundry flowers grow, where annuals and perennials, feathery weeds and colourful exotics, mix and come again each year, one would invent a hedgebank.

As I walk back down the lane at the end of my hedgerow year, a cluster of bright blue-and-yellow bittersweet catches my eye. Near it is a nettle-leaf curled round a cocoon harbouring immature spiders' eggs. An unknown spider, brown and stripey with jointed legs, appears. In the field with the milk cows, the robin, feeding with some blackbirds in their moulting clothes, manages a little fragment of song from the hedge. Snuggled among the bright yellow stamens of a beautiful pink dog rose is a new insect, some kind of flower-bug, I think. A bat flies up the lane swooping on the insects; small and alone, it is probably a pipistrelle, and it reminds me how many more mysteries there are to be unravelled in this everyday wilderness.

Harvesting the hedgerow's airspace

House martin

Spotted flycatcher

Swallow

Species List

The following list gives the common (if any) and scientific names of the plants and animals identified in the hedgerows bordering the lane during the study year. Where there is doubt I have put a (?) after the name. Where I could only identify family or superfamily I have put that name and "sp." or "spp.".

I am all too aware that this list is far from complete, and that the species using the lane vary from year to year. Sometimes plants arrived and vanished before I could document them, and frequently animals disappeared before allowing themselves to be examined or caught.

If the specialist readers (notably those interested in moths and ground-living invertebrates) are disappointed – partly because of an unusually wet year – I hope the generalist will be interested in gaining some idea of the staggering number of plants and animals taking refuge in an everyday hedgerow.

BIRDS

nesting in lane hedges, bank and hedgerow trees:
Blackbird; Turdus merula
Chaffinch; Fringilla Coelebs
Crow, carrion; Corvus corone
Dunnock (hedge sparrow); Prunella modularis
Goldfinch; Carduelis carduelis
Magpie; Pica pica

Mistle thrush; Turdus viscivorus
Nuthatch; Sitta europaea
Robin; Erithacus rubecula
Song thrush; Turdus philomelos
Warbler, garden; Sylvia borin
Wren; Troglodytes troglodytes

using hedges for foraging, social or preening activities:
Bullfinch; Pyrrhula pyrrhula
Greenfinch; Chloris chloris
Pigeon, wood; Columba palumbus
Pipit, tree; Anthus trivialis
Rook; Corvus frugilegus
Sparrow, house; Passer domesticus
Starling; Sturnus vulgaris
Tit, blue; Parus caeruleus
Tit, great; Parus major
Tit, long-tailed; Aegithalos caudatus
Tit, marsh; Parus palustris
Warbler, willow; Phylloscopus trochilus
Woodpecker, great spotted; Dendrocopus major
Woodpecker, green; Picus viridis

occasional visitors/predators:
Blackcap; Sylvia atricapilla
Buzzard, common; Buteo buteo
Chiffchaff; Phylloscopus collybita
Cuckoo; Cuculus canorus
Fieldfare; Turdus pilaris
Flycatcher, spotted; Muscicapa striata
Goldcrest; Regulus regulus
Jackdaw; Corvus monedula
Jay; Garrulus glandarius
Martin, house; Delichon urbica
Owl, tawny; Strix aluco
Redwing; Turdus musicus
Sparrowhawk; Accipiter nisus
Swallow; Hirundo rustica
Treecreeper; Certhia familiaris
Wagtail, pied; Motacilla alba

Warbler, wood; Phylloscopus sibilatrix
Wheatear; Oenanthe oenanthe
Yellowhammer; Emberiza citrinella

MAMMALS
Bat; Pipistrellus pipistrellus:(?)
Fox; Vulpes vulpes
Hedgehog; Erinaceus europaeus
Mole; Talpa europaea
Mouse, wood; Apodemus sylvaticus
Rabbit; Oryctolagus cuniculus
Rat, common; Rattus norvegicus
Shrew, common; Sorex araneus
Shrew, pygmy; Sorex minutus
Squirrel, grey; Sciurus carolinensis
Stoat; Mustela erminea
Vole, bank; Clethrionomys glareolus
Vole, field; Microtus agrestis
Vole, water; Arvicola terrestris

OTHER VERTEBRATE
Lizard, common; Lacerta vivipara

PLANTS
herbaceous
Avens, wood; Geum urbanum
Bedstraw; Galium verum
Betony; Betonica officinalis
Bird's-foot trefoil; Lotus corniculatus
Bistort, common; Polygonum bistorta
Bitter-cress, narrow-leafed; Cardamine
  impatiens
Bittersweet; Solanum dulcamara
Bluebell; Endymion non-scriptus
Bramble (blackberry); Rubus fruticosus
Bryony, black; Tamus communis
Bryony, white; Bryonia dioica
Bugle; Ajuga reptans
Campion, red; Silene dioica
Chickweed, common; Stellaria media
Cinquefoil, creeping; Potentilla reptans
Clover, red; Trifolium pratense
Clover, western; Trifolium occidentale
Columbine; Aquilegia vulgaris
Comfrey, common; Symphytum officinale
Cow-parsley; Anthriscus sylvestris
Crane's-bill, meadow; Geranium pratense
Creeping buttercup; Ranunculus repens
Creeping-jenny; Lysimachia nummularia
Cuckoopint (lords and ladies); Arum
  maculatum
Dame's violet; Hesperis matronalis

Dandelion; Taraxacum officinale agg.
Dock, broad-leaved; Rumex obtusifolius
Dog's mercury; Mercurialis perennis
Enchanter's nightshade; Circaea lutetiana
Figwort; Scrophularia nodosa
Forget-me-not, field; Myosotis arvensis
Foxglove; Digitalis purpurea
Garlic mustard (Jack-by-the-hedge); Alliaria
  petiolata
Gooseberry; Ribes uva-crispa
Goosegrass (cleavers); Gallium aparine
Ground elder; Aegopodium podagraria
Ground ivy; glechoma hederacea
Hawkbit, rough; Leontodon hispidus
Hawkweed, mouse-ear; Pilosella officinarum
Hawkweed, orange; Pilosella (Hieracium)
  aurantiacum
Hedge-parsley, upright; Torilis japonica
Herb Robert; Geranium robertianum
Hogweed; Heracleum sphondylium
Honeysuckle; Lonicera periclymenum
Hop; Humulus lupulus
Ivy; Hedera helix
Knapweed (hardhead); Centaurea nigra
Ladies' smock (cuckoo-flower); Cardamine
  pratensis
Lesser celandine; Ranunculus ficaria
Loosestrife, yellow; Lysimachia vulgaris
Marjoram; Origanum vulgare
Meadow sweet; Flipendula ulmaria
Mouse-ear, common; Cerastium
  holosteoides
Mullein; Verbascum sp.
Nettle, stinging (common); Urtica dioica
Nipplewort; Lapsana communis
Orchid, common spotted; Dactylorhiza
  fuschii
Plantain, greater; Plantago major
Plantain, hoary; Plantago media
Plantain, ribwort; Plantago lanceolata
Ragwort, common; Senecio jacobaea
Rose, dog; Rosa canina
Rose, field; Rosa arvensis
St. John's wort, perforate; Hypericum
  perforatum
Sanicle; Sanicula europaea
Saxifrage, London pride; Saxifraga
  spathularis x umbrosa
Scabious, devil's bit; Succisa pratensis
Selfheal; Prunella vulgaris
Silverweed; Potentilla anserina
Snowdrop; Galanthus nivalis
Sorrel, common; Rumex acetosa

Speedwell, germander; Veronica chamaedrys
Speedwell, thyme-leaved; Veronica serpyllifolia
Speedwell, wood; Veronica montana
Stitchwort, greater; Stellaria holostea
Stonecrop, reflexed; Sedum reflexum
Strawberry, barren; Potentilla sterilis
Strawberry, wild; Fragaria vesca
Thistle, marsh; Cirsium palustre
Thistle, spear; Cirsium vulgare
Turnip, wild; Brassica rapa
Tutsan; Hypericum androsaemum
Valerian, common; Valeriana officinalis
Vetch, bush; Vicia sepium
Vetch, common; Vicia sativa
Vetch, tufted; Vicia cracca
Vetch, yellow; Vicia lutea
Vetchling, yellow meadow; Lathyrus pratensis
Violet, common dog; Viola riviniana
Violet, early dog; Viola reichenbachiana
Willowherb, broad-leaved; Epilobium montanum
Willowherb, great; Epilobium hirsutum
Wood anemone; Anemone nemorosa
Wood sorrel; Oxalis acetosella
Woundwort, hedge; Stachys sylvatica
Yellow archangel; Lamiastrum galeobdolon

TREES AND SHRUBS
Ash; Fraxinus excelsior
Alder; Alnus glutinosa
Beech; Fagus sylvatica
Birch, silver; Betula pendula
Blackthorn (sloe); Prunus spinosa
Cherry, wild; Prunus avium
Elder; Sambucus nigra
Guelder rose; Viburnum opulus
Hawthorn; Crataegus monogyna
Hazel; Corylus avellana
Holly; Ilex aquifolium
Oak, pedunculate; Quercus robur
Osier (willow); Salix viminalis
Plum, wild; Prunus domestica
Privet, common; Ligustrum vulgare
Rowan; Sorbus aucuparia
Snowberry; Symphoricarpos sp.
Sycamore; Acer pseudoplatanus
Willow, goat; Salix caprea
Yew; Taxus baccata

GRASSES
Bent, common; Agrostis capillaris
Bent, creeping; Agrostis stolonifera
Brome, barren; Bromus sterilis
Brome, hairy; Bromus ramosus
Brome, Hungarian; Bromus inermis
Brome, lesser hairy; Bromus benekenii
Brome, meadow; Bromus commutatus
Cocksfoot; Dactylis glomerata
Couch grass; Agropyron repens (Elymus repens)
Dogstail, crested; Cynosurus cristatus
Fescue, red; Festuca rubra
Fescue, sheep's; Festuca ovina agg.
Hairgrass, crested; Koeleria macrantha
Meadowgrass, glaucous; Poa glauca
Meadowgrass, rough; Poa infirma
Meadowgrass, smooth; Poa pratensis
Meadowgrass, wood; Poa nemoralis
Melick, ciliate; Melica ciliata
Melick, wood; Melica uniflora
Oat, wild; Avena fatua
Oatgrass, downy; Avenula pubescens
Oatgrass, false; Arrhenatherum elatius
Quaking grass; Briza media
Ryegrass (hybrids); Lolium spp.
Vernal grass, sweet; Anthoxanthum odoratum
Wood rush, field; Luzula campestris

FLOWERLESS PLANTS
Ferns and mosses:
Bracken; Pteridium aquilinum
Buckler fern; Dryopteris spp.
Dicranoweissia cirrata (moss)
Eurhynchium praelongum (moss)
Fissendens taxifolius (moss)
Hart's tongue fern; Phyllitis (Asplenium) scolopendrium
Horsetail, field; Equisetum arvense
Horsetail, wood; Equisetum sylvaticum
Hylocomium splendens (moss)
Maidenhair spleenwort; Asplenium trichomanes
Mnium undulatum (moss)
Pellia epiphylla (liverwort)
Plagiochila asplenoides (major) (liverwort)
Polypody, common; Polypodium vulgare
Polypody, western; Polypodium interjectum
Polytrichum formosum (moss)
Polytrichum juniperum (moss)
Fungi:
Boletus impolitus

Clavaria rugosa
Coprinus atramentarius
Cup fungus; Peziza rutilans
Exidia albida
Fairy-ring mushroom; Marasmius oreades
Fomes fomentarius
Heliotium citrinum
Honey fungus; Armillaria mellea
Marasmius ramealis
Milk cap; Lactarius pallidus
Mycena capillaris
M. flavo-alba
M. galopus
M. inclinata
M. tintinnabulum
Oyster fungus; Pleurotus ostreatus
Pholiota (Galerina) mutabilis
Psathyrella sp.?
Russula emetica
Shaggy cap; Coprinus comatus
Shaggy parasol; Lepiota rhacodes
Trametes betulina
T. versicolor
Xylosphaera (Xylaria) hypoxylon
Lichens:
Cladonia coniocraea
Cladonia pocillum
Graphis elegans
Graphis scripta
Lepraria incana
Opegrapha atra

INVERTEBRATES
Insects:
Bee, honey; Apis mellifera
Bee-fly; Bombylius major
Beetle (antlike); Pselaphidae sp.
Beetle, variable longhorn; Stenocorus
meridianus
Beetle, wasp; Clytus arietis
Blackfly; Aphis fabae
Bracken clock (see garden chafer)
Bumble bee; Bombus agrorum; B.
lapidarius; B. pratorum; B. terrestris
Bush cricket, dark; Pholidoptera
griseoaptera (?)
Butterflies:
Gatekeeper (hedge brown); Pyronia
tithonus
Green veined white; Pieris napi
Grizzled skipper; Pyrgus malvae
Holly blue; Celastrina argiolus (?)
Meadow brown; Maniola jurtina

Orange tip; Anthocaris cardamines
Painted lady; Cynthia cardui
Peacock; Inachis io
Red admiral; Vanessa atalanta
Ringlet; Aphantopus hyperantus
Small tortoiseshell; Aglais urticae
Small white; Pieris rapae
Capsids; Blepharidopterus angulatus;
Capsus ater; Liocoris tripustulans;
Lygocoris pabulinus; Systellonotus
triguttatus
Carder bee; Bombus muscorum
Carrot aphid; Dysaphis crataegi
Click beetle; Agriotes spp.; Elater balteatus
Cluster fly; Pollenia rudis
Cockchafer (May bug); Melolontha
melolontha
Craneflies; Tipulidae spp.
Cuckoo bee; Nomada ruficornis
Cuckoo bee; Psithyrus rupestris; Psithyrus
campestris
Damsel fly; Agrion virgo
Dock aphid; Aphis rumicis
Dock sawfly; Ametastegia glabrata
Dragonfly, darter; Sympetrum striolatum
Dung fly; Scatophaga stercoraria
Earwig, common; Forficula auricularia
Earwig, lesser; Labia minor
Fever-fly; Dilophus febrilis
Flea-beetle; Halticini or Phyllotreta spp.
Flower-beetle; Oedemera nobilis
Flower-bug; Anthocoris nemorum
Froghopper; Philanus spumaris (cuckoospit
larvae)
Fruit fly; Drosophila sp.
Galls and Gall insects:
Bramble gall; Diastrophus rubi
Gall midge; Cecidomyia veronica
Gall wasp; Andricus kollari
Marble gall; Cynips andrenus
Oak apple; Biorrhiza pallida
Robin's pincushion (Bedeguar);
Diplolepis rosae
Spangle gall; Neuroterus
quercusbaccarum
Garden chafer (coch a bonddu);
Phyllopertha horticola
Grasshopper, common field; Chorthippus
brunneus
Greenfly and blackfly; Aphididae spp.
Ground beetle; Carabus violaceus
Holly-leaf miner; Phytomyza illicis
Hornet; Vespa crabro

Horse-flies; Tabanidae spp.;
  Tabanus bromius (?); Chrysops relictus;
  Haematopota pluvialis (?)
House-fly; Musca domestica
Hover-flies; Baccha elongata; Mallota
  curbiciformis; Melanostoma scalare;
  Scaeva pyrastri; Rhingia campestris;
  Syritta pipiens; Syrphus ribesii; Syrphus
  balteatus; Volucella bombylans
Lacewing; Chrysopa septempunctata
Ladybird, rufus; Coccidula rufa
Ladybird, seven-spot; Coccinella punctata
Leaf-beetle; Chrysomelidae spp.
Leaf-hopper; Cicadellidae spp.
Leaf-miner; Nepticulidae spp.
Midges, biting; Culicoides pulicaris
Mosquito; Culex pipiens
Moths:
  Buff tip; Phalera bucephala
  Depressaria pastinacella (dispunctella?)
  Dunbar; Cosmia trapezina
  Early moth; Theria primaria
  Grass moth; Pyralidae spp. Crambids
  Green-oak tortrix; Tortrix viridiana
  Lackey; Malacosoma neustria
  Magpie moth; Abraxas grossulariata
  Mother-of-pearl; Pleuroptya ruralis
  Nepticula aurella
  Plume moth, large white; Pterophoris
    pentadactyla
  Silver Y; Plusia gamma
  Six-spot burnet; Zygaena flipendulae
  Stigmella distinguenda
  Yellow shell; Camptogramma (Euphyia)
    bilineata
Owl midge; Psychoda phalaenoides
Platygasteridae spp.
Red ant; Myrmica ruginodis
St Mark's fly; Bibio marci
Scorpion fly; Panorpa communis
Shieldbug; Acanthosoma hemorrhoidale
Soldier beetles; Cantharis rustica; C. livida;
  Rhagonycha fulva; R. lutea
Springtails; Collembola spp.
  (Enotomobryoidea & Sminthuridae)
Squashbug; Coreus marginatus
Stable fly; Stomoxys calictrans
Thrips; Thysanoptera spp.
Wasp, common; Vespula vulgaris
Wasp, cuckoo; Vespula austriaca
Wasp, German; Vespula germanica
Wasp; Mutilla europaea
Wasp, ruby tailed; Chrysis ignita

Wasp, spider-hunting; Anoplius fuscus
Wasp, tree; Vespula sylvestris
Weevils; Byctiscus betulae; Phyllobius
  viridearis; P. urticae; P. argentatus;
  Polydrosus cervinus (tereticollis?);
  Rhynchites caerulens; Curculio nucum;
  Apion spp.

Spiders and Harvestmen:
  Araniella curcurbitina
  Dictyna spp.
  Garden spider; Araneus diadematus;
    Araneus quadratus
  Heterodictyna walckenaeri
  Lathys humilis
  Meta segmentata
  Money-spider; Linyphia montana; Linyphia
    triangularis
  Segestria spp.
  Therididae spp.
  Theridion pallens
  Wolf spider; Pardosa lugubris
  Harvestman; Leiobunum rotundum

Molluscs
Snails:
  Aegopinella pura
  Cepaea hortensis
  Cepaea nemoralis
  Discus rotundatus
  Ena obscura
  Garden snail; Helix aspersa
  Oxychilus alliarius
  Oxychilus helveticus
  Punctum pygmaeum
  Succina putris
  Vitrea crystallina
  Zonitoides excavatus
  Slug: Arion ater

Miscellaneous Invertebrates
  Millipede; Polymicrodon sp.
  Millipede; Polyzonium sp.
  Pauropus sp.
  Pill millipede; Glomeris marginata
  Pill woodlouse; Armadillium vulgare
  Scutigerella
  Woodlouse; Philoscia muscorum
  Woodlouse; Porcellio scaber
  Woodlouse; Trichoniscus pusillus
  Worm; Bimastus tenus
  Worm (pot worm); Euchytraeus sp. (?)
  Worm, earthworm; Lumbricus terrestris

Bibliography

BIRDS:

Armstrong, E.A., *The Wren*, 1955

Betts, Monica M., The Food of Titmice in Oak Woodland. *Journal of Animal Ecology*, 24

Burton, Robert, *How Birds Live*, 1975

Coombs, Franklin, *The Crows*, 1978

Davies, N.B. and Lundberg, A., Food Diet and a Variable Mating System in the Dunnock. *Journal of Animal Ecology*, 53, 1984

Davies, N.B., Cooperation and Conflict Among Dunnocks in a Variable Mating System. *Journal of Animal Behaviour*, 33, 1985

Fitter, R.S.R. and Richardson, R.A., *Collins Pocket Guide to Nests and Eggs*, 1968

Flegg, Jim, *In Search of Birds*, 1983

Flegg, J. and Yapp, W.B., *Birds and Woods*, 1962

Lack, David, *The Life of the Robin*, 1965

Lack, D., *Population Studies of Birds*, 1966

Lack, D., *Ecological Isolation in Birds*, 1971

Marler, Peter, Behaviour of the Chaffinch. *Behaviour Supplement 5*, 1956

Newton, Ian, *Finches*, 1985

Perrins, Christopher, *British Tits*, 1979

Reader's Digest *Book of British Birds*, 1969

Shrubb, M., Birds and Farming Today. *Bird Study, 17*, 1970

Simms, Eric, *British Thrushes*, 1978

Simms, E., *Woodland Birds*, 1971

Snow, David W., *A Study of Blackbirds*, 1958

Turêek, F.J., Colour Preference in Fruit and Seed-eating Birds, Proceedings, XIII Ornithological Congress 1963

Witherby, Jourdain, Ticehurst and Tucker, *The Handbook of British Birds*, 1943-1965 (5 vols)

Williamson, Kenneth, The Bird Community of Farmland. *Bird Study, 14*, 1967

Yeates, P., *The Life of the Rook*, 1934

ECOLOGY & GENERAL:

AA-Drive Publications, *Book of the British Countryside*, 1978

Elton, Charles, *Animal Ecology*, 1965

Elton, C., *The Pattern of Animal Communities*, 1966

Hooper, M.D., Hedgerows as a Resource, in *Forest and Woodland Ecology*, (Institute of Terrestrial Ecology), 1981

Hoskins, W.G., *The Making of the British Landscape*, 1970

Jeffries, Richard, *The Hills and the Vale*, 1980

Krebs, J.R. and Davies, N.B., *Introduction to Behavioural Ecology*, 1981

Lorenz, Konrad, *King Solomon's Ring*, 1964

Mabey, Richard, *The Roadside Wildlife Book*, 1978

Mabey, Richard, *The Common Ground*, 1981

Morgan, R.P.C., *Soil Erosion*, 1979

Pollard, E., Hooper, M.D. and Moore, N.W., *Hedges*, 1974

Streeter, David and Richardson, Rosemary, *Discovering Hedgerows*, 1982

White, Gilbert, *The Natural History of Selbourne*, 1977

MAMMALS:

Burton, M., *The Hedgehog*, 1969

Corbet, Gordon and Ovenden, Denys, *The Mammals of Britain and Europe*, 1980

Bang, P. and Dahlstrom, P., *Animal Tracks and Signs*, 1974

Cowan, D., *The Wild Rabbit*, 1980

Crowcroft, Peter, *The Life of the Shrew*, 1957

Eldridge, J., Observations on Food Eaten by Wood Mice and Bank Voles. *Journal of Zoology, London*, 158, 1969

Herter, Konrad, *Hedgehogs*, 1965

Jeffreys, D.J. and Pendlebury, J.B., Population Fluctuation of Stoats, Weasels and Hedgehogs in Recent Years. *Journal of Zoology, London*, 156, 1968

Lockley, R.M., *The Private Life of the Rabbit*, 1985

Mellanby, Kenneth, *The Mole*, 1971

Sheail, J., *Rabbits and their History*, 1971

Southern, H.N. and Corbett, G.B., *The Handbook of British Mammals*, 1977

INVERTEBRATES:

Alexander, R. McNeil, *The Invertebrates* 1979
Boycott, A.E., The Habitats of Land Molluscs in Britain. *Journal of Ecology* 22, 1934
Bradley, J.O., Tremenam, W.G. and Smith, Arthur, *British Tortricoid Moths*, Ray Society, 1973
Bristowe, W.S., *The World of Spiders*, 1958
Burton, John, et al, *The Oxford Book of Insects*, 1979
Cameron, R.A.D., Jackson, N. and Eversham, B., *A Field Key to the Slugs of the British Isles*, Field Study Centre, Aidgap (N.D.)
Cameron, R.A.D., Down, K. and Pannet, D.J., Snails and Ages of Hedges. *Biological Journal of the Linnaean Society*, February, 1980
Cameron, R.A.D. and Redfern, Margaret, British *Land Snails*. Linnaean Society British Fauna 6, 1976
Carter, David J., *Observer's Book of Caterpillars*, 1979
Chapman, R.F., *Insects*, 1969
Chinery, Michael, *A Field Guide to the Insects of Britain and Northern Europe*, 1972
Davis, B.K.N., The Hemiptera and Coleoptera of Stinging Nettles in East Anglia. *Journal of Applied Ecology*, 10, 1973
Cowie, Robert H., The Life Cycle and productivity of the Land Snail, *Theba pisana*. *Journal of Animal Ecology*, 53, 1984
Edwards, P.J. and Wratten, S., *Ecology of Insect-Plant Interaction*, 1980
Ellis, A.E., *British Snails*, 1926
Evans, G., *The Life of Beetles*, 1975
Ford, E.B., *Moths*, 1955
Ford, R.L.E., *The Observer's Book of Larger Moths*, 1974
Ford, R.L.E., *Studying Insects*, 1973
Heath, John (ed), *The Moths and Butterflies of Great Britain and Ireland*, 10 vols (5 in press)
Jones, Dick, *Country Life Guide to Spiders*, 1983
Kerney, M.P. and Cameron, R.A.D., *A Field Guide to the Land Snails of Britain and Northwest Europe*, 1979
Linssen, E.F., *Observer's Book of Insects of the British Isles*, 1959
Lockett, G.H. and Millidge, A.F., *British Spiders*, 1974-75, 3 vols
Mason, C.F., Food, Feeding Rates and Assimilation in Woodland Snails, *Oecologia, Berlin*, 4, 1970
Morton, J.E., *Molluscs*, 1979
Nichols, David and Cooke, J.A.L., *Oxford Book of Invertebrates*, 1971
Oldroyd, Harold, *The Natural History of Flies*, 1964
Runham, N.W. and Hunter, P.J., *Terrestrial Slugs*, 1970
Savory, Theodore, *Arachnida*, 1977
Skidmore, Peter, *Insects of the Cow Dung Community* (F.S.C. test version), 1986
South, R., *Moths of the British Isles*, 1961

Southwood, T.R.E. and Kennedy, C.E.J., The Number of Species of Insects Associated with British Trees, *Journal of Animal Ecology*, 53
Spradbury, J. Philip, *Wasps*, 1973
Stokoe, W.J. and Stovin, G.H.T., *Caterpillars of the British Butterflies & Caterpillars of the British Moths*, 1944-48, 2 vols
Whalley, Paul, *Butterfly Watching*, 1980

PLANTS:

Flowering and general:
Bell, Peter and Woodcock, Christopher, *The Diversity of Green Plants*, 1969
Bishop, O.N., *Natural Communities*, 1973
Clapham, A.R. and Nicholson, B.E., *The Oxford Book of Trees*, 1975
Condry, William, *British Woodlands*, 1974
Edwards, P.J. and Wratten, Stephen, *Ecology of Insect-Plant Interaction*, 1980
Gilmour, John and Walters, Max, *Wild Flowers*, 1973
Grigson, Geoffrey, *The Englishman's Flora*, 1975 (paperback)
Fitter, Richard, and Fitter, Alastair, *Guide to the Grasses, Sedges, Rushes and Ferns*, 1984
Hickey, Michael, and King, Clive, *100 Families of Flowering Plants*, 1981
Huxley, Anthony, *Plant and Planet*, 1978
Hyde, Molly, *Hedgerow Plants*, 1976
Institute of Terrestrial Ecology. *Woodland Ecology*, 1981 Symposium
Keble Martin L.W., *The Concise British Flora in Colour*, 1974 (3rd ed.)
Lousley, J.E., *Wild Flowers of Chalk and Limestone*, 1969
Mabey, Richard and Evans, Tony, *The Flowering of Britain*, 1982
Milthorpe, F.L., *The Growth and Functioning of Leaves*, 1981
Morris, M.G. and Perrins, F.H. (eds), *The British Oak*, 1974
Peterkin, G.F., A Method for Assessing Woodland Flora for Conservation Using Indicator Species, *Biological Conservation*, 6, 1974
Prime, Cecil T., *Lords and Ladies*, 1960
Proctor, M.C.F. and Yeo, P.F., *Pollination*, 1973
Rose, Francis, *The Wildflower Key*, 1981
Rackham, Oliver, *Trees and Woodland in the British Landscape*, 1976
Salisbury, Sir Edward, *Weeds and Aliens*, 1961
Silvertown, Jonathon W., *Plant Population Ecology*, 1982
Tansley, A.G., *Britain's Green Mantle*, 1968
Turril, W.B., *British Plant Life*, 1962

Flowerless plants:

Alvin, Kenneth L., *Observer's Book of Lichens*, 1977

Brightman, Frank H. and Nicholson, B.E., *The Oxford Book of Flowerless Plants*, 1966

Dickenson, Colin and Lucas, John, *Encyclopedia of Mushrooms*, 1979

Frankland, Juliet C., Hedges, J.N. and Swift, M.J. (eds), *Decomposer Basidiomycetes*, 1982 symposium

Harley, J.L. and Smith, S.E., *Mycorrhizal Symbiosis*, . 1983

Lange, Morten and Hora, F. Bayard, *Collins Guide to Mushrooms and Toadstools*, 1965

Ramsbottom, J., *Mushrooms and Toadstools*, 1953

Richardson, David, *The Vanishing Lichens*, 1975

Smith, Annie Lorrain, *Lichens*, 1975

Soothill Eric, and Fairhurst, Alan, *The New Field Guide to Fungi*, 1978

Surcek, M. and Kubicka, J., *A Field Guide in Colour to Mushrooms and Other Fungi*, 1980

History:

Cameron, R.A.D., Down, K. and Pannet, D.J., Snails, Hedges and History, *Biological Journal of the Linnaean Society*, February 1980

Cameron, R.A.D. and Pannet, D.J., Hedgerow, Shrubs and Landscape History in the West Midlands, *West Midlands Arboricultural Journal*, 1980

Hooper, M.D., Hedges and Local History, *Standing Conference for Local History*, 1971

Linnard, William, *Welsh Woods and Forests*, 1982

Rackham, O., *Ancient Woodland*, 1980

CRO Carmarthen (Dyfed County Archives) estate maps and muniments: Dynevor, Cawdor, Taliaris estates. Maps: by Bowen, Kitchin, Saxton and Speed, Emery, F.V., Ogilby's road maps, William Rees.

Index
Figures in bold refer to illustrations